OTHER BOOKS BY MEL LONDON

Getting into Film
Bread Winners
Easy Going
Second Spring
Bread Winners Too (Second Rising)

WITH SHERYL LONDON

The Fish-Lovers' Cookbook
Creative Cooking with Grains & Pasta

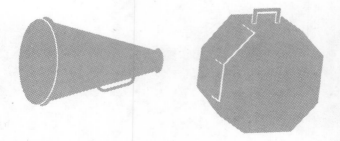

MAKING IT IN FILM

MEL LONDON

SIMON AND SCHUSTER
NEW YORK

Grateful acknowledgment is made to the following for permission to
reprint previously published material:

The New Yorker: Cartoon by Mischa Richter. Copyright © 1984
by The New Yorker Magazine, Inc. Reprinted by permission.

Paramount Pictures Corporation: Excerpt from *The Bardwell
Caper.* Copyright © 1981 Paramount Pictures Corporation. All
Rights Reserved.

Playboy, Inc.: Cartoon by Marty Murphy. Copyright © 1984 by
Playboy, Inc. Reprinted by permission.

Designed by Stanley S. Drate/Folio Graphics Co. Inc.

Manufactured in the United States of America

10 9 8 7 6 5 4 3 2 1

Library of Congress Cataloging in Publication Data

London, Mel.
    Making it in film.

    "A Fireside book."
    1. Moving-pictures—Vocational guidance. I. Title.
PN1995.9.P75L63   1985   791.43′023   85-11876
ISBN: 0-671-60493-7
        0-671-55542-1 Pbk.

Acknowledgments

So many of my film friends have been involved in the "making" of this book, and my greatest fear is that I might omit some of their names. They have given so freely of their time, their photo files, their advice, and they have my deepest gratitude. Somehow, I have always been blessed with an editor who managed to "understand" me and to laugh at my jokes. Charles Rue Woods is, fortunately, no exception, and I am delighted with his guidance.

The filmmakers were there, too, when I needed them: Frederick Wiseman, John Sayles, Herbert Brodkin and Tom De Wolfe, Judson Rosebush and Jeff Kleiser, Larry Dubin, Tom Buckholtz, Bob Pipher, Dick Sylbert, Dick Rauh, Carol Hale and Ed Schultz and my old friend Beverly O'Reilly, Pamela Yates and all the struggling young people at Skylight, Joan and Al Harrison, the staff of EFX, and especially Kaye Armstrong of Flying Tiger.

My thanks also go to CBS Records, who came through when no one else would listen, to Allen Zwerdling, he of the marvelous *Backstage* group, Wynn Nathan and Don Taffner, Chuck Tranum and Doris Gravert, and that old "warhorse" Joe Shaw. I hope, too, that the story of Doug Gowland and his Apple Star Productions will be an inspiration to those who give up a little too easily.

I have saved my "last but not least" for a very special group of people, for this book could not have been done without them. Professor Saul Taffet of NYU, Dan Klughertz of Global Village, and Joan Kuehl of the School of Visual Arts were kind enough to ask me to speak to their classes from time to time. It was there that I met the students, the graduates, and the eventual job hunters who spoke to me of their goals, their doubts, their futures, and their dreams—and who then asked all the hard questions about "making it in film." I can only hope that in this book I have managed to answer some of those questions.

MEL LONDON
Fire Island, New York

To the late Margareta Akermark
(1913–1983)

For her encouragement, for her warmth and
inspiration to all the young filmmakers who
found their way to the Museum of Modern Art—
including this filmmaker when he was young.

CONTENTS

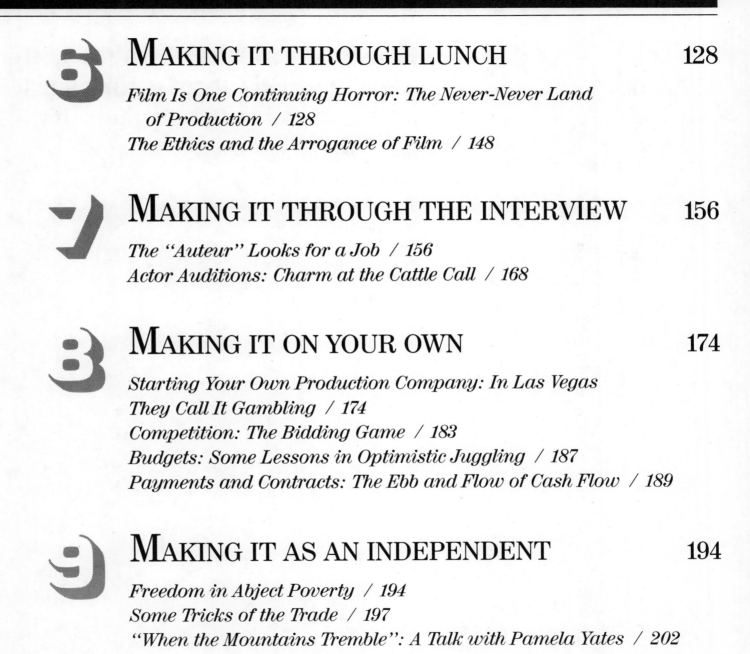

MAKING IT HAPPEN: The most frequently asked questions about getting started and moving ahead in the film industry   208

INTRODUCTION

The Making of *Making It in Film*

It has been almost ten years since the career guide, *Getting into Film,* was first published. And in spite of what my grandmother felt about me, I am no different from anyone else out there. I look with awe at the preposterous speed with which ten years can slip by.

In fact, I can still remember many of the details of my first film and television jobs thirty-five years back. There was the producer who always called me "kid." There were the late night dinners at the Horn & Hardart Automat, three vegetables and a slab of mystery meat, all for a dollar and a quarter—my "reward" for working twenty-four straight hours in order to satisfy a script editor at the network who insisted that I find some way to put a murder into a simple love story! There was the muted hysteria of the television control room as all shows went out over the network live, whether ready or not.

And there was the first awkward entry into film, where people seemed to take their time rather than turning on the lights and grinding out the shows as they did in television. Color stock was rated at ASA 10, and lighting was an all-day affair. Indeed, I *have* been around a long time.

I can still feel a glow at the special points in my film life when some kind of recognition has been given to my work. It is a business that has its own way of constantly reminding us of our humble beginnings. Of course, many details have become clouded and muddled, proving that they must have happened a long time ago.

Thus, when I was invited to write another film book, it was difficult to accept that so much had happened since the first, and that there might be a need for another book about careers in the industry. Just that week I had received the quarterly catalog from Cinemabilia, a wonderful bookstore that overflows with volumes about film and the adjunct media. Listed in the leaflet were *332 new books about film.* All had been published within the past six months or so.

★ Books about Robert Aldrich, Truman Capote, Federico Fellini, Sinatra, Swanson,

Steinbeck, and Streisand, about Stroheim and Spielberg, plus a *Who's Who,* a Who *Was* Who, and a complete book to help you in your studies of film robots.

★ Books about the best Hollywood musicals, the worst Hollywood musicals, the most unusual Hollywood musicals, how the Hollywood musical went to war, a book about Hollywood writers, Hollywood portraits, Hollywood child actors, and Hollywood's first hundred years.

★ Books about photography, pornography, religion in film, rock music, politics, mime, and monsters, not to mention histories about every country that ever exposed a foot of Kodak, Agfa, or Fuji film.

As I looked back, and reflected about a new book, I realized that:

★ *MANY THINGS* had changed in the ten years.

★ *NOTHING* had changed in those ten years!

THE THINGS THAT HAVE CHANGED

★ The *technology* has mushroomed into areas that we could barely imagine in the sixties and the midseventies. From the development of new (sometimes better, sometimes worse) film stock from Eastman Kodak, to the creation and the expanding usage of sophisticated hardware like the Steadicam, lighter cameras, featherweight tripods, electronic film gadgetry, and new lighting technology, the seventies gave us only a taste of what was to be a media revolution in the eighties.

★ *Computers* have come into their own in almost every area of the film world. In animation, laboratory technology, color timing, tape production, and editing, and even in the finance and production areas of budgets, scheduling, payrolls, and administration, the bits and bytes have taken over from us mortals, sometimes to our advantage, occasionally to mess things up much better than we ever could.

★ *Videotape* has steadily blossomed into a strong, sophisticated, and accepted form of communication, as filmmakers have begun to realize that it may be around to stay. The world is now filled with filmmaker/tape experts, communications hermaphrodites who can switch from medium to medium with ease in order to survive. Even Hollywood, too often the lumbering dinosaur of our industry, has begun to discover that the boom in videocassettes has become a vital moneymaker for the studios. The United States/Canadian videocassette rights to *Silkwood* were sold for $1.5 million. This was soon topped by the *preproduction* sale of *Santa Claus—the Movie,* the $1.5 million feature starring Dudley Moore, for $2.6 million! By the time this book is published, those figures will probably fall into the low-budget range. And the revenues from cassettes and discs, now about 15 percent of the returns for a typical movie, will probably also rise dramatically.

★ *Cable and pay TV* markets have also grown, not only for the Hollywood moguls, as detailed in the paragraphs above, but also as another potential entry opportunity for young people. And to show just how quickly things change in our industry, during that short period of time a noble experiment seems to have come and almost gone—QUBE, the technology that allowed people to answer back to their TV screens or shop by remote control. The latest reports seem to indicate that QUBE may well go the way of the Edsel and the vacuum tube.

★ *Music videos* have become a new form of production opportunity for everyone in the industry. We hear of some high-budget productions, but most are on the low end. As such, the field has given newcomers a chance to flex their production muscles and has even developed some "superstar" directors.

★ The *corporate* world has expanded its own audiovisual scope, a trend that started in the early days of the sixties, and has now become a job market that rivals the networks and the film production companies.

It became evident that any new book about film careers had to cover the areas I've listed above. Thus, in the chapters that follow, I have discussed them, fully aware as I write that they will change and change again in the *next* ten years.

Such is the delight, the frustration, and the excitement of our industry.

But there has been one other change in these years, and that one was of a very personal nature. After years of working with companies such as David Wolper and as a partner at Vision Associates, I finally took the plunge and formed my own film production business in 1980, Symbiosis Inc. I was, of course, fully convinced that I would promptly starve to death in this highly competitive industry, and to this day I am still in awe at every telephone call or letter that asks me to produce a film for a client of mine, whether new or old. Thus, I have more fully written about going into your own business and/or making your way as an independent, if this is the route that you'd like to follow in your own film career ("Making It on Your Own," page 174). Possibly you might even learn from some of my mistakes and experiences, as well as from my accidental wisdom in making a success (so far) of the new venture.

AND WHAT HAS NOT CHANGED

There are some things that never seem to change in the film business, while other things move much too slowly.

★ The overpromotion and the "hype" of our industry will always be with us. But it can only affect you adversely if you begin to believe that this is a "glamour" craft, if you actually believe what the publicity flacks say. The day you put on your dark sunglasses (even symbolically), open your

shirt to the waist (for the men), and dangle twenty gold chains from your neck is the day that you're in plenty of trouble. Film is a *business,* a pragmatic, tough, realistic, "bottom line," unsentimental business. And since this is one of my favorite subjects, I have expanded upon it at length in the next section of the book.

There are other areas where film has not changed much over the years. Of course, I suppose that if I were writing about banking or Wall Street or the garment center, I might say essentially the same thing. Or we might find that the profession of law is notorious for exploiting its new college-grad employees in terms of work load and hours, if not of salary. There are major corporations that warn their new staff people that they must be prepared to give up their personal lives. So it should come as no surprise to find that we film people have also become bogged down in moral and financial quicksand, as well as in the exploitation of people.

★ Opportunities for *women and minorities* have moved slowly near the top. The field has remained essentially a male-oriented, white middle-class industry. Certainly there are areas where the lower and middle levels have opened up: production management, editing, production crews—sound, gaffing, camera assistants—some documentary production, small-company ownership, corporate and advertising audiovisual production, a smattering of directorial feature work—all with standards that

are higher for minorities than for white males. Meanwhile, up at the top it has not really changed at all. Nevertheless, in my first book I included a separate chapter entitled "Women in Film," while I did not feel the need for it in this volume. Perhaps that, in itself, is a sign of progress!

Ten years ago I commented that if you looked around, you would find that *all* heads of production at the major studios in Hollywood were men. Shortly thereafter, Sherry Lansing became the president of production at Paramount and the industry made a liar of me. Things change quickly, as I have stated, and for whatever the public reasons given, Ms. Lansing is now a partner with Jaffe/Lansing Productions, and I can say once again: Look around you. *All* heads of production at the major Hollywood studios are *men*!

★ The financial stranglehold on our industry has not really changed. In fact, it is growing stronger instead of weaker as business interests begin to control more and more of the Hollywood output. Notice that Herbert Brodkin (page 122) states that *all* of the powers with whom he deals are either lawyers or accountants. Columbia Pictures was purchased by Coca-Cola, and the businessmen tightened the financial controls even further, aside from decreeing that no *Pepsi-Cola* product was ever to be seen in a Columbia film!

In the area of film commercials, advertising agencies have begun to play an even more vital and decisive role in the final product. And in the documentary and business film, we are dealing with more educated clients, more sophisticated negotiations, more opposition to adequate budgets, and much more creative interference than ever before.

Finally, in the area of little change, there is one more factor of utmost importance to any reader of a career guide in film and, in fact, to *any* budding filmmaker:

★ The *first job* is still difficult to get. It always has been—it continues to be the first great challenge to the young college student and to the career changer who would be a filmmaker. With over one hundred thousand film students matriculated in colleges and universities across the country, there just never seem to be enough jobs for those who want them.

Another factor has appeared in the job market that has made entry even more difficult for the new filmmaker. There are now an uncounted number of people in the field of continuing education, storefront audiovisual neighborhood units, and independent, nonaffiliated students who are studying communications with an eye toward changing careers and becoming film or videotape producers. Interestingly enough, some have been incredibly successful in making that change.

This is a time in our history when people are finding that the first job, the first career that they went into after high school or college, need not be the end-all of their working lives. Career changers are everywhere, and in one directing class that I taught at NYU some years back, the youngest student was twenty years of age, the oldest was *seventy-four*! It is an area that continues to fascinate me, for in my seminars at universities and for the American Film Institute, I have queried students about just that aspect of their goals. In Houston, for example, at an A.F.I. Rice University seminar, there were people who had paid a hefty entrance fee—and had come from as far away as New Orleans, Washington, Des Moines, and Chicago to hear eight speakers cover film as a career!

So the job market becomes more difficult, for these people are also competing for entry-level positions and for the job rungs up the ladder. I was curious. What did all those people *do* during the regular working day? In questionnaires that were filled out at my request, here were some of the professions of the potential job switchers:

Attorney	Journalist
Student	Assistant Film Editor
Day Laborer	Recording Engineer
PR Writer	Graphic Designer
Ships Broker	Warehouse Clerk
Translator	Engineer
Plasterer	Photographer
Word Processor	Nurse
Video Technician	Teachers:
Painting Contractor	of German
Stock Index Trader	of English
Songwriter	High School
Secretary	Public School
Insurance Salesman	Medical Photographer
Oil Executive	Art Gallery Curator

And all of them, when they "grow up," want to be in the film business! This is a reality, but I hasten to add that my purpose in listing them all, in stating that so many people are now attending school as majors in communications, is *not* to be discouraging. I have always felt that beginning filmmakers take a most unrealistic and fanciful view of our field. The schools (many of which use *Getting into Film* as a career guide textbook) are not very much help, since they still tend to avoid the pragmatic and difficult issues of how you get your first job and how you progress from there, while paying an inordinate amount of attention to the historical perspectives of the film industry and the psychological implications of each and every frame of the abundant Hollywood, European, and Asian output.

As those who are unfortunate enough to have sat through my lectures and seminars well know, I find great encouragement in the fact that almost everyone that I have seen, interviewed, and encouraged has managed to place himself or herself in the field. I glow as I watch them progress, however slowly, until their resumes begin to shine with credits and the proudly listed achievements of finished film or videotape projects. But all of them have been willing to work hard—all of them have been willing to "pay their dues."

Thus, the first book was devoted almost entirely to getting that *first* job in the field; indeed, it was intended for those who had not even made up their minds as to *which* film craft interested them most, as well as for the younger college student or beginner who was tentatively exploring the field of communications. The thrust of *Making It in Film*, by contrast, is more concerned with those of you who have already decided that this *is* the industry for you, possibly even having tried out in the first job or two. It is, most of all, a book about knowing how to *advance* your career once you have made the decision to stick with it, come what may. To that end, it is deeply concerned with giving you both the encouragement and the knowledge that will help you move ahead.

THE "WAR STORIES"

Any group of filmmakers, given a chance, loves to exchange experiences. A plane that was twenty hours late in Pakistan. A location that didn't exist after they had traveled for three days over the Andes. The film stock that was lost between Thailand and San Francisco for ten days because someone trusted a government official who said, "Don't worry. Leave it to me"—and it was finally found in Des Moines ten days later. The best restaurant in Hiawatha, Utah. The worst restaurant in Hiawatha, Utah. (The *only* restaurant in Hiawatha, Utah.) The camera that broke down in the middle of the desert. The irreplaceable film scratched by the laboratory. Being arrested. Almost being arrested. Talking his way out of being arrested. Hostile natives (sometimes in New York City). Riots. Revolutions. Festivals. Carnivals. The stories go on all the time.

Listen to any film crew gathered around the dinner table at some less-than-adequate, ungracious, Formica-topped motel dining room. Listen to the same film crew in the best of French restaurants in the middle of some large, sophisticated European city. The "war stories" will continue nonstop, as one veteran's tale reminds the next in line of something that happened to him or her. And buried deeply within each and every story will be a lesson to be learned. It might be a lesson in production. It might well be a hidden tip on how to expedite government approval in some out-of-the-way dictatorship. It might even contain a tip on how to get your next job or even the first one in your career.

Essentially, if I had to describe this new book, I would say that it is made up almost entirely of "war stories," a broad range of experiences culled from a wide range of people who have been successful in our field. Film students constantly ask the same question: How did *they* get started? Was it much different so many years ago? It is natural and it is expected that the beginner should want to know the answers. I was reminded of it again just a few months ago.

I received a telephone call from a young woman who was in her first year in the communications curriculum at Harvard University. She had read my book. She was coming to New York. When she got there, could she see me? Of course she could.

Sitting demurely in my living room, intense, committed, very bright, she finally asked the question:

"Mr. London, I'm already *seventeen*. And I haven't accomplished anything in my life. Does it get easier as you get older?"

My answer, of course, was, "No!"

I have asked these same questions of people who have been successful in the film industry, whether well known to the public and the film aficionados—John Sayles, Herbert Brodkin, Fred Wiseman—or moderately anonymous to the outside world while still successfully doing the things they love best and making a living at it. Their answers and their "war stories" are also between the covers of this book.

In addition, I have questioned my students at each and every lecture—at New York University, at the Annenberg School in Philadelphia, at the New School, and at the American Film Institute seminars in Los Angeles, Washington, New York, Boston, and Houston. It is the answers to *their* questions that make up the bulk of the material in this book. You will find, for example, a chapter entitled "Making It Happen: The Most Frequently Asked Questions About Getting Started and Moving Ahead in the Film Industry," and possibly one of your questions is also covered—and answered—in that section.

If you are willing to stay with me for these several hundred pages, then perhaps I—and the people who were gracious enough to speak with me—may be of some help to you. But if even this short introduction has challenged you too much, and if you are already discouraged by the numbers, the odds, and the fact that this is a difficult, demanding, perplexing industry, then I have one sage word of advice, culled from Frederick Wiseman, the well-known and talented documentarian, taken from one of his Hunter College lectures.

During the question and answer period, a member of the audience stood up and asked,

"What does it take to become a filmmaker?"

Without missing a beat, Wiseman answered, "Marry someone rich!"

"The questioner retorted, "I'm not kidding!"

And the filmmaker replied, "Neither am I!"

MAKING IT IN FILM

MAKING IT IN FILM
Ambitions, Goals, and Dreams

In Pursuit of the Dream

After one of my lectures, I was particularly taken with a questionnaire that had been filled out by one attendee. For some reason, it seemed to capsulize all the fears, the ambitions, the dreams, and the trepidations of the new filmmaker. In direct contrast to the fluff quoted on the preceding pages, his answer to one of my questions was, indeed, very close to the subject of this book.

His name is Harry Litwack, and he lists himself as an "unemployed writer." Now in his midthirties, he is typical of the career switcher who has decided to try a field that seems to offer more gratification than did his previous work as a welfare worker and a teaching coordinator. But he is also mature enough to understand that he will encounter pitfalls along the way.

In a sense, Harry has been lucky. Though he is the author of an unproduced screenplay and four screen treatments, he has managed to get some on-set experience as a production assistant with *Trading Places* and *Taps*. My question read: "What are your most important questions (emotions) about the film field—goals, job opportunities, creative concerns, making a living?"

Harry's answer:

"How to continue:
★ keeping a roof over my head and food on the table;
★ sustaining emotionally, psychically, and spiritually until the next break in my career without giving in to the doubts that say I should put the brakes on myself;
★ finding film work experience that will advance my career;
★ overcoming the roller coaster ride of elation, stagnation, motivation, and boredom while keeping a realistic approach toward making a career for myself in film."

I was particularly taken with his last line on the sheet: "Do you have a job for me?"

Unfortunately, too much of our student time and our study of communications is spent in the weighty analysis and the philosophy of film or overblown promotional hype, rather than in devoting a dedicated effort to understanding some of the problems listed above, the *business* as it affects our professional lives.

A Curmudgeon Looks at Hype

Every morning I sift through the pile of mail I receive to read the letters and circulars that deal with the film industry, including a good share of what I like to call motion picture hype.

Usually the mail brings with it marvelous offers of studio space in Birmingham, Alabama, or Ten Sleep, Wyoming, literature hailing Texas as the third coast, two or three resumes from recent graduates or longtime professionals, ten or twenty film invoices from suppliers (all of them higher than I might have liked), and an occasional puff piece about a new or old film publication. It is in this latter group that I find the greatest threat to a valid understanding of just what our industry is really all about, especially for the vulnerable beginner.

Understand, then, that it is not the *content* of any of the publications with which I take issue.

Harry Litwack on the set of Taps.

Rather, it is the *tone*. I fully understand it when it is used to market our product and when it is directed to the public, who eventually support the industry in the feature field. The overblown image of motion pictures is deliberate and well thought out, whether it be the vapid appearances on television talk shows, shallow, slice-of-life captioned photography in *People* magazine, gossip about the much married and the much bedded, or "planted" pieces telling us the clever sayings of movie stars, many of whom have never had an original idea in their lives.

The problems begin when *we* start to believe our own creative writing about just how marvelous we are. In the susceptible, struggling early stages of our careers especially, this deception threatens our progress by blinding us to some of the realities of a very pragmatic, demanding, "bottom line" industry. As our careers slowly drag themselves along the minefields of reality, we begin to wonder if the fantasy exists at all—or if it ever did.

Look, for example at this prepublication offer for a magazine that was, unfortunately, to have a short life: *The Movies*. If I had had any doubts about how wonderful we are, this paragraph would soon dispel them forever:

"The people, then and now. The bright, dynamic imaginative, often narcissistic, frequently outrageous talents involved in films. How they operate, why they do the things they do, what motivates them, how they got there, how they live. What they like, what they think, what they fear. Who *they* think are genuinely brilliant and talented, and which movies they love."

If you really want to get the full impact of the paragraph above, read it aloud. The surprising thing to me is that the magazine failed so quickly. It was the equal of any piece of fluff literature about the film industry that exists on the newsstands and through subscriptions today. It catered to what has become the overwhelming penchant for gossip, glamour, tinsel, glitter, and pizzazz.

Essentially, then, our own publications promise us what we have been brought up to believe about the film business, what we have been subjected to all of our maturing years, and what many of our film schools do their utmost to perpetuate. The bold type tempts us. We are the fans as well as the would-be filmmakers. *The Movies* will sate us with:

★ The Action!
★ The Excitement!
★ The Glamour!
★ The Color!
★ The Drama!
★ The Legends!
★ The People!
★ The Future!

But in that magazine, as in all the others, and in the continuing flood of promotional mail, one item always seems to be missing:

★ The Business!

The film field has also become glutted with a meaningless vocabulary, as empty and hollow as the promotional literature quoted above. We have evolved a language that rivals the lingo of "computerese," but with much less substance. We can actually read critical articles that tell us a filmmaker has "turned the fluorescent geometry of this institutional corridor into a sort of piston-powered mandala."

To cite another example, in a long article about Alfred Hitchcock, published not too long ago in *American Film,* the critic Robin Wood managed to write: "The introduction of semiotics and structuralism, the politicization of film theory during the late sixties and seventies, the new emphasis on concepts of ideology, the vital and radical input of feminist theory, the growing importance of psychoanalytic theory (especially as a political weapon)—all these interrelated phenomena have ensured that we can no longer look at the films as we used to, as 'works of art' on 'universal' human themes."

A reader of the magazine called the entire article "a wonderful spoof"—and possibly it was. But the literature has been so inundated with "filmspeak" that even a spoof would take on the mantle of reality. "Auteur," "cultural metaphor," "psychic mirror," "minimalism," "reductivism," and an almost psychotic search for "the real meaning" of a film. I do realize that the telephoto lens in Hitchcock's *Rear Window* was a phallic symbol. But calling it to my attention as one of the critical meanings of the film reminded me of Sigmund Freud's marvelous comment: "My dear sir, I *know* that a cigar is a phallic symbol. But it is also a *cigar!*"

I am not denigrating, by any means, the creative aspects of film, nor am I totally against the analysis or criticism of a director's work. The questionnaires completed by students reflect a constant concern with the areas of creativity, integrity, freedom, and independence and a desire to produce personal reflections of their emotions, ethics, or philosophies. And though the collaborative nature of film frequently mitigates against creativity and inspiration (not to mention freedom), I think it's gratifying that we can even feel that ours is an industry that can offer so much. For without the dream, why struggle so hard to succeed?

For me, the most important thing about the masters, whether or not we agree upon just who they are, is their *method* of working, their solution to the everyday problems of film and of production, their thought analysis in bringing their total vision to the screen, whether it be in a feature or in a small personal documentary about the father of the filmmaker. I respect the fact that Hitchcock's sexuality reflected itself in his films. But as a filmmaker, I am more impressed with the fact that he was probably one of the best prepared of directors when he came on the set, and that his ratio of shooting (how much film was shot per elicited final minute) was somewhere in the neighborhood of *three to one!*

For the filmmaker, no matter what his or her status in the field, it is a constant source of frustration when the questions of critics and young students revolve around the *real* meaning of the work up on the screen. Werner Herzog told a *New York Times* interviewer who wanted to know the "true" message of *Heart of Glass,*

"You should look straight at a film; that is the only way to see one. Film is not the art of scholars but of illiterates."

Luckily, there are realists among us. In an American Film Institute seminar, the veteran director Robert Wise was answering questions posed by the young film buffs in the audience. Wise had started as a messenger in the editing department of RKO when he was only nineteen, and eventually he moved into the realm of America's top-flight group of directors with *Blood on the Moon, The Day the Earth Stood Still, Odds Against Tomorrow, West Side Story,* and many, many more. Thus, Wise might be the perfect candidate to philosophize about his work in "film-babble" and undecipherable platitudes. Instead, he is one of the most down-to-earth people in the business.

A young man in the audience that day raised his hand and commented that one could not help but notice the repetition of the pattern of circles on the sidewalk in *West Side Story.* Could Mr. Wise please tell the audience the significance of those images?

Wise stood there, the audience waiting to hear some words of philosophical film wisdom and Freudian analysis, and then he answered, "No, sir, I cannot!"

And Whither Goest Thou?

I have always tried to be a pragmatist about the film industry, and rereading what has gone before, I realize that there is also no small amount of cynicism deep within me. To the people who have come to me for advice, I have always tried to communicate a realistic view about our field, and I have never minced words about the difficulties. But at the same time I have tried not to burst the bubble of the dream, the pursuit of a career in this most fascinating profession. I admire the enthusiasm that I see, while I am still in awe at the vast numbers who want to join us.

Your goals vary, with only one constant always there: to work in film. There are the more practical ones among us, as one student put it:

"I want eventually, as I guess does every aspiring young filmmaker, to be able to make my own movies, with as little hindrance from outsiders as possible. The more exposure I have to independent filmmakers, the more aware I become that the nature of film makes it a peculiarly more difficult medium than any other form of expression. *Money*—and big money—is the stumbling block."

But another student took a different view:

"We shouldn't be thinking about 'making it' financially in film. If we want to make money, we should do it in easier fields."

And still another:

"To produce for the BBC a year-long weekly series on the history of the Western world based upon Samuel Beckett's narrative notion of never being able to arrive at a conclusion about anything."

And my favorite one, a most succinct objective:

"To be the greatest director!"

For each of you, the career path will vary. As I see the resumes that come across my desk each week, I am amazed and pleased at how they grow from year to year. From the initial struggle to fill the page with school and early experience, the "updates" soon push the schooling into a few short sentences as work experience takes over the major part of the summary. Bit by bit, most people seem to make it somehow—in spite of the competition, in spite of the hype, in spite of the arrogance and the lack of feelings of most people in hiring positions.

At this point, the cynics among you will expect me to preach hard work, paying your dues, and the theories of Horatio Alger—in which case you would not have to continue reading any further.

Quite the contrary. I do advocate working hard, for most of us in the film business put in too many hours solving too many unexpected problems, meeting our deadlines, or just making a living. And I do agree that you will have to pay your dues, for if you want to replace those who have spent years paying dues to get where they are, you will certainly have to struggle for it. I also feel that you must know and understand the film business, wiped clear of all the hype and the pizzazz and the philosophy of dilettantes and people who have never exposed a foot of film themselves. And you absolutely *must* have a knowledge of the career paths that will take you to your eventual goal, whether it be the world's most famous (and successful) director or a documentary cinematographer or the owner of your own small (or large), struggling production company.

But I also admit that there is still another factor that will play a great role in changing the face of your resume in your early years in the film business. It is a factor that not too many writers seem to cover, and certainly no professor, to my knowledge, has ever conducted a seminar about it, nor do the universities offer courses in it. It has nothing to do with the homilies of good, clean living that our parents advocated as the key to success. I speak of *chance*. I speak of being in the right place at the right time. But more important, I speak of *knowing*, or instinctively feeling, that you *are* in that right place and that it *is* the right time, so that you might take advantage of it!

Later on in this book you will read a great many words on the subject, as some of the people I interviewed recount their own career paths. Each of us in the profession is a shining example of all the elements I have outlined above—including chance. My own entry into radio came about because my mother-in-law knew the dentist's wife who knew a woman whose son wrote quiz shows. I went into television because the quiz show packagers were among the first to help invent TV game shows. And I switched from television to film because I met my company commander from World War II on a street corner in Manhattan and he offered me a job in his budding film production company. And incidentally, the dentist's wife's friend's son who gave me my first writing job was Nat Eisenberg, who has moved through a long and successful career as a film producer with his own company, NBE Productions! Just the other morning, while at my local bank, I saw this strange factor of chance and serendipity take place once again.

It was a quiet morning and, for a change, the lines were not too long. Ever curious about people, I eavesdropped on a conversation that was taking place at the next window. The customer, it seems, was a hairstylist, and he commented admiringly about the full, bushy, luxuriant head of hair that the teller sported. The customer, by way of explanation, mentioned that he had baby-fine hair and he always looked with some envy at a full head of shiny hair.

The teller, it seems, was a budding actor, and since it was a quiet, not-too-busy morning, he had time to speak of his background, working in stock, in showcase productions, making the rounds. Well, the hairstylist had a client who happened to be a casting agent and who was constantly on the lookout for new, young talent. In fact, the hairstylist went on, the agent was currently looking desperately for an actor who could play a teenager. The teller smiled, the bank transaction now completely forgotten. Why, he had just played a teenager in summer stock that past season. And he did look much younger than he really was. (He did.)

Fine, the stylist said. Just bring your photo and resume to the bank tomorrow and I'll stop by to pick them up and deliver them to the casting agent.

I left wondering if I had witnessed the beginning of a bright new career.

Nat B. Eisenberg, right, one of the author's oldest film friends, who began in the early days of live television and now owns his own successful film company, NBE Productions.

MAKING THE NEXT DECISION

Is There Life Outside N.Y., L.A.?

Too often we tend to be too narrow in our thinking about just where we would like to pursue the early stages of our film careers. Especially for the beginner, this can be a serious block in the pursuit of that goal. We think first of New York and California (while those on the West Coast think of *California* and New York). Possibly we even think for a moment about second cities such as Chicago, Detroit, Dallas, Boston, or Atlanta.

There is no doubt that New York is the major film center for the production of documentaries, commercials, and the business film, as well as the key focal point for the gathering of network news. California still ranks first in the production of features and television sitcoms, along with a small amount of commercial production. And the other cities I've mentioned (including Washington, Miami, San Francisco) are doing a fair share of local, national, and international filming for corporations, agencies, and travel-oriented clients.

The film companies and the people who work in the industry are now based everywhere, and along with the astounding growth of tape production, a broad range of services are currently being offered all across the country (and around the world). Just look at the lists.

There are production companies in Putney, Vermont; Orem, Utah; Lewisville, North Carolina; Metuchen, New Jersey; Barrington, New Hampshire; Pomfret Center, Connecticut; and Woodinville and Brown Deer, Wisconsin! There are people working in film in Palatka, Florida, and in Wakonda, South Dakota. Some are successful. A great many are struggling. And most are happy to be away from the tensions of the city. As Bob Richards, of Em Com Productions in Minneapolis, told an interviewer for *Backstage*, "Working in the Midwest reminds me of the America that Norman Rockwell used to paint, where people had time for one another."

In fact, after forty years and sixty countries on six continents, after uncounted air miles, too many canceled flights, too many rental-van breakdowns, endless discussions with security people as to why we just can't put the film stock through the X-ray machine, and infinite pursuits of the perfect sunset, I have evolved a well-proven theory that the world is *filled* with motion picture crews. And the most important part of that theory is that they can be recognized in an instant!

I'm not speaking of the crew that plants itself in the middle of some busy urban intersection, equipment, vans, lights, and people strewn all over the sidewalk, crosswalk, and roadway, while everyone seems to be doing nothing in particular. Rather, I am referring to the more common situations of daily life—in restaurants, at airport waiting rooms, at luggage check-in areas—where those of us who are in the film industry can spot another film crew instantaneously.

Sometimes it is quite obvious. We arrive at the sidewalk check-in area of any airport, big or small. It is early morning. It is always early morning. It is always too early for any decent human being to be awake and at an airport. Next to us, a van pulls up to the curb and some sleepy people unload thirty-two well-worn Halliburton cases, tool kits, long boxes that were never designed to pack easily, and six or eight personal suitcases that have seen better days. Someone counts. Someone checks the count. The skycaps hurry over, for thirty-two pieces of luggage represent a substantial tip. They, too, can recognize a film crew. The skycap counts. The assistant checks the skycap. To the watcher, the credo of the film crew is obvious: *Never trust anyone.*

Or—we hurry through the airport at Bogotá, Colombia. It is the middle of the afternoon rush hour and planes are leaving for all over South America and the rest of the world. It is that hour of South American hysteria, the corridors filled with people carrying badly tied cardboard boxes, babies squalling, garbled announcements made one after the other, and the two-way flow of traffic at its most horrendous peak. There, standing on a long, snaking line for a flight to some godforsaken jungle location, are six people. Somehow, we see them. We comment. They must be a film crew. Why? No reason. Attitude? Dress? A glazed, hypnotic look around the eyes? It is impossible to describe why we would pick them out in all the turmoil and chaos of the departure wing of the airport. We go over just to check. They are, indeed, a film crew from Rome, on their way to Bucaramanga. We chat briefly and leave for our own flight to Buenaventura, now only three hours late for departure.

Or—the restaurant is crowded. It is *American Lunchtime* (see *"Making It Through Lunch"*) in Indianapolis or Grand Rapids or New Orleans. At a nearby table there are eight people gathered around their menus. There is nothing to distinguish them from anyone else in the room, though they might well be in work clothes. But one person sitting at the table has a light meter case attached to his belt. He must be an assistant cameraman for a film crew. He is. They are. And again, we spot our own and nod to them in passing.

Or—we arrive in Lima, Peru, at one A.M. We are scheduled to depart the next morning at six A.M. (!) for Cuzco to film Machu Picchu. The schedule is tight, as it always is. The luggage is unloaded. Three pieces are missing—*including the case with the film stock!* Somehow they have been off-loaded in Bogotá, but the office there is closed. The airline couldn't care less. The customs people are tired and want to go home. The production manager goes off to the coffee shop to find a telephone and attempt to reach Bogotá one more time. There, sitting at the half-clean tables and drinking tepid coffee from cardboard cups is a group of six exhausted people who are obviously waiting for an early morning flight to somewhere. The production manager recognizes one of the men, someone he has worked with back in New York. They are a film crew! They have just finished shooting a commercial in Peru and are waiting to return to New York. In fact, they have twenty rolls of film stock left over from the job. And, of course, we can have them all and pay for them when we return. We gleefully make the six A.M. flight to Cuzco. When we return to Lima, the luggage from Bogotá has been forwarded and we now have *forty* rolls of film. Later that day, an emergency shipment from New York arrives, sent in answer to our urgent cable, and in it are twenty more rolls of film stock, bringing our supply up to *sixty* rolls!

The customs officers are now convinced that we are smuggling drugs in all those sealed cans, but we finally convince them that the seals were put on by Eastman Kodak and that we are, indeed, an innocent documentary film crew there to do a travel sequence.

There are times when the whole world seems filled with nothing *but* film crews. We are sent to Australia to film the annual horse extravaganza, the Melbourne Cup, and so is every other film and television crew in the entire world, it seems. Placed atop the main grandstand, we are but one of sixty or seventy crews, elbow to elbow, camera to camera, lens to lens, each one of us jockeying (no pun intended) to get the best spot for the finish of the race. A million dollars in film equipment and personnel for two and a half minutes of crowded horseflesh.

There is an added note of irony to the last story, by the way. When we arrived at the race course early in the morning, we decided to choose a horse at random and follow it through the day, in the stables, the grooming, saddling, warm-up, mounting of the jockey, and then the race.

For no reason at all that anyone can remember, we chose a lovely chestnut named Gatum Gatum (number 21). By the time the race had begun, we had logged hundreds of feet of background color. To make the sequence perfect, *Gatum Gatum won the race!* The horse was proudly marched to the winner's circle and covered with garlands of flowers. We sped down to photograph the proud owners, the jockey, and the lovely horse, who had paid a handsome twenty to one. Then we realized that in our

There are hundreds of filmmakers who would never move to the production centers of Hollywood/New York. Tom Buckholtz operates his busy production company in New Orleans, filming commercials, documentaries, and music videos.

excitement, our preparation problems, and our enthusiasm, *no one* on the crew had bothered to place a bet on our chosen horse!

We are, indeed, everywhere. Documentary film crews, television news and sports tape and film crews, feature film crews, commercial production companies, independent producers. For an industry that claims to have so few job opportunities, it is amazing just how prevalent we are. We seem to come from everywhere in the world.

Possibly one of the best examples of a filmmaker who chose to live and work away from the New York/Los Angeles axis is Tom Buckholtz, who has his own small company of seven people in New Orleans. He explains, "I set up business in New Orleans with the belief that good work sells harder, and clients aren't concerned with the address of a production company . . . in terms of work, my reel speaks for itself."

He's worked for Procter and Gamble, for Burger King, and he's produced three MTV assignments for Journey. When I spoke with Tom, he was also working on a film about the Louisiana Cajuns, with a grant from the American Film Institute. He's traveled to Europe eight times for film projects, and he works in Central and South America, as well as in New York, Los Angeles, Boston, and Texas, just as the rest of us do.

"I wake up and look at the Mississippi. I can see it from the levee that runs along my property. I live upriver from the city, on an old sugar plantation. My production company has an office on Magazine Street, right in the thick of uptown New Orleans. I can walk outside my house or my office and look at this terrific city and feel its realness."

In our last telephone conversation, we discussed the job markets outside the major areas. Tom commented, "You have to pick the life-style you like. Don't worry about where the filmworld is. You gotta be happy first!" Tom also feels that since New Orleans is not one of the major markets, the people who work in film are used to putting in a lot of extra effort to make things work and to stretch the budgets. And in the long, tedious postproduction periods, he adds, "New Orleans has some of the best and strongest coffee in the world . . . enough to keep everyone awake to get to the end!"

Possibly the most interesting thing about this expanding phenomenon and the growth of the tape/film industry into smaller areas is the remarkable range of services that are offered to potential clients. People like Tom Buckholtz offer exactly the same professional talents available in New York or Chicago or Los Angeles, and he is correct in saying that "good work sells" and thus clients are not interested in the location of a producer or the production company. But in looking at the listings, I find that the smaller companies—all of them outside the cities of prime production—now offer just about *everything else* a client will ever need to fill a communications need:

★ Animation—cel, clay, collage, stop motion
★ Computer-controlled animation
★ Training and sales video
★ Business films and documentaries
    Educational
    Government
    Political
    Social
    Religious
    Sports
    Fund-Raising
★ Commercials
★ Multi-image slides and filmstrips
★ Postproduction in film and videotape
★ Music production and scoring
★ Editing
★ Negative cutting
★ Scriptwriting
★ Political media consultation
★ Acting workshops
★ Casting services
★ Location scouting
★ Teleconferencing
★ Sound recording and transfers
★ Interlock screening
★ High-speed photography
★ Aerial and underwater photography
★ Optical effects
★ Set construction and prop rental
★ Equipment distributors
★ Lighting packages and personnel (gaffers, grips, and so on)
★ Feature trailer production
★ Transcript typing
★ Research

Now, I am *not* trying to send you out of New York or Los Angeles just to get rid of you! I am just trying to say that we too often narrow our parameters, and thus we narrow our opportunities. And I suppose I am speaking as much of the film producer who thinks only of New York/Los Angeles as I am of the beginner who is trying to find his or her way *into* the field in the first place and then is looking for the path that will lead to *making a living* in the business of film. If you want to knock on the doors of New York production houses or the television studios, or if a Beverly Hills swimming pool is your motion picture goal, I certainly wish you the best of luck, while I remind you again that the rules of the game are very tough indeed. Do it. It's just that for some of my readers I know that the *idea* of making films is more important than *where* you eventually end up making them.

I recently went through an experience that taught me, as a producer, just how true those words can be. My film editor for the past few years was a remarkable young woman named Suzanne Jasper. Well trained, experienced, imbued with an unusual intelligence and a sense of film joy, she was the salvation of our small company when I dropped thousands of feet of disconnected film and sound tape on her doorstep and she returned to me the most remarkably edited documentary continuity. My clients loved her. *She* made *me* look good. I settled in for a long period of filmmaking with an editor who proved the old saying, "You can always save it in the editing room!" *And then she moved away!*

Suzanne moved back to *Bat Cave, North Carolina*! And I, with another film that had to be edited for a long-term client, was faced with the task of finding an editor to put together forty

KARL SCHURMAN

One of the author's favorite film editors, Suzanne Jasper, who now works successfully out of her editing room in Bat Cave, North Carolina, not far from Hollywood Road on Highway 74.

rolls of footage and cut it down into a perfect fifteen minutes that would make sense to the eventual audience—and that people could watch without falling asleep. With my own training and background, there was no choice but to do the talent hunt in New York, and I searched diligently for someone who might edit the film.

The results were, to put it bluntly, a sheer and unmitigated disaster. The secret of film collaboration is the chemistry of the people, and our chemistry was H_2SO_4 combined with $KCLO_3$. I was unhappy. The client was unhappy. The new editor was unhappy. One of the functions of being a producer is to make choices. This time I was wrong. And the film was slated to be recut. But—by whom?

It occurred to me that Suzanne might be the right person, but she had left me. Possibly she might still want to do it. But in Bat Cave? No one in the entire film industry, to my knowledge, had ever edited a film in Bat Cave. What kind of reputation would our small company have when we answered a potential client's questions with, "Oh, yes, our editing room is in Bat Cave, North Carolina!"

But that is exactly the decision I made. Suzanne and I had long consultations about how we would manage the music selection (in New York), viewing and selecting from the work print (in Bat Cave), producer/editor interlock (Bat Cave), client interlock (New York), and mix (New York). We worked out a schedule to select dates for Bat Cave or New York. And I shipped a six-plate Steenbeck editing machine down by truck, where Suzanne's converted bedroom became the Symbiosis editing room, complete with racks, viewer, trim barrels, and row upon row of neatly labeled white boxes that contained our unfinished film.

And—it has worked! The whole idea has worked. When the machine breaks down, which it sometimes does, parts are ordered from The Editing Machine Company in New York, or it is repaired via long-distance telephone discussions with a technician in the Big Apple!

Best of all, the first film out of Bat Cave was a huge success. Given the added concentration factor of being isolated in the mountains of North Carolina, the innate intelligence of the editor, and the countless late night calls to discuss minor points, the film was hailed by the clients (and this producer). We all decided that Bat Cave wasn't such a bad production center after all!

We are now cutting our fourth film down there, and we have even discovered a nearby local dirt lane that is called Hollywood Road!

As the film industry grows in all fifty states, many more young people are beginning to start their careers nearer their homes or colleges, with an eventual (if hazy) look toward New York or Los Angeles in their film futures. Given the huge increase in film production in their state, Texans now call their area "the third coast." Chicago, always a vital production area, has seen a substantial growth not only in film, but in a booming videotape industry.

Just a few weeks ago I received a letter from Holly Pritchard, a young woman who had been brought up in Raleigh, North Carolina. On a location trip to Charlotte, we managed to meet for about an hour to discuss her background and her goals. After graduation from Wake Forest University with a major in radio-TV-film and a minor in English, Holly gained some experience at the local television stations. But knowing that she had to move out eventually, and not particularly anxious to go up to New York, she discussed other opportunities with me. We settled on Atlanta, and a short time later the following letter arrived:

"Your advice was invaluable to me and you will be happy to know that I am making the move to Atlanta. I spent a productive week there knocking on the doors of production companies and TV stations. I was very fortunate to meet with a number of important people who encouraged me to move to Atlanta. I have no specific job, but several companies are interested in using me for free-lance work. . . .

After my hard week in Atlanta, I discovered for myself the importance of your advice: Go ahead and make the move. I am certain that 'making the move' will provide me with many exciting experiences in film."

Of course, Holly's story has no ending as yet. But somehow I am convinced that she will find her way into and up through a film career, whether she stays in Atlanta or eventually moves to a larger communications center. I have been in contact with students, graduates, and beginning filmmakers who are now working in Charlotte, Washington, Honolulu, Boston—and even in Glasgow, Scotland, and in Australia!

What I am trying to say is that those film

crews we met in Bogotá and the cameramen lined up across the top of the grandstand in Melbourne, and even the ones who were sitting next to us at lunch, were not necessarily based only on the East and West coasts of the United States. They come from just about anywhere today! And they all make films.

Thus, in discussing the career paths that you might follow, my major objective is to get you to expand your horizons when you think of the first stumbling steps toward a place in our industry. And in the same vein, trying to broaden the prospects available to you, I must ask another rhetorical question.

Is There Life Outside the Feature?

A few years back, I read with interest a *New York Times* interview with a woman I had known for many years. She had been a documentary filmmaker who was quite talented, sensitive, and dedicated. At the time of the article, she had just completed her first feature film, and opportunities for women in features being what they are (infinitesimal), the newspapers and magazine writers were having a field day with interviews about her coming film.

Paul Hartwick and Glenn Przyborski have worked out of Pittsburgh for the past ten years. Their only complaint is that "after all those years, 48 awards, and 176 clients, some agencies can't even pronounce our company name: Hartwick/Przyborski Productions!"

I was quite delighted for her, for I had watched her struggle to get to that point, and I felt a glow of reflected pride in seeing her reach a pinnacle in her career. Then I read a paragraph that turned me off and made me rather uncomfortable.

In recounting her background before this first "break" in her career, she mentioned her documentary experience, but in a rather harsh and denigrating series of statements. After all, she was now a feature director. The past was past; problems of dealing with "real" people, the headaches of location shooting, and the attempts to achieve reality when the camera was an unwanted intruder were all behind her now. Hollywood had called.

She is not alone. In seminar after seminar, and all across the country, I have heard some of my guest speakers laud the feature while relegating the rest of the film business to second-class citizenship. A writer in Houston once told the audience that he had begun his film career by doing scripts for business films and commercials. However, having just completed his first feature, he could admit that he had *only* done the other work out of necessity "to pay the rent."

It is probably not necessary to point out that there are thousands of filmmakers involved in feature work who are having difficulty paying their rent. Speak to most of the actors out in Los Angeles, if you don't believe me. On the other hand, there are thousands of us out there in the film world who have made a resounding success in the other areas of film work, and many of us wouldn't change our careers under any circumstances.

As you begin your career, it is important to realize that the *majority* of the people who work in our industry are *not* working in features, whether by necessity or by choice. Unfortunately, there is a perception among us that there is only one higher reality in the world of the motion picture, and that reality is the feature film. This is sheer nonsense.

Too often, especially for the beginner, this is the result of just not knowing what else exists out there in the world of film. Having been inundated with magazine articles, newspaper stories, professional college lectures, and the dilettantism of the thousands of film books mentioned earlier, the young filmmaker sees the features as the *only* shining beacon at the end of the boulder-strewn career path. In addition, the pragmatics of thinking about how we get a job is somehow pushed to the back of our minds. Allen Zwerdling, an old friend and the publisher of *Backstage,* put it well in one of his columns some time back:

"There are no employment placement bureaus in our field and there is a plethora of film graduates armed with diplomas without any knowledge of the practicalities of getting work. . . . The graduates head for Hollywood or New York and beat their heads against the walls trying to break into the areas of the business that can't keep the majority of the experienced professionals employed full time. . . .

It is really a heartbreaking situation, a perennial one, seeing hundreds of young people trained to work in the film field without the slightest knowledge of how to get their feet wet. The blame lies mostly with the colleges and universities teaching students how to appreciate the art of Brian De Palma, George Lucas, Steven Spielberg, Francis Ford Coppola, Roman Polanski, etc., but never hinting that Sedelmaier, Gomes, Horn, Sokolsky, Scott brothers are even around."

A great many more names come to mind as I think of the people who have "made it" in the "other areas" of film, some of them friends, others whose names I read over and over again or whose films I see and admire. Some may be familiar to you, others you may never have heard of. It is not important, for there are probably a thousand more that should be added to the list: Francis Thompson, Frederick Wiseman, Alan and Susan Raymond, Barbara Koppel, Pamela Yates, Hillary Harris, Alexander Hammid, Bob Giraldi, Lucy Jarvis, Steve Elliott, Jim Manilla, Charles Guggenheim, Elinor Bunin, Norman McLaren, Len Lye, Carmen D'Avino, John and Faith Hubley, John Grierson, Bill Jersey, plus a name that comes out of the past and the early days of the documentary, Robert Flaherty.

They all make films. They work happily (and many times with difficulty) in the world of the documentary, the commercial, the business film, television, animation and graphics, short subjects, music video, and in their own independent film companies, offering a variety of services to an expanding world of communications.

For those who have decided, however, that the theatrical world is the *only* goal worth considering—and that directing is the major objective—keep in mind that the path may never be a straight one. I will expand upon this theme in the next chapter, but I might well remind you now that directors don't generally begin as directors, nor are producers necessarily trained in the technology of film. Feature job categories are filled by a great many people who started out in commercials, in documentaries, and in professions far removed from the motion picture field. As I've mentioned, the key Hollywood and TV producers and financial moguls are generally lawyers and accountants. For example, Hugh Hudson (*Chariots of Fire* and *Greystoke*) started his career as a director of television commercials. So did Richard Lester. Other examples come to mind:

★ Howard Zieff, who now directs features, started his career as a still photographer with a very special eye for character roles.
★ Robert Benton began as a screenwriter.
★ John Sayles was a novelist prior to producing and directing his own films.
★ Noel Black was "discovered" after he had produced and directed a delightful short subject, *Skater Dater,* which went on to win an Academy Award.

We are also in an era where many actors pay their dues in summer stock, in short films, and on the stage, fighting their way up to stardom and then deciding that being a director might be more rewarding emotionally, if not financially.

Is there life outside the feature? Indeed, there is a vital and gratifying life for thousands of us, a vigorous and active and rewarding life in film, if you care to look. We travel—I have worked in sixty countries to date—and we meet some of the most interesting people in the world. And we work very, very hard. Just look a bit further than Hollywood, even if the film books and the film classes seem to ignore us altogether:

★ We work in documentaries and in social films.
★ We work in commercials and in the advertising agencies that develop the concepts.
★ We work in business films, training films, educational films, promotion films, and political films.
★ We work, these days, in video and all its component parts—in cable and in music video and in every area of communications, including video conferencing.
★ There are many of us in television, in the program areas, in newsfilm and newstape, in development, and even in the fields of sitcoms and television features.
★ We make films in clay animation, in collage and cel animation, in stop motion, and we paint on film.
★ We work in film sales and in syndication and distribution.
★ The people of your generation have been raised with computers, and the area of computer animation is filled with young people who have new ideas.
★ We are working at in-house communications divisions of major corporations, some of them with equipment so sophisticated that it puts the small television stations to shame.
★ There are filmmakers who produce the trailers for features, those condensed ministories that tempt us to part with another five bucks to see a failed work of art.
★ Some of us work in medical films, both for the professional audience and for the general public.
★ Some of us produce films for the government on a federal, state, or local level.

Which reminds me of a story. Some years back I received a call from a man who wanted to see me about a job. Since I have an open door and I love to give advice, however wrong I may turn out to be, I asked him to come up one quiet afternoon to tell me of his background and to bring a sample film, if he had one. He indicated that he had been a filmmaker for ten years, so I assumed he would certainly have a short film to show. He arrived on time and we chatted. He was about thirty-five and seemed to know the business well. The past ten years had been spent making films for the Central Intelligence Agency. I was fascinated. I didn't realize up to that time that the CIA even made motion pictures (rather naive thought, I suppose).

"Fine," I told him. "Now let's look at one of your film samples."

He twisted uncomfortably in his chair and finally said, "Well . . . uh . . . I don't have anything to show you."

I was a bit annoyed, since we had discussed the sample on the phone. "But you told me that you've made over fifty films during these past ten years."

"I know," he answered, "but they were all for the CIA and they're classified top secret. I can't show them to you!"

Yes, there is a film world out there with thousands of us struggling in areas that we sometimes forget about when we are studying the philosophy and history of film. And each of these areas represents either a career choice or a rung on the ladder to wherever it is we may be going.

Not only is there life outside the feature, but there is also a world outside that of the director. Look at the list on page 30. Each of the people involved is providing a service, a talent, or a profession to the making of films. Some may do it for the rest of their lives and love it. Others may move up or down or sideways in pursuit of a goal. For every director, there are thousands of us who edit, who do cinematography, writing, production, music, makeup, set design, graphics, and all the preproduction and postproduction work that brings a finished motion picture to the screen, be it the large screen of Radio City Music Hall in New York or the small screen of a television set placed in a classroom in Paradox, Colorado. Film is a collaborative effort, and it takes a lot of us to make it work.

The trick in moving up the ladder—no matter what your eventual goal—is to know when to make the move and how to take advantage of that move. The trick is to find work, to become active in the industry no matter what your job path, no matter which part of the industry opens its doors to you. The feature? Possibly, but

rarely. Why not look more carefully at some of the *other* opportunities?

Commercials and Advertising: The Industry Twins

"Frankly, I would rather my students go out and drive a cab than make commercials!"

—FILM SCHOOL INSTRUCTOR

Unfortunately, that's exactly what a large number of film school graduates and beginners in our field end up doing! For if there is a conception of the bottom rung of the career ladder in the minds of most film school professors and their students, it is television commercial production.

It is not my function to destroy a dream, for I have heard that dream described to me too often by young filmmakers. Fueled by the hype of an industry, frequently nurtured through four years of film school plus another year for a masters degree, the goal takes one of several forms, all based on role models:

★ the European "auteur," along with critical acclaim from an adoring public.
★ the Lucas-Spielberg-Coppola-Scorsese Hollywood success story following graduation.
★ the De Palma-Corman-Sayles "I'll do it my own way" school of filmmaking.

Of course, for some the dream is attainable, and the feature film becomes the beginning, the middle, and sometimes the end of a career. Occasionally a nod is also given to the documentary, for it represents to the beginner the perfect medium in which to communicate ideas and to help change the thinking of the world.

I am well aware of the fact that Terence Malick and Paul Schrader came out of the American Film Institute program. I have also read with interest articles in esoteric film magazines about Lucas, as well as other USC grads like John Carpenter and Randal Kleiser, or the recent NYU success stories of Coen, Jarmusch, and Seidelman.

And if we are to look for the perfect combination of serendipity, timing, pure luck, hard work, and talent, the sale of the screenplay of *Under the Volcano* to John Huston must surely be a prime example. Guy Gallo, a teaching assistant for an underground lecture course in American film history, had written a screenplay of Malcolm Lowry's novel two years before, while still a graduate student at Yale Drama School.

Through the recommendation of a professor at the school (remember the role of contacts?), Huston heard about the screenplay. Normally, in "real life," Huston would have heard about it, nodded about how "nice" it was, or ignored it completely, and Gallo would have continued to teach. But who ever said that film is real life? In this particular case, it turns out that Huston had been wanting to do the book as a film for over *two decades* but had never been able to find a way to translate the book to the screen. He took an option on the script and the film was produced. In a later interview, Gallo admitted that film school can teach a certain amount of the filmmaking craft, then added, "But it helps to be naturally stubborn. And to have a fairy godmother!"

Thus, with stories like these constantly taking up the pages of newspapers and film magazines, it is no wonder that the dream is constantly dangled before the young film person. And with the strong emphasis of their training, based almost entirely upon the writing and production of features, and to a lesser extent the documentary film, it is no wonder that there is an obvious disdain for the commercial film world, as well as an almost total disinterest in the acquisition of the technical knowledge so necessary for almost any type of film or video production. One writer called it "aesthetic elitism," and I think the term is most appropriate.

For the majority of graduate film students, as well as for people who have begun to pay their dues on the lower levels of our industry, this rejection of the more "commercial" areas of film and tape has resulted in a sudden, startling realization that most of our talented people are either unemployed or struggling desperately in the free-lance market to build a reputation and thus a career.

A part of the blame, of course, is due to the fact that we just have too many people looking for the available jobs. Look, for example, at the number of waiters and waitresses in Hollywood restaurants who are all trained as actors, and who are all waiting for "the big break." The unions remain tightly closed because so many of their people are not working at any given time. Dick Sylbert's estimate (page 71) that 111 of 135 California designers are out of work at any given time is matched by the cinematographers, the editors, script supervisors, and most of the other guilds and unions in the field. I do admit, then, that there are a great many of us looking for too few jobs, and I can also add that ours is a terribly incestuous business, in which a few of the same people get most of the work.

But in the very earliest stages of a career, a part of the problem lies in *setting your sights too narrowly*. If you come into our business with the firm opinion that the feature is the end-all (and one done with total independence and artistic freedom at that), and if you agree with the quotation at the beginning of this section, if film school was an "art" school instead of a place to get a grounding in the pragmatics and the technology of film, and if you look with contempt and loathing at all those "commercial" filmmakers, there is a good possibility that you might well be driving the next taxicab that I take to the airport on my way to a location in Fish Haven, Iowa.

It is interesting to note that there have been some grudging admissions of change, especially from the communications schools. One large eastern college has just begun to think of adding music video to its curriculum, now that it seems to have become a part of the business (and is not too terribly commercial). While regretting their change in attitude, the faculties admit that such change is necessary if they are to promise more to the graduates than a grounding in film history and a record of unemployment.

Those of us who have always been proud of being the pragmatists in our industry continue to preach that it is more important to get good, solid, on-the-job experience on any set in any city or location than to be the best informed film history student on the works of Eisenstein or Hitchcock or Bergman. The reasons are quite simple, if you will only listen to us:

★ You are not locked in to one job, one path, one part of the industry.

★ No one in this insane business ever knows where a career path will end. Just look at the examples of some of the people who were interviewed for this book! I read the other day that Sherry Lansing began her career as a *math teacher*!

★ It is important to keep working, to keep aware of the industry changes and the technological advances. It's a tough thing to do when you're not working while holding out for art film production.

★ In just being there, your list of contacts will grow. The workers in our industry are like gypsies (or "itinerant workers," as director Hal Cooper once described them to me). We move from one place to another, from one part of our industry to another.

Commercial directors end up as feature directors. Agency producers leave to join film production houses. Feature directors move into music video. Talented documentary filmmakers like the Maysles brothers have made an impact on the commercial world. Other producers of documentaries like Claudia Weill have opened up new markets by making their first features. Screenplays seem to come from everywhere, and some of them actually get produced.

The important thing, however, is that our most successful people make it a point to *keep active* in the field, denigrating nothing and accepting the fact that there are areas of our business that differ from their eventual dreams and aspirations. Whatever they are doing at the moment, *all of them* are producing films or making videotapes, along with the concomitant complexities of production, with the excitement of the medium, with its rewards, its frustrations, and sometimes with the recognition that goes with it all.

There has been a change in attitude toward the television commercial in one other important area. Over the past twenty years or so, the postwar generation has grown up and become old enough to join the film industry. Spawned on a steady diet of commercials that filled every small gap in television programming, there has been an inherent acceptance by this group of the ten-, the twenty-, and the thirty-second spot as a film form with its own definition of "art." And because of the techniques that have been developed and exploited by the television commercial, we have seen some remarkable changes in other areas of film production from the documentary

to the training film to the feature. For a generation brought up on the commercial's fast-moving message, a slow-paced feature film will be rejected out of hand. I have always contended that this young generation of audiences can see and digest a subliminal flow of quick-cut images much more quickly than their parents, because they were weaned on stories that had to be told in sixty seconds, later to be condensed to thirty seconds when air time became more expensive, and now squeezed even further into ten-second spots, with storyline, music, actors, optical effects, product recognition, and, above all else, a message!

For the people who work in the field of television commercials, the experience, the training, and the discipline of having to tell the story in so short a time is something that stands them all in good stead when they move into other areas of film. Where the average film school sample is generally much too long and repetitious, the commercial barely has time to deliver its meaning, much less make a viewer run out and actually buy the product or take action through the message. It is good training for the filmmaker, no matter what the eventual goal. And it might also surprise some people to learn that producers, directors, writers, and owners of their own independent companies sometimes decide to *stay* right in the commercials field to make their own superb reputations (and an awful lot of money) in the world of the ten-, twenty-, and thirty-second spot!

Though no one story is typical of any other, here in the field of commercials, as well as in the rest of the film industry, Bill Fertik might be

taken as a success story that follows an almost perfect path. Known both for his commercial work and for his production of documentary films, Bill is a producer/director/writer who won an Academy Award in 1974 for his lovely film *Bolero,* funded by the National Endowment for the Arts.

Currently he is head of his own company, with a staff of six people, and his original idea was to become an actor, but:

"My mother threatened to kill me if I became an actor. . . ."

He studied writing at Syracuse University, took his masters in film writing at NYU with the late Haig Manoogian, a man who encouraged a great many young filmmakers to go on for careers in the field:

"Marty Scorsese was in my class, and even while I was in school, I was writing screenplays for television segments on Ben Gazzara's *Run for Your Life* and the show *I Spy.* At the same time, I was writing screenplays that were being optioned by the majors—until they found out I was only eighteen years old, and suddenly lost interest!"

While still in college, Bill worked for a small production company and then went to Grey Advertising as a producer/writer. Did he like it?

"I *hated it!* But I got my big break there while I was producing a commercial for Duz. The cameraman was Mike Elliott, who cofounded

EUE Productions, and he was one of the stars of the field. On the set, he had put the camera into position and I walked over and said, 'You have the camera in the wrong place!' "

Mike looked at him, as you might imagine that *any* well-known cameraman might stare at a young agency producer who had told him to move the camera.

"Oh, yeah?" Elliott snarled. "Then you move the camera and show me."

Bill moved it, the shot was taken, and the next day they saw the dailies. Elliott said nothing. But at two A.M. that morning, he telephoned Bill and said, "Fertik, you want to get rich? Come sign with me!" He had, indeed, liked where the camera had been moved, even by a twenty-two-year-old.

"I was twenty-wo, I looked fifteen, I weighed 148 pounds, and I grew a mustache to look older. When I went out to Hollywood with Mike, they wouldn't let me in the stages at Burbank. I looked like some kid who was trying to sneak in!"

Interestingly enough, Bill Fertik never studied camera technique, which I suppose is the major reason for going on this way. It is another classic example of how one of the best-known people in our field managed to move up the ladder in his own way, fully realizing that in another situation on another stage, a Mike Elliott might well have thrown someone like Bill Fertik right out into the street! The timing was right. It has to be right.

Bill Fertik (center) on location in Israel. The field of the television commercial has developed its own "stars" of production.

"I suppose the camera was a natural talent. I had a Brownie when I was a kid and I took pictures all the time and I developed and printed them myself. My grandfather was a primitive painter, my father was a trained commercial artist who took me to Sheepshead Bay in Brooklyn on weekends, where we both painted. My mother was an English teacher who insisted that I write every day, which I still do. . . ."

The question, then, was how to put the background together where everything would help. Film obviously was the answer.

"At first I packaged small films that no one else wanted to do. I did entire music films for between $7,000 and $15,000 each. I shot them, edited them, did the art work on an animation stand, the music, the writing. Everything. And I shot at as low a ratio as possible because film stock and developing are expensive."

As for advice to young beginners, Bill Fertik suggests much the same routes that most of us take. For the potential cameraman, the camera supply house, packing orders at practically no pay, learning about cameras with an eye to eventually taking the assistant camera test:

"We get a hundred resumes a month! I find that most people are looking at film for the wrong reasons. They're star struck. Glamour is only there for a couple of minutes a day. The rest is hard work! You can spot the ones who genuinely like film."

Once you get the job, Bill offers a piece of advice that might well go in the section of this book dedicated to production problems. Never trust your memory!

"Write it down. Have lots of pencils and lots of paper . . . and I don't mean little scraps. Carry your pad with you and never put it down. One mistake can cost $30,000. Suppose you don't write down the flight number and you get it wrong . . . you can lose an absolute fortune!"

From the point of view of the client, we get still another feeling about the television commercial. Bill Early, manager of TV/film services at Armstrong World Industries, straddles two worlds in his work at the company. Many of his commercial jobs for local dealers are produced right in house both on film and on tape. For the national spots for Armstrong, however, he utilizes an advertising agency with its armament of writers, art directors, and account supervisors. Thus, he sees this world from both ends. He calls it a "copycat" business:

"It is not uncommon today to see commercials that cost upward of $80,000 to $100,000 and more. Until this year, virtually all soft drink commercials and more of the fast junk-food commercials had large casts of beautiful young people who were singers and dancers . . . and all the commercials looked like Broadway productions. They all looked so much alike that it was difficult to remember which was Mc-Donald's and which was Burger King. Most of them were dreadfully wasteful and imitative of

something good that had been done before. Someone does something special that works, and a thousand other creative geniuses follow with something just like it. . . ."

Unfortunately this is true, and costs have been rising as a result. By the mid-1980s the average cost of producing a commercial from storyboard to air was *$193,000*! But these high budgets might well be a blessing in their own way for the filmmaker who is just starting out.

The mere fact that the industry is competitive, the very nature of its "copycat" creativity, opens up new doors for those who are just beginning:

★ The commercials field is aware of every invention, every new idea, every piece of new equipment in order to be the first to use it—or to copy its use if they are not the first. The Steadicam, new helicopter technology, computer graphics, new optical effects, and new videotape editing techniques are generally used *first* in the production of commercials.
★ Escalating budgets make the use of new techniques practical and available. Where the average budget of the business film has only moved up to between $75,000 and $100,000 for a twenty-minute production, commercials have long since passed that figure for only twenty seconds.

I remember that this was the case even twenty-five years ago, when we were producing travel films for a major international airline. At that time they paid us $60,000 to travel a full crew to the South Pacific, spend four weeks there filming the beauties of the region (always remembering to "shoot above the garbage," as my cameraman used to comment), and then finish the twenty-eight-minute subject back in New York. We did the job with a crew of four and even made a small profit. Following our location shooting, a plane arrived carrying the crew from a production house that was to make a sixty-second spot for the same airline—and about the same island. Fourteen people disembarked from the plane, the job took two weeks, and the price paid to the commercial producer was equal to our budget for the twenty-eight-minute film. Which brings up some other points about commercials, if we are to be realistic:

★ The locations for commercial shooting have expanded to include the world.

Bill Early wryly says that it's another reason that the costs have skyrocketed:

"Some of the spoiled children of this business have very expensive tastes in travel. Some writers tend to think of great summertime ideas in midwinter (and vice versa). Some producers, star directors, talent, account men, and art directors can't make themselves comfortable anywhere but in California, and at accommodations no less than the Beverly Wilshire Hotel or the Bel-Air."

How, then, is *this* an advantage to the young filmmaker? I think the answer is obvious.

Since location shooting has its own problems, its own techniques, its own area of film experience, just being on location—whether it's Tallulah Park, Georgia, or Paris, France—can give you a new view of film and help to expedite your own location shooting in years to come.

If you've read the preceding carefully, you have probably noticed yet another comment that is particular to the production of television commercials. There are an awful lot of people involved! The entire job market is, in a sense, controlled, directed, and creatively supervised by the advertising agency. For some filmmakers unable to work in a mutually collaborative effort, this can be a severe "turnoff." At the risk of repeating myself, I am again reminded of the quote that is used over and over in the film world: "If you see two people gathered around a Steenbeck or a Moviola, they're probably cutting a feature. If you see *twelve* people gathered around, they're cutting a ten-second spot!"

Agency executives and commercial film producers agree with the assessment. An old friend of mine—found again after many lost years wandering in the film field—is Joe Shaw, senior vice-president and director of TV commercial production services at Dancer Fitzgerald Sample, one of the largest of America's advertising agencies:

"Being an agency producer is like being in a rowboat with six people and trying to get them all to row in the same direction at the same time!"

Joe Shaw and I talked about "old times" one

afternoon, for I had known him many years ago when he was a cameraman in the film and television industry. Originally he got his start in the mail room at the American Broadcasting Company, where he described himself as "the fastest collator in the place." Alongside Joe in those days was Rod MacLeish, who did the job of pulling news stories off the Teletype machines. Now, as senior vice-president at the agency, Joe meets many young people who come there for jobs in commercial production:

"A lot of people come here and want to be commercial producers. I ask them if they want to be *filmmakers* or agency producers. And I try to make them understand that there are a lot of hands that produce a TV commercial, in addition to the people at the production company: the art director, the copywriter, the client advertising manager, the account supervisor, and the producer who works at our agency. . . ."

In addition to that, before the commercial even goes into production, it has to be accepted and approved by the continuity people at the three networks, the client's legal staff, and by the agency lawyers!

Nevertheless, the commercial world—both at the advertising agencies and in the production companies—has boomed, and changing technologies have been noted very quickly:

★ Most large agencies now have their own videotape facilities, some of them the equal of anything the networks can offer. Young people moving up in the job market have a superb opportunity to get hands-on experience doing auditions, test tapes, optical effects, and teleconferencing.

The industry has also grown and changed so much in the past twenty years that it has begun to develop its own "star" system of people who not only command high fees, but have begun to move back and forth into music video, features, and their own high-budget commercials. And because of the competitive nature of the marketplace, hungry, new, eager, talented filmmakers and production people continue to enter the field and make their marks quickly, sometimes fading just as quickly as others take their places. It is not the most stable of worlds, and it makes for an inordinate amount of insecurity on the staffs of large agencies. On top of that is the fact that some clients change agencies with the frequency of moves in a backgammon game. Though loyalty does exist on the client level, it is not one of advertising's strong suits, and with the loss of a big client we also find the shaking out of jobs.

Added to all of this is the need to understand that the product is "king"; countless hours of studio time can be spent just in getting the right highlight on a glass of beer. One unfortunate model began to lose her hair after doing countless takes for a shampoo commercial. My friend Bill Early has put it succinctly in an oil painting that he did, and it now hangs in his office at Armstrong. It shows a large set, filled with all the production people who make up the crew—director, script supervisor, client seated in a director's chair, lighting and grip crew, prop people and camera crew, and there, on a cyclorama, sitting in all its glory, is a small can of "the product" about to be photographed!

I remember directing a toothpaste commercial for a large agency. We finished the bulk of the shooting by three in the afternoon, not at all bad, I thought. Then we spent *eight more hours* filming the toothpaste being squeezed from the tube, because the art director didn't think that the little tip at the edge of the toothpaste would look good on film. So I can understand why much of the field is a "turnoff" to film school graduates who have joined a production company in the hope of making social documentaries! But if this is a discussion of changes, let me comment on two more that might well help the young film person:

★ For a long time the agency art director was the prime mover of the television commercial—until the agencies found out that they frequently were not versed in on-line production problems. Storyboards didn't always work out the way they had been envisioned. This has opened up still more opportunities for production-trained people to take charge.
★ Of all the areas that have opened some opportunities for women, the advertising agencies have probably led the field.

The motion picture industry has not been notably effective in providing top jobs for the talented women who are trained, capable, and ready to work hard. For each "example" that we read about in the newspapers, there are twenty thousand more who cannot climb past the job of production assistant or editor. In my own union, Directors Guild of America, only 5 percent of the members are women. Where once Sherry Lansing was the one exception always quoted to us when we complained about the lack of women in charge of production, even she has left to form Jaffe/Lansing Productions and now *all* Hollywood production moguls are *men*.

Advertising, on the other hand, has opened its doors much more widely by comparison. I will not write of it as a perfect and ideal panacea, for many areas of discrimination still exist. Since the clients of the agencies are corporate world executives, it is still a business domain filled with "old boy" networks, and women who have struck out on their own have found it difficult to break the country-club, golfing Sunday chauvinism.

At first, though, the jobs of producers, art directors, and copywriters opened up to women in the areas of products specially devoted to the female consumer. But the lines have blurred in past years, and women are now found on every level of agency production and through the entire product line. The executive suites have also opened somewhat, and we now find vice-presidents of production, copy, and even legal clearance. In addition, within the last ten years or so, we have begun to see women starting their own agencies.

The agency/commercial world has its own hype, just as the rest of our business has, and some would have you believe that the advertising world is perfect. There has been some progress, to be sure, but as one woman who is the head of her own agency stated, "You still have to be twice as smart to succeed as a woman in advertising."

And if we investigate the "star" system I mentioned earlier, you'll find (by accident, of course) that all of the top directors, the ones who command from $2,000 to $7,500 per day, are men!

Finally, let me cover another area of interest to those beginning a career in this field. Changes in commercial production have also been seen in its growth out of New York and Los Angeles. With costs rising so rapidly, and with filmmakers beginning to produce their work all across the country, television commercials are now a part of the industry in Miami, Dallas, Chicago, Omaha, and all the other cities that I've listed in an earlier chapter. We can find them everywhere. Their growth has also been fueled by the inability of local producers and agencies to pay the sums demanded by film and tape "stars" on the two coasts.

In the smaller markets, *ingenuity* must take the place of money. Bill Early uses the example of the $200,000 commercial that calls for a sidewalk cafe in Rome, as a chorus of singing waiters delivers a tray of Tony's Pizza. On the other hand, a tight close-up of a luscious piece of pizza backlit to show the steam rising as a hand removes it from the tray and feeds it to the camera might be even more effective, not to say more reasonable to produce, and I must repeat that money does not equal creativity.

On the lower end of the budget, and out of the major production areas, excellent work is being done by filmmakers and videotape pro-

ducers, all of them making samples with which they expand their business or move to another, larger market. It is a good training ground on which to try out innovative ideas without the flood of money that floats productions in major cities (not always with the most effective results).

For a young filmmaker faced with constant production problems, having to answer the almost hourly questions that crop up in preproduction, production, and postproduction, the commercial gives good, practical experience. And this, after all, is what the essence of the film industry is all about—be it feature or training film or television spot. In a lecture about broadcast advertising at Temple University, Bill Early posed some of those questions, and they might well be considered for *any* film or tape production in which you are involved:

★ Do we really need a set, or could we shoot it on location?
★ Do we really need original music, or could we do as well with stock music?
★ Or no music?
★ Or sound effects?
★ Or a single instrument?
★ Or silence?

Thinking about these things can lead to a great and different idea.

We live, we have grown up, in a world of advertising, and there is no way to avoid it. Allen Zwerdling quoted an ad he had read in a copy of the Hollywood, Florida, *Mirror,* and it probably best describes our society today, all of it re-

flected in a booming television commercials industry, peopled by a generation who have grown up and who live comfortably with it:

"Why is it a person wakes up in the morning after sleeping under an advertised blanket on an advertised mattress and pulls off advertised pajamas, takes a bath in an advertised tub, washes with an advertised soap, puts on advertised clothes, sits down to a breakfast of advertised coffee and cereal, and puts on an advertised coat, rides to the office in an advertised car, writes with an advertised pencil . . . then refuses to advertise, saying advertising doesn't pay; and later, when business isn't good enough to advertise . . . advertises it for sale!"

Many of our brothers and sisters have found a way to combine the particularly American phenomenon of advertising with their burgeoning film careers. The market exists, as we all are aware, and it is changing and it is growing. If the filmmaker can accept the severe limitations and the very special requirements put upon his or her work by the structures of the very special commercials business, then this is also a field worth considering in your growth and in your movement through the film field.

If you have already considered pursuing the field of television commercials, either with an advertising agency or with a production company, then I send you on your way with a very pragmatic quote:

"When Willie Sutton, the bank robber of the thirties, was apprehended, one of the reporters asked him why he robbed banks. Willie answered, "Because that's where the money is!"

If, on the other hand, you are still somewhat in doubt, if this long chapter has not convinced you that the field might be worth pursuing, even if no one says you have to stay in it forever, I leave *you* with a paraphrase from a very well known television commercial: "Try it! You may like it!"

The Sponsored Film: Career Path Stepchild

Bear with me, if you will. Read the following list quite carefully. In projecting *your own* film career path and dream of the future, are there any experiences that *you* might like to duplicate?

★ I love to travel. I have worked on films in over *sixty* countries on every continent in the world. I have made four trips to Australia, eight to Asia, over fifty to Europe, and twenty or more to South America. In the United States, I have unfortunately missed three states in my travels (Idaho, South Dakota, and North Dakota).

★ As a part of those travels, I have filmed the Rio Carnival in Brazil, the Lincoln Heritage Trail, the Festival of Diwali in India, the Melbourne Cup in Australia, the river festivals in Kyoto, Japan, and Indian Celebrations in Peru, Ecuador, and Colombia.

★ I have a curiosity about how people work and live. I have filmed in coal mines, atop bridges that were being built. I have gone through jet pilot's school (and failed because I have no depth perception!), and I have worked right alongside farmers as they fertilized their crops and as they harvested wheat and corn in the Midwest. I have lived and worked with citrus growers in the West and with the people who make steel, aluminum, automobiles, and electronics.

★ I have worked with some of the most interesting people in business, entertainment, politics, and social programs: ex-Hitler armaments minister Albert Speer, ex-actor Ronald Reagan, Bernie Cornfeld, Chester Morris, Dorothy Gish, and the presidents and CEOs of some of America's largest conglomerates (as well as the unsung who make those corporations work).

★ I have a social conscience and I like to think that my films may, in some way, help to make this a better place in which we all can live. I have worked in the worst of slums in Asia and in South America, as well as here in my own country. My films for hospitals and social welfare agencies have helped to raise millions of dollars, and my own Academy Award nominee on the subject of

Parkinsonism and chronic disease collected over six million dollars that helped build the new wing of St. Barnabas Hospital in the Bronx. Some films have helped to find parents for foster children, others have taught breast-feeding values to Indian women in South America, and others have raised money for foundations that support the blind, the deaf, and other handicapped groups.

★ I am not particularly a sports enthusiast. This comes after too many young years as a sportscaster on radio, growing more and more disenchanted as the seasons progressed. Nonetheless, as a filmmaker I have worked on documentaries about soccer, skydiving, cliff diving, ta-kroh, Thai boxing, archery, surfing, swimming, track, baseball, and scuba diving. I have even produced a documentary about a sport that is always described as "like watching the grass grow"—the America's Cup.

★ I used to be a "white knuckle" flyer. But now, having logged over three million miles in the air, I love to fly. I have flown in helicopters, usually piloted by war veterans who know how to take a film crew down below tree level as we snake along a river. Filmmaking has put me in small planes to fly down below the canyon level at Rainbow Bridge, and I have been in flying boats, training jets, in the cockpits of DC-8s, 747s, and single-engine, high-wing general aircraft.

★ I am basically a coward. I do not like trouble. I have learned on my film jobs that you have to smile a lot to talk people out of either maiming or killing you on the spot. However, everything creates a marvelous story for film classes when I return. And while these incidents happen, I convince myself that *it is really happening to someone else,* not me. It helps me to survive. I have filmed in Vietnam during the war, and have been arrested in Cambodia (just managing to get out of the country on the only DC-3 that came into Siem Reap and landed on a strip cut out of the middle of a rice paddy).

I have been in an airplane whose engine conked out while still in the air— and we only had *one* engine. Luckily we were over the airport at Buenos Aires! I have had a howling mob throw rocks at our film crew in Pakistan and have had to talk two vicious drunks out of attacking our cameraman in Germany because they resented our photographing their beer joint, and I smiled a lot as a man with a loaded .45 automatic pistol pointed it at me and told our crew to get out of a slum in Ecuador. (Which, of course, we did!)

I can probably think of more. Much more. But my objective is not to give you a resume or to boast that I have more stories than you do. The point I really want to make—what everything listed above has in common—is that *every one was a sponsored film!* Every one of those motion picture projects—every one in which I could involve myself with life-styles that were instructive, exciting, adventurous, or fun, and probably a hundred more, were paid for by a corporation, a government, a foundation, or a national or international social welfare agency!

I hope that the list will open your eyes to the potential waiting for young filmmakers who want a life-style that includes travel, meeting people, and adventure (some of it bland, some of it more threatening). Somehow along the way, in our reading, in our discussions, in our film school curricula, and even in our thinking about our careers, the sponsored film seems to become a stepchild. Whether it is because we used to call it the "industrial film," bringing to mind images of factory assembly lines, or because of the awful classroom sessions in grade school, when we saw films that featured the company president or the chairman sitting behind a desk and sonorously preaching at us about the production of plastic clothespins, a career in the sponsored film industry was frequently underestimated. Even to this day it is equated with audiences looking up at the reel to see how much time is left to sleep undisturbed.

It would be simple merely to say that the sponsored film is changing rapidly. Whether we call it an industrial film, a corporate film, or by its broader, more accurate term of "sponsored," which denotes the film has been paid for by someone other than the filmmaker, it is a form that has had potential for innovation and film creativity from its inception. Certainly it is changing—and it is offering still more opportunities, as I shall discuss later on. But Robert Flaherty's *Louisiana Story* was a sponsored film (Standard Oil). The remarkable and entertaining (a word we seldom use with sponsored films) *To Be Alive,* presented on three screens at the New York World's Fair and produced by Francis Thompson and Alexander Hammid, was also a sponsored film (Johnson's Wax). In fact, *all* films presented at exhibitions and world's fairs are sponsored—whether by governments or corporations or foundations. They are paid for by someone else, and the filmmaker is hired specifically to do that production—and, in many cases, is paid quite handsomely for it.

My own films, as well as those of others who have made a living in this world, are a catalog of companies and organizations that have decided to communicate a message to an audience, many times a totally non-commercial message, by paying for a film production in some of the most interesting places around the globe:

★ a film on sports around the world (Pepsi-Cola)
★ two documentaries about Thailand (Eastman Kodak)
★ *Celebration,* with Lorne Greene, about the life stages in various societies on six continents (Bissell)
★ a film on rural health care and breast-feeding/immunology, shot in Ecuador (Pan American Health Organization)
★ travel films in fifty countries (Alitalia, Pan Am, Viasa, Varig, Qantas)

If you but look at the list of categories for the American Film Festival (pages 75–76), you begin to see the vast scope of this most remarkable field. Corporate image, sales training, travel, agriculture, fund-raising and social documentaries, education, guidance, environment, art and dance, life-style, and even pure experimentation and the use of new technology such as IMAX are all a part of this world.

There has been an almost unnoticed change that has taken place in this area of film. Though women and minorities are still fighting their way to the top echelons of the corporate executive world (in spite of what the corporations would like us to believe), many of these same companies have begun to accept filmmakers who are not white males. Especially for women, opportunities for producing corporate films have opened up tremendously in the past ten years, both in the area of outside production and as a part of in-house corporate video and film. Women are forming their own companies; some are equal partners with men, others have made their marks as directors, editors, producers, and writers, all as a part of the production teams that work to communicate corporate ideas.

Within the corporation itself, the world has opened up for people who are still gathering the experience that will help them move ahead in the world of film/tape. At companies like American Express, Avon, Sears, Standard Oil, American Can, Armstrong World Industries, Dow Chemical, and hundreds of others, both in the blue chip and the small company category, there has been a remarkable explosion of business communications, especially in the area of videotape.

★ The Bell System, before its breakup, had one of the most sophisticated tape production and video network systems in the country.

★ Avon Products produces and sends monthly video messages to 500,000 sales reps across the country and boasts the largest corporate video network (18,000 VHS machines!) in the corporate world. They project future in-house production will expand to between *seventy and one hundred shows* a year!

★ American Express uses an in-house division to send its messages to 225 offices around the world, to thousands of employees, to its stockholders, vendors, and prospective customers.

In addition, all of this has meant a substantial growth in the business potential of production houses, in postproduction facilities in tape and film, and in the free-lance market.

★ Teleconferencing and interactive programming has also become a tool for the corporations.

Here is yet another area in which you can choose your location from almost anywhere in the country. Production companies exist everywhere. The corporations themselves, many of them in outlying areas of the United States, also provide a training ground, a way to expand your film knowledge and craft, and an excellent opportunity to produce your sample films, *all of them paid for by the company for which you work.*

It doesn't matter whether you are a part of the field in a production company or in an independent area, whether you are employed by a corporation, a foundation, a social welfare agency, or a government organization: they *all* use film, they *all* use tape. They frequently have equipment that is more "state of the art" than the networks. I remember being astonished at the audiovisual technology at Standard Oil and Sears in Chicago when I compared it with the rather dingy, seedy, almost antiquated studios of a major network affiliate in the same city!

On the other hand, some companies are just expanding, and their audiovisual people learn very quickly to do major productions with minor facilities and equipment. These corporations and organizations are also good training

Teleconferencing is being accepted by more and more corporations as a means of letting executives speak to one another. This is a Video Nine conference from their studios at KETC in St. Louis, beamed to twenty-five U.S. cities for the Edward S. Jones Company.

grounds for people who want to learn, to become more innovative, and then to move on, having learned all they can from the experience. And as new technologies are accepted by the companies and the audiovisual departments are expanded as a result, the job market naturally increases. Producers, writers, directors, editors, and video technicians all find that the experience is there to be had. And again, remember, if you will, no one tells you that you have to stay there until your pension becomes due and they ease you out with a farewell dinner and a gold watch at the age of fifty-five!

There is one area of change that I have but touched on, and upon which I would like to expand. Though we have always had our innovative and experimental filmmakers in the sponsored film—Len Lye, Carmen D'Avino, Hillary Harris, Wheaton Galentine, Charles Guggenheim, Francis Thompson—there were times when their new film styles were not too easily accepted by the stodgy corporate world. The usual comment was, "Well, *I* understand it, of course, but will the audience understand it?" Or the words given to the producer at the beginning might have been, "I want something different, but not *too* different!"

It was the reason that we saw film after boring film that looked the same, had the same stentorian tones of the baritone narrator (always men, by the way) and the constant repetition of medium long shots.

Interestingly enough, even in those days there were innovators who fought hard to change the look of the business film. It was not easy. In some instances it is still not a simple thing to convince a committee that a film would be boring if we followed their dictates. We are still, in some areas, making the "industrial" film, and many of our jobs include the filming of client assembly lines, those repetitive, computerized, impersonal production facilities of which they are justly proud. But here is where the filmmaker begins to use his or her ingenuity. For even in machines, there have been filmmakers who have gone past the roar of the lathes and presses, the repetition of the product being manufactured, to show the sponsors *and* the audience that there is another way to see, if we care to look more closely.

Cameramen like Bernie Hirschenson, Michael Livesey, and Jon Fauer have brought an "eye" to the world of the business film, and many sponsored films (including some by the author) have been screened before audiences at the Museum of Modern Art and other museums around the world. A most remarkable film produced in Holland entitled *Glass* was one such film, and it played theaters across the country as a short subject, delighting audiences who were never really aware that this was a sponsored film.

Wheaton Galentine's *Treadle and Bobbin* took place entirely within the confines of *one* Singer sewing machine. And just recently, on a trip down to South Carolina, Jon Fauer spent half a day with just one spinning machine at a cotton mill; the final photography, all of it abstract, was cut to an organ prelude and is a moving work of art.

In each film, no matter what the subject matter, there is a learning experience for the eager young filmmaker: about people, about how to see differently, about color, about form, about rhythm, and about how the technology can work to make the picture on the screen come to life for an audience.

The sponsors of these films have undergone remarkable changes in their thinking and in their acceptance of new forms and unusual film language; they also have become aware of the fact that you can't bore an audience for long and have them accept your message or even feel kindly toward what it is you are trying to say.

Rather than rejecting the new forms—the graphic developments, the extreme close-up instead of the long shot, the effect of collage and painting on film—and the use of unusual locations in place of sterile re-creations in the studio or the office of the chairman, corporations and other sponsors are actually *encouraging* innovation. In my own career, I have found nothing but approbation from my own clients when I have suggested new techniques and new technologies. The experimental film of yesterday has become the film form of today in the sponsored film—and young filmmakers would be wise to take note of it.

There is a market for jobs, a growing market, mostly because there is a need to communicate on large and small screens as never before. Mark Chernichaw, executive producer of audiovisual communications at Avon, commented in an interview, "We're living in a print-illiterate society. Most people want their information spoon-fed. So instead of the memo in the mail, which two out of ten people will read, everybody's interested in electronic media."

And an old friend, Ed Schultz, a partner (with Carol Hale) in New York's Cinemakers, Inc., articulates this from the point of view of the filmmaker:

"In the sponsored world, everyone is trying to tell a story to an audience or to communicate a message—whether to the public, to employees, or to their executives. We use contemporary visual language to articulate that message for them. We're the Cyrano de Bergeracs of the corporate world!"

MAKING IT UP THE LADDER

After the Entry Level, Another Entry Level?

"In this business, every pebble you drop makes waves that can overturn a chariot. You never know when the guy you were mean to today turns out to be your boss tomorrow. . . ."

—SUZANNE JASPER

While I was still in college, I thought that I might want a career in the theater, though I was an accounting major and was rudely interrupted in my schooling by a large world war. As a seventeen-year-old, my experience was limited to several leading roles in camp musicals and a part-time job at the Shubert chain of legitimate theaters in New York checking coats and selling the watered-down orangeade at intermission. The advantages, aside from making all of ten dollars a week, were being close to the theater and all its glamour, and seeing my favorite shows over and over again, perched on the steps of the mezzanine. I think I saw *Pal Joey* (with Gene Kelly) one hundred forty-one times, *Best Foot Forward* (with June Allyson and Nancy Walker) one hundred seven times, and *DuBarry Was a Lady* (with Ethel Merman) only eighty-four times.

The disadvantages were that I never saw the end of the first or second acts, since I had to leave the theater before intermission to haul the orangeade six blocks down Eighth Avenue, and I had to get to the check room before the show ended. In addition, the orangeade that slopped over the carrier each night managed to turn my raincoat bottom into a solid, congealed wallboard. But—I was in (or near) the *theater*. And I was only seventeen.

I was reminded of all this while reading a short biography of Dustin Hoffman. Somehow, we all get the impression that the stars in our business, be they actors or directors, just somehow "got there." In his struggles as an actor, Hoffman checked coats at the Longacre Theater (the article didn't mention the orangeade), washed dishes, did a stint as a custodian of a dance studio, worked in the toy department of Macy's, and continued all the while to haunt auditions "with a zeal that bordered on obsession." Much, much later, Hoffman used those early days and the frustrations and panic of looking for work when he starred in the motion picture *Tootsie*. The entire opening sequence of rejection, disappointment, and the struggle upward in a most difficult business was based upon his own experiences.

One of the most asked questions by students and young filmmakers is, "How did *they* get there?" Well, if we analyze just how "they" got there, we find rather quickly that this field of film has an infinite number of career paths, not one of them at all like the professions of law or accounting or medicine. It would be marvelous and terribly helpful to the beginner to be able to say that you merely started as a gofer, moved up to production assistant, then to production manager, to assistant director, and finally to director, or that you progressed from equipment rental house technician to assistant cameraman to cinematographer.

Instead, there is an astounding and baffling variety of paths, each one leading to a serendipitous second step and none of them following any logic at all. I have been saying for years that there are no rules, and that in itself becomes the best and the worst factor dealing with moving up in our field. Where, in fact, do you even begin?

★ Dede Allen (editor of *Reds, Bonnie and Clyde, Rachel, Rachel*, and *The Hustler*) began her career as one of the first female messengers at Columbia Pictures.
★ Robert Rehme, chief executive officer of New World Pictures, started as an usher in Cincinnati, moved to theater management, and went to United Artists in the public relations department.
★ Our own editor, Suzanne Jasper, got her first job in our business (after schooling in fine arts) by being hired for *Saturday Night Live* for a Madeleine Kahn sequence. Her job? *To wave her arms and make a flock of pigeons fly on cue!*

If you look at the career paths of most of us in the field, you begin to see that, most of all, *there is no pattern.* This is probably the best piece of advice that you can keep with you while you move into the film business and make your way among the minefields. Even though some jobs may not seem to be moving you forward, they may be invaluable to you in later years. Accounting for me was the salvation in my budget projections. A technician who can repair a tape recorder on some isolated location is a boon to a producer who has hired him or her as a sound person for a shoot. For example, here are some of the ways that friends of mine have moved up in the field:

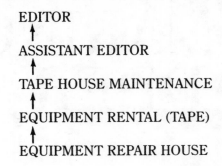

EDITOR
↑
ASSISTANT EDITOR
↑
TAPE HOUSE MAINTENANCE
↑
EQUIPMENT RENTAL (TAPE)
↑
EQUIPMENT REPAIR HOUSE

Here's another, in a different category:

DIRECTOR OF COMPUTER GRAPHICS
↑
ANIMATOR
↑
OPERATOR, COMPUTER GRAPHICS HOUSE
↑
GRAPHICS COURSE/ART COURSE
↑
IBM TRAINING ON COMPUTERS
↑
COLLEGE MATH (MAJOR)

Note, of course, that the last example seems to follow a more logical path. But here's one that teaches an important lesson. The person involved began at a television network on the very lowest level. But as his career progressed, he moved to another network, and then *back* to the first one. By doing so, he managed to skip several rungs up the ladder:

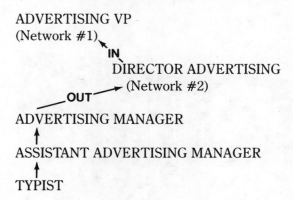

ADVERTISING VP
(Network #1)

IN

DIRECTOR ADVERTISING
(Network #2)

OUT

ADVERTISING MANAGER

ASSISTANT ADVERTISING MANAGER

TYPIST

The biggest problem in getting ahead in our field comes when we try to lay down some rules, to define well-worn paths, to ignore the serendipity of the field and the well-worn (but vital) advice that you have to "pay your dues" before you can move up. Every time I have preached a rule, a letter has come to tell me that it was time to break that rule. For example, I have always said that ours is an industry in which a recruiter will *never* come to the campus to hire you. They do it in computer engineering, in law, in some parts of the medical field, and in large corporate structures. But they will *never* do it in film.

Having just finished a lecture at Northwestern, where I solemnly made that pronouncement, I boarded an airplane to Los Angeles and sat next to a young woman who told me her story. She was, indeed, in film—and how she had gotten to where she was at that moment was a classic case in point.

She was graduating from Harvard Business School when *a recruiter* from MGM came to the campus. They needed a person who might want to work in the financial department of the company, and they promptly hired her. Elated, euphoric, her first film job garnered with little problem and certainly without the traumas that beset the rest of us, she and her mother drove to California over a period of a week, enjoying the unfolding of the countryside, anticipating her new job in Hollywood.

When she arrived, she went directly to the offices of MGM and announced herself, asking for the man for whom she was to work. The receptionist was startled and obviously distraught, finally blurting out that the gentleman was no longer with the company. *He had been fired the previous week!* At which point, the young woman burst into a torrent of uncontrollable tears.

Another executive, passing her in the hallway, asked her about her problem, and between sobs she told her story. The man invited her into his office, consoled her as best he could, and began to make calls to friends of his who worked in the field as producers or owners of their own companies. After several calls, he connected. Yes, some friends *were* looking for a person who would work on a very low level. No, they couldn't pay very much since they were just starting out and only had a staff of three people. And would a Harvard MBA even be interested in such a job? (She would.) An interview was arranged. She was hired as low woman on the totem pole in the struggling new production group.

The company was Lorimar! It is now one of the best known and most successful producers of television sitcoms. It has grown into a publicly owned corporation, with its stock traded on the Over-the-Counter market. And *she* is now a full-fledged producer with them. Sitting on the airplane, she recounted the story and told me that she was just returning to Hollywood after producing her first television feature film!

At another lecture, this time at New York University, I made another of my pronouncements, a golden rule for job hunting in the film industry, and a tenet that is well known by all professionals: *You will never find a job in the want ads!* Two days later, a letter arrived from a young woman I had interviewed about a year back. Her name is Leonora Lorenzo and she lives in the Washington, D.C., area:

"My story begins with a happy ending. Defying the painstaking experience of most job seekers, I secured my *very first* job in video production from the want ads in the *Washington Post* newspaper. And, defying all the odds (not to mention the gods), that is also how I landed my second (current) position in the field!"

Perhaps the most encouraging thing for the young filmmaker to hear is that Leonora had no experience at the time, "short of enjoying a night out at the movies," but her previous experience as a writer/researcher of grant proposals got her the job of researcher with a small production company. And though she was hired to do research on development work and film grants, "there was very little time for me to do that work. The company had a backlog of productions demanding immediate attention. So I researched and wrote my first scripts, *produced and directed my first shoot, and ultimately edited and marketed my first pieces, all within a ten-month period.* [Italics mine.] I was no longer completely inexperienced."

There is just one more small section of her letter that I would like to quote, for it puts to rest yet another piece of job-hunting dogma: *The only way to get a job or move ahead is by using your contacts. It's not what you know, but who you know:*

"Although my pursuits ended successfully and happily, some of the intervening moments were disillusioning and even forced me to abandon my quest for a while. Ironically, I found the least successful method of job hunting to be networking—using contacts. Even the few contacts that I had in the field could offer nothing to this inexperienced (yet eager) newcomer. . . . I decided that networking was valuable to those who have a track record and who have built up an arsenal of colleagues/associates on whom they can call."

There are two important points to be made in Leonora's saga. First, you will find over and over again that the experience you've gained in some completely remote area of your life is the key to getting a film or tape job. For Leonora it was her experience in writing grant proposals—and the timing of finding a company that needed a researcher to do just that for their film projects. For others, it may be a favorite sport that creates the job opening for a film that is about to begin—on the subject of track, archery, hot-air

Some filmmakers have made their reputations with specialty photography in specific areas, such as food. Here, Paul Hartwick of Hartwick/Przyborski Productions in Pittsburgh utilizes his unique abilities as an art director on a shoot for HBM/Creamer and their client, Foodland.

balloons, or street games. Hobbies listed at the bottom of a letter or a resume may catch the eye of a producer about to embark on a trip down a white-water river, up a mountain in the Himalayas, or on a long voyage aboard a twelve-meter yacht in preparation for the America's Cup. Fluency in a particular foreign language might also be the door opener, whether it be Urdu for a film about India or Italian for a film about the cooking of Italy. I would never leave on a trip for South America without having at least an assistant cameraman or assistant director who speaks fluent Spanish.

The second point is, perhaps, more subtle, but important nonetheless—the area of networking. Certainly it is wise to contact the people you know as you go up the ladder. Certainly it is okay to be in a hurry to get up that ladder. I am known as one of the most impatient of men. On location I pace a lot. I want everything done *now*. As Tina Gonzalez, one of my producers, described me, "Being on time means being ten minutes early. Being late means arriving on time!"

So I understand only too well the impatience of the career seeker. But my friend Don Taffner says, "On your future—you can't say that the miracle is not going to happen—sell the script right out of school—direct a feature at age twenty-four—because it *does* happen on occasion—but the chances are that it won't happen!"

Don Taffner is an old friend and one of the most successful people in the field of the television sitcom. He is executive in charge of production for *Three's Company* and *Too Close for Comfort,* and he is in charge of worldwide distribution

A scene from Man About the House, *starring Richard O'Sullivan, Paula Wilcox, and Sally Thomsett, the British original of ABC's* Three's Company. *Don Taffner, distributor of the British program and executive producer of the American version, has become one of the most successful syndicators in the television field.*

and syndication for all the shows produced by his company. Unlike Leonora, who is just starting out, Don has been in the business for over thirty years. He is one of the most delightful and upbeat people I know, and we talked one early morning at his company's exquisite headquarters in uptown Manhattan.

"In their rush to get somewhere, young people are not aware of the fact that there is a sort of 'projected philosophy' that works in your favor as you grow in the business. . . ."

As you progress, he says, there are a great many people who are in your peer group and who are also just starting out. They are with you in the lower levels at the networks, in the film companies, and in the advertising agencies:

"As you go along in the field, you all grow together. Your peer group soon becomes the one that contains the 'power brokers,' the people who begin to designate who sells, who gets somewhere, who produces the sitcoms, who becomes successful. You are all growing together, and you have an entrée to one another through the mere fact that you started out together."

Of course, there is the matter of timing and the need to recognize it:

"There comes a time when you have to take advantage of all this. There is a right time, a time when the people who grew along with you are now at the top. And *that* is the time

that you have to 'make it' or it's too late, for as they disappear, their places are taken by the younger, up-and-coming group, who do not know you, who have their own peers growing along with them, who have their own new ideas, and who consider you 'old hat' and passé."

And, of course, this new group begins to choose their *own* people to whom they give their favors and with whom they become friends and cogrowers, until they, too, give way to yet another new group.

For those of us who have been in the industry for many years, nowhere is this more evident than in the field of the commercial (and the advertising agencies, their Siamese twin) and in the area of network television. "Superstars" appear and disappear with the rapidity of a high-speed computer program, reminding me of the Andy Warhol quip that, with our penchant for constantly finding something new, "one day, everyone will be famous for fifteen minutes!"

Yet this is the way that the "seniors" in the film business manage to be heard by decision makers, how they sell their scripts, or get their shows produced, or find funding for their films. And all of them made their way up a crooked ladder, generally starting out in a part of the field far removed from what they are now doing.

Don Taffner feels, for example, that there are not enough people who are even aware of distribution and sales in our industry:

"When I call the universities and tell them

that I have an opening in my company for sales/distribution/syndication, they hang up on me."

It's another case that proves that the schools don't teach you how to get a job.

"For the schools, directing, producing, graduating as Martin Scorsese are the goals. But many of the younger people that I've hired for the stockroom, or to work the telex, or be a summer replacement for a secretary, are now in production or selling programs overseas, selling syndication or to the networks, and putting their own packages together."

He is a great believer, proven by his own remarkable success, that those scripts and shows that are being sold by his salespeople also help them meet a great many others along the way:

"I don't even have messengers deliver things—within limits, of course. I ask my salespeople to take them personally. More things can happen walking the streets than sitting in your office. Delivery of a film to A gets you past the receptionist to B and C and D—all because you personally delivered a print."

Just being there lets you say hello to a familiar face in the hallway, lets someone introduce you to someone else.

"Don't spend twenty-four hours a day chasing the rainbow. *Get back in the trenches for twenty of those hours.* You might find the person in the trenches right alongside of you who will eventually help your career!"

If we examine Don's career along with all the others that younger people look at, and ask, "How did they get there?" the stories cascade one atop the other, the funny coincidences are uproariously recounted, and we begin to realize that all the paths depend upon the factors we have been discussing: serendipity, talent, hard work, and being able to recognize an opportunity when it arises.

After college (St. John's in Brooklyn), having no idea of what he wanted to be when he "grew up," Don took a lower-level job at the William Morris Theatrical Agency and worked his way from the mail room to agent. In the mid-fifties a show called *Foreign Intrigue* was being produced overseas and delivered to the United States for eventual network distribution. At the time, Don was the agency messenger/contact who was sent to the airport to pick up the film. Thus, when William Morris expanded into European network distribution, Don was obviously the expert on foreign film production, *having been the only one ever to go to the airport to pick up film from Europe!*

In 1963, by now an expert (and a real one), he started his own company by representing overseas broadcasters interested in buying American shows. But then American producers began to open offices in Europe, and Taffner began to meet competition, and the Europeans no longer needed American representatives here in the United States. Thus, he switched and began to sell *foreign programs in America.* He tells, with relish, about his first sale, an Australian production called *Skippy the Bush Kangaroo:*

"I sold it to Kellogg by convincing them to think of the show as *Lassie,* except that the pet was a kangaroo instead of a dog!"

Eventually he branched into syndication, selling market by market instead of through the networks, and he formed his own syndication company based on the theory that he might just as well be doing it for himself as for someone else. Today, instead of turning over the shows to the networks, he:

★ brings the property to them
★ retains financial control
★ syndicates the shows through his own company
★ retains foreign rights, also for syndication

The enormous success of *Three's Company* and *Too Close for Comfort* attests to the fact that it has worked out well. For the beginner in our field, looking avidly at how *"they* did it," it is another prime example of moving a career through paths not frequently mentioned when we read of the "glamour" of the film business and how Lana Turner was discovered while she was sitting at the soda fountain in Schwab's Drugstore on Sunset Boulevard in Hollywood.

A Talk with John Sayles

If we had met on the West Coast, and if writer/director John Sayles lived in Beverly Hills instead of Hoboken, New Jersey, we might have had lunch at Ma Maison or Spago, surrounded by the jingling gold chains that dangle between fully open shirtfronts. The only customers would have had telephones at their tables, the better to speak to their agents between bites of pâté.

Instead, we met one brisk winter day at the Gaiety Delicatessen in the theater district of New York, as the other customers were gulping their salami and pastrami before hurrying to the Wednesday matinee. We sat back in the corner, unrecognized by the noisy crowd, occasionally hassled by a barking New York waiter who kept repeating, "Tell me when ya wanta order. . . ."

I wore my goosedown coat against the chill, but John wore only a white, short-sleeved T-shirt, his usual "uniform" in any kind of weather. ("It drives my crews crazy. I never get cold!") The luncheon had come out of an exchange of letters during the time that he was editing *The Brother from Another Planet* and after I had read an article in *Newsweek* magazine that John had written (in May of 1983).

I have always had great respect for John Sayles as a filmmaker who has broken with the Hollywood mold, has continued to live in Hoboken while doing most of his work on the East

Cinematographer Ernest Dickerson peers into the camera and director John Sayles looks on at Harlem's Baby Grand while shooting The Brother from Another Planet.

Coast, and has remained independent in an industry that thrives on collaboration and "deals." I was especially taken with his advice to young filmmakers, for he substantiated so much of what many of us have been saying for so long. He feels that too many people just send out letters pleading for someone to hire them: "The trick is to get out there and *make something happen!*"

Make something happen! John Sayles started as a novelist, his interest in filmmaking limited to an occasional trip to the local movie theater.

"While I was working on my first novel, I was living on food stamps, working in factories, in hospitals, as a day laborer. At the same time that I was laid off from a job in a sausage factory, I had a story accepted by the *Atlantic.*"

The story was expanded into a novel, which he sold for $2,500. He wrote two novels and a short-story collection, which became film properties. On the strength of his fiction writing, he got an agent, who suggested that he head out to the West Coast "to meet producers," and he landed his first job with Roger Corman, rewriting a film called *Piranha,* a tale of ravenous fish that ate little children's feet! His feelings about Roger Corman are very much the same as most of the filmmakers who have worked with him:

"The beauty of Roger Corman was that if he hired a screenwriter to write a movie, he was going to *make* that movie. He didn't have twenty scripts under development. Roger also wouldn't take vague things. He was one of the most specific people I've ever known."

Finally, John managed to accumulate $40,000, and he decided to make his first independent film. "No one," he says, "was going to knock on my door and ask me to direct."

Actually, he had written *Lianna* before *Secaucus,* but the first work was put on the shelf until a later work might click, something that happens often to writers both in the motion picture industry and in the publishing world. *Secaucus* was chosen first, for a very pragmatic reason.

"The story of *The Return of the Secaucus 7* was determined by the budget! I had $40,000 of my own. What could I make for $40,000? I knew a lot of good actors, all of them non-SAG. But all of them were about my age—thirty years old. I didn't know a single actor who was eighteen. And I didn't know any who were sixty."

There was only one road to follow, of course. John Sayles would make a movie all about thirty-year-olds. But the budget was also too small for travel to exterior locations or for expensive per diem costs, so:

"I decided that we'd have a bunch of thirty-year-olds sitting around! And where could I put up a cast and crew cheaply enough to keep the budget from being devastated? Well, I had worked in summer stock and I knew some-

thing about the tricks of living on a budget. I worked out an arrangement where I could put everyone up for $800 a week!"

He also knew that shooting in 16 mm was cheaper than 35 mm, and if he was lucky enough to eventually get a distributor, he could worry about blowing it up through the liquid gate process later on.

"I found another $20,000 in deferrals for postproduction—labs, mixing, titles—making the budget $60,000. And I deferred another $60,000 to the actors and technicians who worked on the film."

At the time that *Secaucus* was produced, not too many independent films had been successfully finished and distributed. *Northern Lights* and *Heartland* had had moderate success. And, some years before that, I can recall a remarkable independent called *Cold Wind in August,* with Lola Albright, which was produced in black and white for a little over $100,000—even then a remarkably low budget. *David and Lisa* was, perhaps, another prime example. And there were a few others. Interestingly, we might think, then, that raising so small an amount of money by Hollywood standards would be a simple task:

"The one reason you have trouble raising even a small amount of money, like two million dollars, is that Hollywood companies don't want to be associated with a two-million-dollar picture. They want to be associated with nothing less than ten million dollars!"

The morning after *The Return of the Secaucus 7* opened, the first call came in from Hollywood. John Sayles decided to remain an independent.

"My first experience at directing was something that *I* had financed, so I had freedom. I could have made the film and put it on the shelf, and no one would care. . . ."

After *Lianna* and *Baby It's You,* John Sayles received one of the "genius" grants from the MacArthur Foundation, with a guaranteed income for five years, to be spent in any way he chooses.

"I don't live with security in mind. For example, I put my own money into my films because I couldn't possibly ask other people to put their money in if I didn't contribute my own. If *Brother* makes money, I might take a year off and write."

The Brother from Another Planet was budgeted at $340,000, an infinitesimal amount by today's blockbuster standards. And although it limits the technical freedom of the film, working with this kind of a budget also tests the creative and imaginative faculties of the people who work on the film.

"I can't say, as they do in Hollywood, 'We need this shot. I don't care what it costs.' I don't have the economic freedom to decide that I'd like a crane shot. But then again, I write the script myself, so I can decide how to make do with less."

A good example is a critical sequence in *Brother* that takes place in a subway in New York City. Normally, it would be an expensive way to shoot the sequence. Instead, the entire section of the film was shot at the Subway Museum in Brooklyn. They added the ubiquitous graffiti to the car, and with proper camera movement and sound, no one was able to tell that it was not shot underground on the sprawling, noisy subway itself.

For two hours our conversation ranged over a variety of film subjects. I have covered the subject of screenwriting and the sale of screenplays in another section of this book. In that area of film, John Sayles also offers good advice, just as he does on beginning a career and climbing up the ladder. How does someone make it happen?

"I found that I learned more about my writing skills from editing and by working as an assistant editor. Editing teaches you about structure, and structure helps both your writing and your directing."

He feels that he also learned his craft as a writer by working as an actor. Thus, when he writes a role, he looks at every part in the screenplay as if he were going to play it.

"I also think that the script supervisor has one of the best jobs in the film industry if the goal is to become a director. He or she works closely with the entire creative group on the film—the director, the cinematographer, and the editor."

BOB MARSHAK

Joe Morton plays "the brother" in this Sayles film, an extraterrestrial who travels up the Hudson to Harlem after crash-landing on Ellis Island.

The subject of "networking" and making contacts early in your career keeps coming up again and again. Don Taffner mentioned it strongly. John Sayles feels that it's just as important. You begin your work for little money or even no money at all. But on the job you meet others who are working on features (or documentaries or commercials), all the while getting to know key members of the production team. And does it work?

Peggy Rajski, coproducer and production manager for *Brother*, has a background as a director and producer in videotape and multimedia programs for corporate clients, having produced business films for Mobil Oil, Pepsi-Cola, and Otis Elevator. She worked for John Sayles on *Lianna* as production manager.

The other coproducer for *Brother* is Maggie Renzi, and she doubled as unit manager and acted the role of Noreen, the social worker, in the film. She originally met John Sayles when she played the role of Kate in *Secaucus,* and she was the assistant for preproduction of that film, served as unit manager during the shooting, and was assistant editor and publicist during the postproduction phase.

Ernest Dickerson, the director of photography for *Brother,* originally graduated from NYU Film School, has photographed short documentaries, music videos, and *Joe's Bed Stuy Barbershop,* featured in the New Directors/New Films series in 1982.

Mason Daring, who composed the music for the film, began his career as an entertainment lawyer and legal analyst! He also com-

BOB MARSHAK

Peggy Rajski, producer and production manager; John Sayles, writer/director; and Maggie Renzi, coproducer and unit manager, on the set of The Brother from Another Planet.

posed the music for John Sayles's *Lianna* and *The Return of the Secaucus 7.*

The script supervisor for *Lianna,* Adam Brooks, is about to direct his first feature, *Almost You,* as is Carol Dysinger, who was the first assistant director on the same film. They, in turn, will probably use the people whom *they* met on the other John Sayles productions, most of whom worked for very little money or deferrals of their salaries. Somehow, they are all making it happen.

In addition to his one final bit of advice, "Don't expect to make a living at it," John Sayles has some very sage words to say to those who write asking him how to get into the film business. "I don't think I've gotten into it yet," he answers, "but I do make films."

He suggests that you look carefully at the filmmaking specialty that you want to pursue eventually and then "do something about it!"

★ He counsels that you make up your mind about what you really want out of working in films. If it's the glamour and the money that supposedly go with the career, and if Hollywood makes the only "real movies" in your way of thinking, then get out to the West Coast and try to break into the "club."

★ If there is a film specialty that interests you, get to work doing something related to it:

- If you want to be a cinematographer, look for a job as a film loader, camera assistant, or an operator. Take a job in an equipment house to learn about cameras. Buy some equipment—tape or even 8 mm—light something and go shoot it.

- If you want to be an editor, look for work rolling up trims and rewinding film. Ask if you can use the editing machine late at night or on weekends and cut something. Find some outtakes that are no longer being used or fill material and cut scenes together. Offer your services as an editor to student filmmakers at the local colleges or universities, or to the independents working in your area.

- If you want to write, you have no problem. Write. Write stuff. Lots of it. Show it to actors. Show it to producers. Show it to agents. Most won't even take a look, but at least the work will exist and you'll be getting better at it.

- If you want to direct, direct something. It may be theater, film, tape. If you can't finance your great idea on the basis of a screenplay or your non-reputation as a director, make it yourself—on Super-8 or tape, with the best actors you can find for free. Then use *that* as a sample to raise the money for the real production. Think of it as a rough draft that you may get to polish later in 16 mm or 35 mm.

- If you're an actor, and nobody is hiring you or your friends who are actors, try producing a play or a small film to be in. And if you know other actors, writ-

ers, directors, editors, and technicians, find one another. Film is a collaborative medium. It can be done.

- Most of all, if there's something that you don't know that you need to know, *go learn it!*

John's final words of advice are the most succinct and direct, and every young filmmaker should take careful note:

"You may have to subsidize your acting or your directing or your writing for a long time. You may have to put your hard-earned money (or your inherited fortune) on the line, and you may well lose it. If you're not willing to take the chance, then stay out of the racket!"

He also recommends that you keep from getting so caught up in the future that you forget your quality of life today. One morning, you may find yourself on some godforsaken location at 5 A.M. It's cold out there and your job is to lug the cable from one set-up to the next and then the next and then the next. Meanwhile, the director, an egomaniac who probably knows less about the film business than you do, is talking to "some guy who couldn't act his way out of a paper bag" and telling him the motivation for slashing up the next coed:

"And you're hating it. You just hate it. And you're convinced that this is not the *real* film industry, and that someday you'll be rewarded by getting your break into the real industry. Well, believe it or not, this *is* the real industry," and he adds with a smile, "especially if the doughnuts are stale!"

More Training—or More Experience?

It would be a lot more acceptable for entry-level and minimally experienced people if our industry were "cleaner" about the way in and the roads ahead. Today, especially with the proliferation of film schools (many of them quite good), communications courses, and the choice between taking job after low-paying job, the decisions get more difficult. Who is to say that a continuation of training will not lead to an eventual contact to help your climb, or that a school sample film will not open the path to Hollywood? Especially after the history of film school grads such as Spielberg and Lucas or Scorsese, the odds have changed. And the decision whether to continue training or get more experience is made more difficult.

On the other hand, the very fact that film does not offer only *one* path, and the remarkably serendipitous experiences that make for magazine articles and "war stories" told around the location dinner table, are all part of the reason that most of us just don't give up—and that many of us manage to make it in spite of the odds that seem all but insurmountable. We see it in the actor who is convinced that he or she will be "discovered" tomorrow (and sometimes is), or the writer of the unproduced screenplay who lies waiting for an angel (who is sometimes found), the unopened office door, or the just mailed letter after which a first job may be offered (and sometimes will be), or the accidental meeting of just the right person who will move you from starvation to stardom (and sometimes does).

The serendipity of film is one of the reasons that a chapter such as this might never end if I were to keep relating stories that crop up over and over again. Whether the subject is well known (or even famous) or just a beginner looking for a first break, the lessons are there for all of us to see. Whether the experience achieved in the early days was garnered at school or in the field makes no real difference, for all the first jobs are generally lower level, and each one teaches something that is of value later on in our careers. And if we are eventually lucky enough (or unlucky enough) to be interviewed, each magazine reporter will inevitably ask the same question. And each student who attends our lectures and seminars will ask it again: How did *he* begin? Where did *she* get her start? How did *you* get into the business?

Somehow, it helps to know that Aaron Spelling, creator of *Dynasty, The Love Boat, Family,* and producer of the successful feature film *Mr. Mom,* told an interviewer for *American Film* magazine that he had always wanted to be a director, even during his early days at Southern Methodist University. But "the closest we came to Hollywood was when Dorothy Malone was our homecoming queen . . . and it was all downhill after that!" After coming to New York and living on bologna sandwiches for three months, he took a bus to Los Angeles, and after three more months landed his first job—*as a reservations agent for Western Airlines!*

Again, if we listen closely, we hear the word "fate"—the luck of being somewhere at the right time and knowing how to take advantage of it. The manager of an "all-girl orchestra" called to make a reservation for eighteen people, and he offered Spelling the job as "band boy," in addition to doubling as amateur talent scout for the show. As Spelling tells it, "Even though it was five dollars less a week than I was making, I immediately grabbed the job. What the hell, I was back in show business!"

I was particularly taken with the story because my own background (hidden until this time) includes a stint as director of a television show featuring an "all-girl orchestra," which was transmitted *live* over the Mutual Network as *The Hour of Charm*(!).

It was in the early days of black-and-white television, and the budget (and the salary) for the show was practically nonexistent. The experience, however, of doing a weekly live show with almost no rehearsal and only two cameras, a full orchestra, two vocalists, and three commercial breaks (all live) was one of the reasons that my future film work managed to survive through other budget disasters. We learned to work with almost nothing, and yet we managed to get remarkable production value—and more "war stories" to add to our treasure chests and with which to bore future classes at film school.

One Sunday afternoon, for example, we

came up with the exquisite idea that we would cover the screen with a rolling layer of misty smoke while the cellist played the last few bars of "The Swan." Of course, we didn't have any money for a real, honest-to-goodness smoke machine. In its place, we filled a bucket with hot water and, at the proper moment, the stagehand would plunge a large piece of dry ice into the water to create a rich cloud of smoke. We had done it many times before on dramatic shows to create fog. There was no reason on earth why it wouldn't work this time.

The show went on the air, the cellist played her solo, and as we came to the end of the song, the ice was dropped into the water-filled galvanized bucket and smoke immediately poured out. Slowly, we dissolved to the camera that was covering the smoke and the screen was filled with the sounds of the cello and the lovely, billowing transition. The camera that had been photographing the cellist—the only other camera on our show—was then released to set up for the live commercial that was to follow, a sponsor who sold grated Parmesan cheese.

However, I cannot read music. And obviously no one else in the control room could, either (even though we were all involved in a music show), and when we were ready to dissolve to the smoke, the cellist *continued to play.* The music had not ended, and, in fact, she was still thirty seconds away from the conclusion of the piece! And no camera was there to transmit it. The smoke kept billowing across the screen—and suddenly the ice froze in the water and the smoke stopped—all of it *live* on network television!

No one moved. No one did anything. All across the country the audience watched as a frozen piece of ice sat in the bucket and the lovely music of "The Swan" continued right to the end, to be relieved finally by an announcer holding a small jar of Parmesan cheese and smiling broadly!

I suppose there is one other fact that must be written if I am to complete the story. It occurred to me as I wrote these last paragraphs, smiling broadly at the recollection of frozen ice in a galvanized bucket. It's true that I was a full-fledged director, and I had a credit at the end of every show, so that my dear mother could call her friends together and glow with pride. But *my salary was practically nonexistent!* These were the early days of live television, and I was told over and over again how lucky I was to be involved in the new and booming field. (And I was.) But I was paid twenty-one dollars for each sponsored half hour plus seven dollars and fifty cents for each commercial on the show. Even in those days of two-dollar dinners at the Horn & Hardart Automat, I couldn't survive. So I made my "real" living as an instructor at a radio school, where everyone else was trying to break into the field and do it for nothing! But I was a director! And I relished the experience.

So in deciding whether you are going to plunge into the job market to be properly exploited, continue with your education in another school, or take still more communications courses, you might keep in mind that the garnering of experience and the collection of hard film wisdom is not limited either to the "real world" or to school. I think that the college film crew,

working on a class project on New York's Bowery or in a cable car on Powell Street in San Francisco or in a cramped apartment location on Chicago's South Side, will also come home with tall tales of getting the job done under the most trying of circumstances. And all of it will be filed away and collected for future recall.

The biggest problem arises in school, however, because of a situation that is not present in the working world of film—*everyone* in the class is jockeying for the position of director, while in the real world there is but one director on each set, and we accept that fact as we do even the most menial of production jobs. Let me tell of a case in point.

A few months ago I received a telephone call from a young woman who was in her masters program at film school at Columbia University in New York. We chatted for a few moments, and then she told me that she had called for a specific reason: Did I know of anyone who might want to work on her school thesis, for which she was producing a short film? I wondered aloud about the others in her class. Didn't they want to help?

"Everybody at Columbia is interested in screenplay writing and direction. No one wants to dirty his or her hands on production!" she answered. Then, in sheer frustration, she blurted out, "Imagine! I'm in film school and *I can't even put a crew together for a film!*"

Until a very few years ago, I was adamant in my feelings that I would always accept a film person with four years of hands-on experience over someone who had spent the same length of time in a communications school. I am no longer quite so certain. Having hired and worked with some of my ex-students as well as graduates of other film schools, my answer now would be, "It depends . . ."

★ It depends upon how you spent those four years (or more)—was it in the philosophy of film or in "hands-on" work with cameras, crews, lights, and location problems?

★ It depends upon what I feel is your commitment to film and to the life that it demands from those of us who love the field but accept the problems, the lack of personal life (for many of us), and the importance of paying our dues early on. (See "Making It Through the Interview," page 156.)

★ It depends not only upon your background and interests, but upon the sample that you offer as a standard of your work.

★ And, being a pragmatist, it depends most of all on timing and whether or not a job is open at that moment!

About a year ago I ran into a film problem that was not a standard one, but one that required an unusual commitment from people without much experience in the field who were willing to "pay their dues." During the editing of one of my films, I found that I was quite dissatisfied with the results as they unfolded during the weeks of collating and putting together a documentary about the fashion industry. In concert with my clients, I decided that I would stop the project, *reconstitute* all the footage, and begin again!

For those who are new in the field, the reconstituting of film footage must certainly be one of the most boring, tedious, repetitious, and banal jobs in the entire world of motion pictures, as well as being the most expensive way to edit a film. After having cut apart twenty-seven rolls of film, some of it as small as three and four frames, we were now asking people to put it all back together again—by the numbers printed along the edges! It is certainly something that we don't teach in film school, nor do professionals ever let themselves think about it in more lucid moments. Yet someone had to do it.

I spoke to the teacher of a class at a local film school, and she recommended three of her best students. In turn, I explained to them that the job would entail finding AA00301 and putting it back with AA00302—and that all of it had to be done accurately, both picture and track, or we could not hope to reedit the film. There were three volunteers, and for three weeks, using whatever free time they had, they were locked in a windowless (but air-conditioned) editing room trying to find a tiny trim labeled AA00301 in order to splice it back with AA00302! We sent in refreshments and sustenance. We called from time to time to give them courage. And they finished the job—and they did it superbly! In over twenty-seven rolls of reconstituted footage, there were only three minor synchronization problems!

To put it mildly, I was impressed. Thus, during the past year, I have made it a point to use each of the three in other categories in order to give them experience in the field and to provide some income while they attended the last year of schooling. One young man has worked with me as a production assistant on location for a series of films that were produced for a client. And I have plans to use him again for another series of films to be produced this year. One of the young women has worked for me as a full-fledged assistant editor on a documentary and is slated for another job within a few months. And the third person, another talented and committed woman, has been offered a free-lance production job on one of my tape projects slated for the end of this year.

In a sense, then, all of them have managed to combine both school and experience, and all of them have garnered their first professional production credits. More important, all three of them have, in me, the best of recommendations and testimonials for any future employer.

When I speak of more training or more experience, I am really referring to the frequent "solution" for the young person not finding a job right out of film school and the terrible feelings of rejection as the hunt continues. Too often, they ask: Do you think that I ought to go back to school to get more training? And too often, the excuse for going back to school for a masters degree and then a doctorate, or to "take some more courses," brings the beginner back into the comfort of the school environment, along with its protective atmosphere and its insulation from the real world.

The universal question returns: Oh, yeah? How are you going to get experience when you have none—and everyone wants someone who is experienced?

There are several ways:

★ Because of the constant rejection, most job

Henry Martin, left, who carries a Ph.D. in music, and Wally Bottger, a one-time trumpeter in the Harvard band who gave up law for music at the age of forty-five, formed Bottger-Martin Productions to write jingles for commercials. In an industry noted for its intense competition, they have already written for several national and regional accounts.

hunters do not spend an adequate amount of time planning their strategy or following up on phone calls and letters. Ex-students probably spent more time at school studying for exams or participating in athletic programs than they do now in writing letters, making calls, and meeting eventual job contacts.

★ If you are going to try to make it in the New York market or in Los Angeles, one way is to begin there and to *stay there.* As John Sayles says, "join the club" right away. But in doing so, stop limiting your potential to only the production houses and the television networks. Your experience can include jobs in the following areas, many of them leading to an eventual production job with a company or an independent producer—or even the formation of your own film company. Remember—each of them will provide contacts:

> Advertising Agencies
> Animation Houses
> Equipment and Supply Houses
> Laboratories
> Film Model Makers
> Studios
> Tape Preproduction and Postproduction
> Editing Services
> Art and Titles

There are job opportunities in everything from entertainment law to music composition, arranging, and recording to finance, insurance brokerage, and all the technical support services that make up the well-coordinated film crew. Most important is the key to all of this: Not one of the jobs need be a dead end forevermore, unless you like it so much that you decide to make it your life's work. If you look carefully at the diagrams on pages 50 and 51, you begin to see that just letting your imagination run rampant can do wonders for your career path.

In this morning's newspaper I read again of the job switch, as a new company doing commercial jingles was formed by two men with very diverse backgrounds. Walter Bottger had worked as a lawyer with some of America's most prestigious law firms, a special prosecutor investigating corruption, and a sometime trumpeter in the Harvard Band. His partner in the new firm, Bottger-Martin Productions, Inc., is Henry Martin, who has a Ph.D. in music, taught it at Princeton University as a doctoral candidate, and has written a textbook due for publication. Nowhere is there any experience in film, and yet they have entered an area of our industry in which over two hundred companies compete, with about 90 percent of the music jingle business going to about fifteen companies!

At an NBC reunion held recently, eighty vice-presidents told interviewers that they had started out as pages at the network! As Allen Zwerdling, editor and publisher of *Backstage,* told me one sunny afternoon in his office high above Manhattan, "I tell people to forget the philosophy of filmmaking and *learn to type*!" He continues by commenting that most ad agency top-ranked women started as secretaries and most men now in the position of vice-president began their careers in the mail room.

Zwerdling has still another theory for those who want eventually to return to the major production areas but don't want to work in the menial areas of the job market:

★ If you're from out of town, go back and start your own company in your hometown. If you come from there, you know the people, you grew up with them. Use the contacts of your own, your friends, your parents, your relatives, and contact the used-car lots, the supermarkets, banks, and the discount stores.
★ Make local spots for very few dollars—make 150 of them, and then cull the two best ones.
★ Come to the big city and visit the ad agencies and show them your samples.

Again we hear the advice: *samples.* Can you show us your work? If you are working in cable for very little money (or no money at all), can you make the time to produce a sample? If you have spent four years in school, what have you got to show for it besides the diploma and a note from your college professor? The two men of whom I wrote just a few pages back, Walter Bottger and Henry Martin, went into the jingle business and immediately put together a reel of music samples, all of them especially created for *nonexistent* products. There is the beginning of a happy ending for the story, incidentally. At the time of this writing they had already done music for English Leather, Charlotte Ford Clothes, Apple Bank, and other commercial accounts.

I have also mentioned that there is a way to continue the job hunt, gathering experience wherever it exists, *and* to continue your training and the development of your skills. All across the country there are courses and seminars that are offered to both the longtime professional and the beginner. Properly chosen, they give you the opportunity to:

★ increase your skills
★ make industry contacts
★ keep abreast of the new developments
★ discover new areas of opportunity
★ learn about techniques and tips developed by other professionals
★ discuss your own ideas and problems

From a very pragmatic point of view, some of these seminars, courses, and meetings might well be tax-deductible, but only under these two circumstances:

★ The sessions are needed to maintain or improve skills required in your employment.
★ The sessions meet the express requirements of your employer.

If you can meet either one of these two criteria, all registration fees, cost of travel, meals, and lodging are deductible.

Here are just a few categories of training that are open in these days of a booming communications business. Some of them—or none of them—may be right for you. You might decide to continue your career on the single path of work experience; or these options may open new vistas, making you feel more secure while you search for a role in the industry. It is a most personal choice.

COMMUNICATIONS SCHOOL. I will only touch on this briefly, for I have already commented extensively about my feelings. The one piece of advice that I can leave you with is this: If you come out of film school without a decent sample, whether of writing or production or film that you've made all by yourself, then you may well have wasted four years of your valuable time.

CONTINUING EDUCATION. Many colleges, universities, and private schools are now offering extensive courses for those of you who are working in other fields and who want to learn the film business. Registration is fairly easy, and the courses are generally open to all nonmatriculated students. Some courses are held at night, others on weekends, some during an intensive four- or five-week summer session. Some offer certificates. Others are merely a good way of expanding your knowledge. The most impressive thing to me is the wide range of subjects that can now be pursued in the continuing education programs:

Film Techniques and Technology
Film Production
Lighting for Film
Computer-Assisted Videotape Editing
Film Editing
Budgeting for Film
Directing for Film
Special Effects
The Role of the Producer

Independent Film
Multi-image Production
Writing for Film
Writing for Television
Advanced Film Theory
The Production Manager
Acting for Film
Music and Sound Direction
The Art Director
Business and Legal Problems
Producing Documentaries
Corporate Media Production
The Advertising Agency
Promotion and Publicity

These are but a few of the subjects, for nowadays you can even find continuing education courses on the philosophy and criticism of the film world, in addition to specific lectures and one-term courses covering the films of Fellini, Keaton, Lubitsch, Tati, Wilder, Hitchcock, De Sica, and Rossellini. For the adult filmmaker-to-be, and especially for someone who may be practicing as a lawyer or accountant or manufacturer, this is a marvelous way to "get your feet wet" and to find out if, indeed, the film business is for you.

Some time back, I received a letter from a man who asked my specific advice about continuing education. Michael Malloy is thirty-five, has spent the better part of his life in the insurance business, and has always had a deep feeling for the motion picture business. He wrote asking my advice about his coming to New York to take a summer course in film production at NYU's Department of Continuing Education. It would

mean a severe financial drain and a big change for someone of his age to even consider moving from one career to another.

I suggested that he contact one of my oldest film friends, who now teaches at the school, Professor Saul Taffet—and that he, Mike, would have to make up his own mind. During that summer session I lectured to Saul's class and said hello to Mike—and then later that year received a letter from Pittsburgh, where he lives.

"Given the facts as I presented them to you, it probably was semicrazy to go to a five-week workshop. To refresh your memory, I was in a financial mess. . . .

The course, however, is well worth every cent . . . first and foremost is Saul Taffet, without question the most remarkable man I've ever met. Secondly, the hands-on opportunity quickly separates the talkers from the doers. The demands they put upon us to make a film with four or five other people you've only known for a few weeks cause one to either sink or swim. If you sink, you go back to widgets. If you swim, you're still not ready to do *Gone With the Wind II*, but you've answered the main question with which you went to the program: Can I do it?

The hard work is exhilarating. If you had told me that I was going to be working that hard before I went, I'd probably have chickened out. I did it. I survived, and I'm now a better person and filmmaker (?) for it.

Lastly, but probably of equal importance to all of the above, is the great feeling of camaraderie you get for those fellow lovers of film who survive the course with you. Knowing that there are others out there who share my passion for film and filmmaking makes me feel less alone. Until I went to the continuing education course, I was beginning to think that my family and friends were right, that I'm a hopeless dreamer and that filmmaking is only for some elitist California group. The workshop was the best experience of my life."

I suppose that I have always been deeply sympathetic to the people who have attended my lectures in the continuing education courses, mostly because I realize just how difficult it must be to pursue a full-time job during the day and then come to class in the evening or on weekends to pursue another, albeit overwhelming, interest.

But there are other courses of instruction open, depending upon your future goals and how you have decided to pursue them:

SEMINARS AND WORKSHOPS: Just as in continuing education, these workshops allow you to choose the single subject that interests you most, and occasionally they require very little time—generally an hour or two, or possibly a whole day. Others take place over a period of ten weeks or more and require that you devote yourself full time to the workshop.

★ American Film Institute has offered workshops and seminars on a variety of subjects. Best of all, these sessions have been given all across the country—in Washington, Los Angeles, Dallas, Houston, Chicago, and New York. The subjects are fascinating and right "on target" in terms of answering the most prevalent questions of young filmmakers. In addition, given the diverse and impressive membership list of A.F.I., the guest speakers and participants usually contain some of the best "names" in the industry: executives, producers, directors, writers, and other working filmmakers:

- Selling Your Feature Film Project to a Studio or Independent
- Directors on Casting
- Filmmaking Grants: How to Finance Your Film and Video Idea
- Film Score: The Music of the Movies
- Acting in TV Commercials
- Acting for the Camera
- Anatomy of a Made-for-TV Movie
- How to Act and Eat at the Same Time
- TV Program Development Workshop
- Writing for the Screen
- Financing and Marketing Techniques

★ American Film Institute has recently joined with ABC Motion Pictures to create a unique Producer's Residency Program. Only two people will be selected each year and will spend ten weeks at ABC Motion Pictures, working in a different department each week of the tenure: production, development, advertising. The most important thing to remember is that this program is *not* for beginners, but for people with some experience. For example, the first resident who was selected in 1983 was Joseph Benson, who studied film at Boston University, Massachusetts Institute of Technology, and Hebrew University in Jerusalem. He also managed a production company that produced commercials and business films before joining the American Film Institute at their Center for Advanced Film Studies.

★ The Center for Advanced Film Studies in Los Angeles is also run by the American Film Institute in a most glorious campus setting. I have had the pleasure of conducting a seminar on careers in film at the center, and it gave me one important guideline—everyone there is interested in the feature. Discussions about documentaries, commercials, business films, or other forms of film are met with great disinterest.

★ The Directing Workshop for Women is yet another innovative program run by A.F.I., funded by The Ford Foundation, The National Endowment for the Arts, The Corporation for Public Broadcasting, the McMurray Foundation, SONY, and the Hunt Foundation. It was established in 1974, and each year as many as twelve women are selected from various areas of film, television, and theater and given the opportunity to direct two projects on videotape.

★ Possibly one of the best known of the workshops is Robert Redford's Sundance Institute in Provo Canyon, Utah. Fearing that Hollywood was squelching new ideas in the quest for "the bottom line," Redford formed Sundance in 1979, in collaboration with film and industry colleagues who agreed with him that new talent had to be nurtured in a system that was unlike what had been developing in the motion picture capital. It has been described as a cross between "a spiritual retreat and a strategic movie-maneuver camp," where 450 scripts are submitted for potential production and only 7 are chosen by a board that is composed of both business and creative people from the industry. For its June workshop, Sundance becomes an intensive production facility for as many as twelve filmmakers, over forty resource technicians, up to twenty actors, and members of the technical film crew. The artists-in-residence have included some of the most talented people in the film industry: Sydney Pollack, Robert Duvall, Waldo Salt, and, of course, Redford himself. In an interview with the *New York Times* (October 23, 1983), Redford summed it up: "I'm not against Hollywood. I don't want my own studio. I'm just trying to do something else with Sundance. What I'd like to do here is make art the core, and see if business can get around that. I don't know if it's going to work, but that's the way I want to go."

INTERNSHIP PROGRAMS: Possibly the best known of these is the program supported by the Directors Guild of America, which chooses talented young people to work with feature film crews in order to gain experience. The program has been so successful that I now note that the DGA trainee even garners a credit

at the end of the film. There are other internship programs available, most notably those run by the networks and the local television stations, especially during the summer months, when vacation slots have to be filled. They are notoriously low-paying jobs (and sometimes are filled by "volunteers"), but they provide excellent contacts and experience for beginners. Many young people have served as interns and have returned to the television station as full-time employees after graduation.

The list is by no means complete, nor could it ever be. New programs are constantly being developed, while older ones fall by the wayside because of lack of funds. Many of the American Film Institute programs, for example, have been cut back due to the drying up of government support during the past few years. But other internship programs seem to spring up as unions suddenly decide that they will eventually need an influx of new blood, or as production companies and television stations find that new openings occur on the lower levels. As for seminars and workshops and schools offering courses, the list would fill a book twice the size of this small volume. The "alphabet soup" of communications groups alone offer a never-ending list of exhibitions, from the NAB (National Association of Broadcasters) to the VPA (Videotape Production Association).

Should you continue to pursue your film education, either while working in the industry, while still attending college, or while working in another industry entirely with the hope of eventually becoming a filmmaker, keep these important points in mind:

★ If the class is being taken to improve or hone your skills, what is the background of the person who is teaching the course? Is it a practical hands-on history or twenty years of theory?

★ Ask if it's possible to attend a class run by that teacher. Certainly no school or professor could object. This is especially valuable advice for acting students, since class participation and the interplay of student with instructor is of utmost importance.

★ How many people are in the average class? Is there enough time for everyone to be heard? If it is a hands-on situation, does everyone get a chance to work with the equipment? In fact, is the equipment the most modern—cameras, editing machines, tape decks?

★ How do you react to a classroom situation? How well do you work with others? Possibly, for your specialty, private lessons might be worthwhile, though the cost will rise astronomically.

★ Before you enroll, have you considered that the experience might be gotten in some other way? Would you be better off sweeping up trims in a real editing room or working in a camera rental house than attending class?

★ What is the cost versus the benefit? This question is important not only for continuing education courses, but also for seminars, exhibitions, and workshops. Many trade exhibitions, for example, have several admission scales—a small one just for the exhibition hall, then added fees for attendance at the workshops and seminars. It pays to look carefully at how the dollars mount up when you compare them to the benefits that might accrue.

★ What is the duration of time of each class, seminar, workshop? Most important of all, can you comfortably manage your time for work and supporting yourself and still take on the added burden of class, an intensive production project, and homework?

★ If you decide to do it, make the best commitment that you possibly can. Do it.

What About the Unions?

Somewhere, sometime, somehow, in the dark and distant future of your career, you *may* have to join a union. On the other hand, you may spend a long, fruitful, gloriously successful film career without *ever* having to join a union. For the beginner in film, the question of union membership comes up over and over again, usually with some trepidation and no small feeling of anxiety. With union leaders constantly threatening a writers strike and negotiations falling apart with the Directors Guild, with all the industry horror stories about how impossible it is to crack

the unions, the best advice that I can give is to stop worrying.

For the most part, Hollywood is the toughest union town, particularly in the feature end of our business. With so many of their members out of work at any given time, it is reasonable to expect the unions to protect the people already on their rolls. Perhaps the best single example is the Screen Actors Guild, where about 15 percent of their membership accounts for almost 90 percent of the annual income for actors! Yet, new people keep coming into the union, and they all have rules that can eventually be met.

The beginner, however, still working at the first and the second film job, can actually make a career climb *without* union membership. There might well be a time, of course, when the next potential job will require you to crack the union of your craft. And in that case, an early knowledge of the requirements, the job categories, and the specific rules and regulations will help to ease the way, though this will in no way guarantee that you will be accepted. *The Producer's Master Guide,* one of the production reference books that we use in the industry, takes *180 pages* to list the unions, give their rules and regulations, their minimum wage scales, and the specific agreements under which their members work with other crafts in the motion picture field.

Some unions are more lenient than others. Some have beginner and internship programs, others have apprentice entry positions, and still others are tightly closed to the outsider. There are some things that you might do during your

early days in this field:

★ Get to know the union of your choice. Do it even while still in school.

★ In some cases, there are two unions that cover the same category in different parts of the industry, such as the International Photographers of the Motion Picture Industries (I.A.T.S.E.) and the National Association of Broadcast Employees and Technicians (N.A.B.E.T.).

If your eventual goal is editing or cinematography or scenic design or publicity or writing, there are unions and guilds that cover these categories and about *two hundred others*. You will not initially be going into a union at the top level—as a full-fledged director or director of photography. So get to know the categories in each union of your choice. And either through the use of a reference book, a call to the union, or by letter, find out the *categories* from top to bottom.

For example, the motion picture editors area of I.A.T.S.E. lists categories that include:

Supervising Editor
Supervising Librarian
Music and Effects Editor
Assistant Editor
Editing Room Assistant
Librarian
Assistant Librarian

And if we look at the N.A.B.E.T. listing for film, videotape, and television, we begin to see how vast the field really is and how the job categories are much more extensive than we first imagined when we discussed the people who are important to our productions. In the commercials and network television categories alone, N.A.B.E.T. gives the following list:

Director of Photography
Camera Operator
Camera Assistant
Second Camera Assistant
Still Photographer
Mixer (Sound)
Recordist
Boom
Gaffer (Electrician)
Best Boy
Generator Operator
Third Electric
Key Grip
Second Grip
Dolly
Third Grip
Inside Property Master
Inside Property Assistant
Third Property Person
Outside Property Master
Special Effects:
    Explosive
    Non-Explosive
Set Builder
Assistant Set Builder
Makeup Artist
Assistant Makeup Artist
Hairdresser
Assistant Hair Dresser

Jon Fauer, on location in "the golden triangle" on the Thailand-Burma border for the feature film Comeback. *Fauer, a graduate of Dartmouth Film School, went up the ladder through production and documentary films to become a cameraman in feature films while still in his early thirties.*

Wardrobe/Stylist
Assistant Wardrobe Stylist
Script
Editor
Assistant Editor
Video Lighting Director
Video Cameraman
Technical Director
VTR Operator
Video Utility
Video Engineer
Video Monitor Operator
Apprentices in every category

I.A.T.S.E. breaks down the categories into smaller units—script supervisors, editors, and so on—but essentially all locals in all unions have broken down the job listings right to the entry levels.

However—and this is a big However—when the time comes to join the union, there will be a way. Either the entry level will open up at the right time, or you will get a job in a category with a production unit that *requires* that you belong to a union—and under the Taft-Hartley law they will have to let you in—or you will find that the union of your choice is more open to trainees and apprentices than you might have imagined. *Somehow we have all gotten in.*

And until then? Until then, you will be able to work in film and you will be adding to your credits—and you will learn that the whole world is not Hollywood (even though some of my friends on the West Coast would disagree with this).

The last time he was in New York, as art director and production designer for Francis Ford Coppola's *The Cotton Club,* I spoke at length with Dick Sylbert about the problem. Dick is perhaps one of the best known art directors in the feature field (*Chinatown, The Graduate, Reds, Catch 22),* and he came up through his work with the Metropolitan Opera, and then NBC "as a designer in what they called the Golden Age of television (about 1951). Frankenheimer and Lumet and Mulligan and Pollack and Marty Ritt—and everybody was everybody's assistant. We were all friends and we all worked on projects together."

Note if you will the way that the peer groups start out together, each one rising to the top later on in his or her career to become the power brokers of our field. We talked about Hollywood and the unions:

"I would say that there are about 135 California designers on the roster—111 of them are out of work at any one time. Of course, there are ways to do it out there. Today, about 50 percent of the pictures made in Hollywood are nonunion. And it's getting close to that in New York. *That's where you start!*

It's not easy, but it's easier in New York than in California. There's no system like the New York system in California. In New York, people all know one another. But it's deadly out in California because they try to keep everyone out. The only thing you're allowed to do in California is get an A.F.I. trainee, an observer. But in New York City we have these wonderful kids—we must have had fifteen or twenty of them on *Cotton Club.* We

had young women working as electricians—they're all taking their N.A.B.E.T. exams."

What surprised me was the statement that the New York union (in scenic design) was more liberal in its thinking, especially after two friends of mine had failed their exams three times in a row.

"Well, the New York union is an old theatrical union and it started in the thirties—and by the time television came around, they couldn't supply anybody. They just were not prepared for TV production from 1950 to 1956.

New York has always had the attitude that if we want people who are qualified—and *if* they qualify through Yale or regional Theaters—then they feel *better in the union than out.* The market will take care of who works and who doesn't. It's not our problem. Our problem is to make sure that anyone who qualifies should get a card in the union. And there's no seniority system."

Once again, it is the area in which you work and the specific film field in which you want to pursue your career that will make a great deal of difference as to the ease or difficulty of eventually getting into the union of your choice. But look again at Dick Sylbert's statistic that about 50 percent of all features in New York and in Hollywood are now nonunion. This, along with the free-wheeling documentary and business film field, a part of the commercial field, and the entire range of government, educational, medical, and local television films and tapes makes for a remarkable amount of jobs that are open to people who do not belong to the guilds or unions. In addition, Dick adds, as we all do:

"Remember that other cities are starting film industries—Houston, studios in North Carolina, Miami is becoming a hub, Chicago. There are 'right to work' states where anyone can get a job—Texas and all through the South."

But even for those who gravitate to the West Coast, where Hollywood is the center of the feature field, or to New York for its broad range of commercial, documentary, and feature work, there are job opportunities that open up constantly. Production has boomed on the East Coast ever since the administration of Mayor John Lindsay, when filming on the streets of the city became a joy, with full cooperation of a new film commission and the disappearance of the constant "payoffs" necessary to work on location. And, as with every boom, the job market opened up for everyone, including beginners. It is still not easy—it will never be perfect—but somehow I find that young people I have known over the years *do* get jobs and *do* get into the unions when the need arises.

I can only quote my talk with Dick Sylbert to prove that I am not the only one who feels this way:

"Hang in there. The good people will float up! Ulu Grosbard was a production manager when I met him. Even if you're just running around with a walkie-talkie, there's a lot you can learn!"

Film Festivals: Are They Worth It?

A few years back, a film student called and asked if I might help with a problem that he had. It seemed that he had just shown one of his films to the people at PBS, and they were most interested in televising his work on a show devoted to new filmmakers. Unfortunately, the film was ten minutes too long, and the producers had told him that they could not screen it at its present length—over forty minutes. If he could cut ten minutes out of the film, they would consider it again. Could I help? he asked. I could try, I answered. And we made an appointment for one quiet afternoon.

I watched the film with interest, as I do any student work. It was fairly good, though terribly repetitious, and I found several spots where we could easily cut the ten minutes and bring it down to length. So when the lights were turned on again and he nervously looked at me, I suggested that there was one piece that seemed to be repeated two or three times, and if we merely put a scissors to a specific sequence, we would bring the picture down at least ten and possibly fifteen minutes. For a moment he was silent, and then he stood up and grabbed the film from my hands, walking quickly to the screen room door. He opened the door and glowered at me.

"Repetitious?!!" he said angrily. "Repeti-

tious? I want you to know that this film won the red ribbon at the American Film Festival!" And with that, he was gone, his film clutched tightly to his chest.

I still laugh when I think of the incident, for I can understand his feelings about garnering a first film award, even though he will eventually learn to accept criticism of his work (I hope). There is no doubt that all of us, as we make the long climb through the film world, will become known as "award-winning filmmakers," and many of us win our first recognition at the festivals while we are still in school or in our first years in professional production. There is a glow that automatically comes with a first award, and I can still remember my own first blue ribbon at the American Film Festival (a few years before the young man took his red ribbon, of course). And these many years later—after the filmmaker loses count of the honors—there is still a glow of pride when notice of a festival award comes in the mail.

However, pride and ego aside, the question that I would like to pursue at this point is much more pragmatic: Are they worth it in your career climb? And if so, just how? Somehow, we go along in our film lives just *accepting* the presence of festivals, the constant entry into competitions all over the world, without ever asking ourselves just how they can help us get ahead.

During an interview on a radio show in Minneapolis, the cohosts discussed my own Academy Award nomination and then asked the question: "Are the Academy Awards hype?" I answered, "Of course they're hype. But they're *good* hype. Anything that will get people to see more films or to buy more films is good for the industry." Ten years later, I still feel exactly the same way.

Therein is where the lines are drawn. All your festival awards, all your gold medals, crumbling certificates, art nouveau statuettes, ribbons, plaques, and naked Mercury on a pedestal, will probably do you very little good when you are selling your talents to your peer group. Eventually we all have festival awards. It is part of the game. Why should we be impressed with yours?

In fact, there are award ceremonies that are so incestuous these days that one advertising agency executive called them a fraud, since the industry flexes its own egocentric muscles by giving one another awards for excellence. The Emmy Awards are another case in point. Who wins most of them? The networks, of course, in a sweepstakes to see who can garner the most statuettes in one long night of self-congratulations. Somewhere around 3,500 people vote for the Academy Award nominees, yet the results bring millions into the coffers of the producers and the motion picture houses. The ad executive I quoted earlier hit it right on the head when he said: "Our agency engages in it because it makes us seem successful. And because we win. But it's strictly a new business procedure for us, and we publicize our winnings. People think we're great. . . ."

"It's strictly a *new business* procedure. . . ." If you keep that phrase in mind, no matter how cynical it seems at first, then the festival world can be seen as a valuable, terribly important

"*What this place needs is a film festival.*"

adjunct to the pragmatism of "making it" in film. Thus, I have always entered festivals—as have most filmmakers—and I continue to do so, even with many years of experience and a loyal client list that generally assures continual work. There are a number of business advantages to winning:

★ On the higher levels—the Academy Awards, Cannes, and so on—the winners are assured of greater distribution and acceptance. The producers, the directors, writers, and editors of winning films suddenly find that the telephone will not stop ringing.

A participant in a Los Angeles seminar that I conducted for the American Film Institute a few years ago put it correctly when he told the story of two assistant editors. One had worked on *Star Wars* and had job offers through the next two years. The other had worked on *Heaven's Gate,* the largest financial flop in modern film history, and found that he could not get work. And we are speaking of two *assistant* editors! So the "major leagues" obviously equate awards with income.

★ If you are dependent upon financial grants from foundations, public television, and the other funding sources, your application will read much more convincingly if you can list awards for CINE, American Film Festival, FILMEX, or Columbus. And if you have managed to achieve some wins in Europe, so much the better.
★ If you are in the very commercial world of

business films or advertising or production of television commercials, then awards become even more important to your future. Your clients love to put them on their own walls, just as you do your own plaques and certificates. In a sense, it shows the rest of the corporate world that they chose the right producer for their film.
★ Hanging on your own wall, the award display is a first view to a new client, proving that you have had recognition by people in your own field.

To that end, when I was a partner in a small film company some years back, we festooned the walls of our screening room with our awards—hundreds, filling every space, and including five Academy Award nomination plaques. When a visitor was due to arrive, we always made certain that he or she would be ushered into the screening room to wait for one of the partners. This would give them several minutes in which to survey the golden harvest, just enough time to impress them thoroughly with our expertise. We sold ourselves as being the best in the field. We genuinely believed we were the best. And the awards that we displayed only proved the point to a newcomer.

★ Festivals give a young filmmaker an opportunity to screen his or her film for a public audience, to be judged, and possibly even to be talked about.
★ Festivals keep the experienced filmmaker active in the industry, add to an already

strong reputation, and open the veteran to new filmmakers and new techniques.

One of the most important points is the need for selectivity, both in choosing the right festival and then the best category in which to enter your film. Most of the professional festivals are terribly expensive in terms of entry fees (not to mention the trip to the festival, should you win an award and want to receive it in person). Where entry fees were once as low as $15 per film, they now float on an escalating scale, depending upon length in most cases, and the cost per entry can run from about $50 for a 2-minute film to somewhere around $150 for a motion picture that runs between 50 and 115 minutes. Other festivals charge a flat fee up to about $100 for any film or videotape that is entered, with lower fees for slide presentations and filmstrips. Many have become so commercial that they now accept Visa and MasterCard credit cards!

There is one bright spot in all these escalating costs, however. Many festivals have special entry fees for student and amateur films, and it pays to check this out before you submit your entry. You might also check out the rules very carefully (usually in very fine print on the back of the entry form). Some festivals still use the technique of charging for an original entry, then *charging again* if your film is "lucky" enough to get into the finals.

There are certainly enough festivals from which to choose, and many of them specialize. For example, the Nissan Motor Company sponsors an annual Focus Award in the categories of filmmaking, documentary, animation/experimental, screenwriting, sound achievement, and film editing, with prizes running from $1,000 to $4,500 in scholarships for the winners.

There are now festivals geared entirely toward tape production, such as the Global Village Annual Video and Television Documentary Festival. For the feature and the unknown director, New Directors/New Films, sponsored by the Film Society of Lincoln Center and the Museum of Modern Art, has been the scene of the first public screenings for a great many filmmakers, including John Sayles. There are also the "standard" festivals that all of us know, and where we have gotten many of our early awards: CINE (Council on International Nontheatrical Events), the American Film Festival, the Columbus Film Festival, and San Francisco Film Festival.

Unfortunately, the only book that gives a complete listing of festivals all over the United States and Canada now costs $110 a copy! You might be able to find it in the library; it's called *Festivals Sourcebook* (Gale Research Co., Detroit, Michigan). It covers its 720 pages with just about every festival, fair, and community celebration in the two countries. But even at such a stiff price, it does not list festivals around the world.

The best way to find out where to enter your film is to check the trade papers and magazines and refer to the annual production directory published by *Backstage,* in which a brief listing of festival dates, addresses, and contact names is included.

I also mentioned that the category in which you place your film may have a great deal to do with your chances for taking a prize. For example, in most festivals there is a category that is called "Public Relations" or "Corporate Image." Usually this is the category where the most expensive, glossy, high-powered films end up. It is generally where we find Exxon, General Motors, and others in the blue chip 500. Low-budget films somehow seem to fall by the wayside, however talented the filmmaker and however well done the subject. Thus, a motion picture done for a large agricultural corporation or a manufacturer of tractors, even though it has a corporate image theme, might do much better as an entry in the "Agriculture" category.

There have been many times when one of our films has been eligible for two or even three festival categories, and we have thought carefully about just where to place it. Thus, after you have decided which festival to enter—possibly one devoted entirely to science films, student work, agriculture, marine subjects, advertising, health films, or sports—look carefully at the categories. For example, here is the listing from the American Film Festival, one of the longest running of the group and one of the most influential in the documentary and short film world.

ART AND CULTURE
Fine Arts—architecture, painting, sculpture
Crafts and Hobbies
Performing Arts—dance, drama, music
Cinema/Television Photography—history, techniques, styles
Literature—dramatizations, language arts
Fiction Films—narratives

Children's Entertainment Films—includes teenagers
EDUCATION AND INFORMATION
Elementary/Junior High School Instructional
Anthropology and Ethnography—including urban anthropology
Religion and Society
History and Archaeology
Social Studies
Science and Mathematics
Nature and Wildlife
Sports and Leisure Activities
MENTAL HEALTH AND GUIDANCE
Mental Health—psychiatry and psychology
Teacher Education—philosophies, goals, methods, reforms
The Disabled
Guidance/Career Education
Human Sexuality—relationships, sex education
Family Relations/Parenting
CONTEMPORARY CONCERNS
Environmental Issues—ecology, pollution, city planning
Energy/Nuclear Issues
International Concerns—social, economic, political
Citizen Action—community organization, political reform, civil rights
Social Issues—social problems, current events
Human Concerns—commentaries on society and human nature
Life-styles
Profiles—autobiographies and biography
FEATURE-LENGTH DOCUMENTARIES
BUSINESS AND INDUSTRY
Management and Sales Training

Industrial Training and Safety

Motivational Films for Business Use

Labor Films—employee relations, union history, work issues

Technology—industrial and scientific processes

Travel and Tourism

Public Relations

Public Information, Commercial—sponsored by business corporations

Public Service, Nonprofit—government and nonprofit agencies

HEALTH AND SAFETY

Medical Sciences—for professional audiences

Health Education—for general audiences

Addiction—alcohol, drugs, tobacco

Nutrition

Safety and First Aid

FILM AS ART

Animation

Visual Essays

Humor and Satire

Somewhere in that almost endless listing there must be a category for the film you'd like to enter. Other festivals add even more specific categories, such as entertainment short subjects and science fiction, and the Rochester International Film Festival is for "movies on a shoestring."

Recently we entered one of our films for Sunkist Growers in the CINE Festival and won a Golden Eagle, which promptly took its place among the others on our wall as well as on the wall of our client at Sunkist, Jack Heeger. Flushed with victory, we entered the same film in the annual Agricultural Film Festival spon-

sored by the Cooperative Information Fair in Phoenix, and we received a lovely certificate on which was printed the word "SECOND" in bold, red letters. To make matters even more frustrating, our film came in second after getting *99 out of 100* points on the judge's scoring sheet.

We who have been around a long time, we who are jaded and nonchalant, we who really don't care about festivals (we keep saying), opened the package and shouted, *"Second?* How come we only took second?!!!"

So much for being blasé.

MAKING IT THROUGH THE CHANGES

The Technological Revolution: How Long Will the State of the Art Be the State of the Art?

When we were kids, we used to imagine what might happen if George Washington were to reappear in our society and suddenly be confronted with radio (we didn't have television), an airplane flying overhead, electricity, or even the common automobile. The story of Rip Van Winkle was impressed upon all of us, for when he awakened after his twenty-year sleep, everything had been transformed around him. Well, we might as well face the fact that a film producer, having slept soundly through the past ten years, might well awaken to the same feeling of disorientation and confusion.

Eavesdropping on a conversation, the producer might be shaken into reality by hearing someone explain, "What we've done is hooked up an Ultimatte to the output of the Rank Cintel Flying Spot Scanner to transfer the video. We're doing matte inserting and creating matte windows right out of the Rank onto our first-generation one-inch."

Without doubt, the computerization of the motion picture industry and the concomitant explosion of tape production is, at first glance, the most obvious change in the way that we produce the end product, be it feature or ten-second spot. "Twenty-four frames per second" has given way to RAM (random access memory), ROM (read only memory), and a vast, ever-growing language entirely based upon the bits and bytes that are now upon us.

But with the avalanche of articles, new school courses, and even a television series of instructions all based upon the computer, we sometimes lose sight of the fact that the revolution has affected *every* part of our industry, and much of the development has taken place outside the realm of microchip high tech. For those of us who have been in the field for many years, the changes have been amazing, even in the areas of equipment and techniques that have become standard in our production armory. Without even touching the realm of computerization or tape, the advances have crept into our field and we now accept technologies and improvements that would have been gratefully embraced in the earlier days of film:

★ As simple a thing as a motor-driven zoom lens is something that is now used universally. Suddenly the zoom has smoothed out, saving the sanity of assistant cameramen, directors, and cinematographers, and through its efficiency saving producers up to thousands of dollars in film stock!

★ The very *size* of our film equipment—as well as reduction in weight through invention of new materials—has created more mobility, greater potential for achieving our film objectives, and a noticeable shrinking in size of the film crew, especially for the independent and documentary filmmaker.

★ In the area of sound mixing, years ago, from three to ten tracks were mixed one reel at a time, and each time a mistake was made, *the mixer rewound all the way back to the beginning of the ten-minute reel.* If he made a mistake in the last ten seconds, back he went to frame number one. There was no such thing as STOP and START!

Technology in the film industry has come a long, long way since the hand-cranked camera. Even young film students might recognize one or both of the "cameramen."

The technology offers a variety of "camera platforms" for today's film and tape crews. Colt Helicopter's A-Star provides a stable yet maneuverable ride, and the motorcycle designed for ABC Sports' New York Marathon by ENG's Alex Carey is an ingenious improvement over the convertible car or truck.

There is no doubt that, on the one hand, all these technological advances have been very much like the old Horn & Hardart Automat slogan: "Less Work for Mother." The ease of using featherweight equipment, for example, allowed me to travel with cameraman Jon Fauer on a six-country South American trip—just the two of us—doing synchronized sound on a C.I.A.–developed Nagra (the SL), with an Arriflex SR-16 and one case of lights!

The further technological breakthroughs of Eastman Kodak and other film laboratories have also eased the way for the producer, especially the person just starting out, and particularly those of us who do not have $20 million budgets for our films. At one time, blowing up 16 mm film to 35 mm theater-screen size would have been unacceptable. The grain factor alone would have turned an audience away. The advent of the liquid gate blowup process has meant that low-budget features now have a chance to be produced without the horrendous hemorrhage of cash that bleeds the budget with every foot of 35 mm color film that we expose. Today, a large number of lower-budget features have been shot in either 16 mm or Super-16 mm and are then blown up to 35 mm for release. Among them:

★ *Angelo My Love* (Robert Duvall)
★ *Lianna* (John Sayles)
★ *Smithereens* (Susan Seidelman)
★ *The Weavers* (Jim Brown)
★ *Come Back to the Five and Dime Jimmy Dean, Jimmy Dean* (Robert Altman)
★ *Girlfriends* (Claudia Weill)
★ *Chan Is Missing* (Wayne Wang)

Of course, with each technological innovation two things happen in an industry such as ours:

★ We reject it out of hand and never use it at all.
★ We fall in love with it and begin to use it too much.

In that sense we are no different from the rest of history. After all, everyone knew that Columbus would fall off the edge of the world. And the airplane would never get off the ground. Everyone knew that the horse was better than the automobile, and besides that, the horse needed only hay and oats to keep it going (with an end product that didn't pollute and was excellent for the garden!).

We film people, in turn, frequently have a problem in judging the value of a new invention and determining whether it will really help our output, whether its cost balances its creative or visual effect, and whether it is even *right* for us. Many of us have been "doing our thing" in our way for many years. It has worked before, and there's absolutely no reason, we say, that it can't continue to work without considering another way of doing it.

When the development of liquid gate blowup was finally honed to a predictable level of quality, I had a discussion with some friends of mine who were in the advertising agency business and in network television. The subject came around to costs and the escalating budgets in our industry. I commented that since their end

product was eventually broadcast over television and was subject to quality reduction on the average home set, less-than-adequate color balance, and the vicissitudes of transmission interference, why did they not shoot their commercials and promotional material in 16 mm film and then blow it up to 35 mm?

At that time, one of my own films was playing at New York's Radio City Music Hall, on the world's largest screen. It was a short subject that I had produced for Coca-Cola around the world, and it had been chosen for distribution by United Artists as a curtain raiser for the feature presentation in theaters across the country. I invited them to the theater, all six of them, and they watched the film in silence. There was no blowup grain. The color was perfect. The audience even applauded, and we all went out into the street.

They were amazed. One agency executive commented, "I'm sold." The network art director said, "I'm glad I saw it. I never would have thought a blowup would look that good. I'm a convert!"

Every story has a moral, and this one is no exception. It is now twelve years since that screening. Everyone who attended *still* uses 35 mm color film. No one in the group has ever tried to blow up 16 mm. Each one has reasons, I suppose. For the agency people, using 35 mm is "professional," and anyhow, they get 17½ percent on top of their expenses. For the art director, there is the very pragmatic reason that opticals are more easily done on 35 mm. But even in the simplest of film productions, the larger, more expensive stock is still the choice, though many of my friends *have* moved over to tape for some of their work.

On the other hand, many of us—even the same people I've described above—will fall madly in love with a piece of technology or a development in the film field and use it until it becomes a part of every one of our productions. Our friends and competitors, seeing us embrace the new invention, also "must have it," and it becomes an industry necessity, whether we need it or not.

I am not speaking of such pragmatic developments as walkie-talkies, spot meters, light-weight tripods, or faster film stock.

★ There was a time when every moving shot, in order to be steady and smooth, would require the laying of tracks. If the shot went on for two hundred yards of dollying, the tracks would be dutifully put down and the heavy dolly moved on to it for the long push. It is still done in many productions, but a few years back Garrett Brown invented a most ingenious piece of equipment that would eliminate the tedious, time-consuming, and expensive laying of dolly tracks. He called it the Steadicam.

It was first publicized when it was used in the original production of *Rocky;* the run up the steps of the Philadephia Museum of Art by Sylvester Stallone was filmed entirely with the hand-held, body-mounted Steadicam in one smooth, remarkable, and effective movement.

Brown received the Academy Award in 1978 for his invention, and immediately another

Cameraman Ted Churchill has made his reputation as one of the foremost experts with the Steadicam. His feature films have included Ghostbusters, The Cotton Club, *and* The King of Comedy, *as well as a long list of commercials and documentaries.*

film explosion took place. *Everyone had to have it.* I don't think there was a commercial made in those days that didn't use the Steadicam, and other cameramen, like my old friend Ted Churchill, became expert in its use and subsequently found that they were in constant demand from producers in features as well as in commercials. There was a short time when almost every producer or ad agency would find a way to use the Steadicam, even for a scene of a hundred-year-old woman sitting on a porch and just rocking. Just as the zoom lens created a constant moving in and out of all shots (and caused a thousand film editors to moan that nothing ever stayed still any longer), so do inventions like the Steadicam become "chic" and overused.

Brown then began working on an invention that he calls the Skycam—a *flying* computerized camera that is controlled by an "elevator joystick." It flies at twenty miles an hour with separate controls for panning, tilting, zooming, and focusing, all the while suspended in the air by flexible cables. Brown himself says that it's for "those shots of which directors have dreamed heretoforwithunder," and he calls it the "ultimate video game"!

Just about the time this book was to go into the final stages of production, a news article informed me that the Skycam had passed its first professional test in a film directed by Hal Ashby and shot by Caleb Deschanel—*The Slugger's Wife* (Columbia). Needless to say, the entire production crew was ecstatic about the results—a view of a baseball game seen almost from the point of view of the baseball itself! Knowing what happened with the invention of

the zoom lens and the excesses committed thereafter, and knowing about the attitudes of filmmakers who *must* be ahead of the trends, can you now imagine what will happen with Garrett Brown's newest invention? He apologizes in advance for all the gratuitous zooms, flights upward, and stomach-wrenching drops that are about to take place on film!

The key for the filmmaker who operates on a budget (most of us), or who is just starting out in the field and trying to balance the dollars against screen impact, is to know *when* to use the new "state of the art" equipment, whether or not you can afford it, and most important of all, whether or not it is right for your production even if you *can* manage to squeeze it into your budget.

As the technology "improves" (if we give the benefit of the doubt to the constantly changing technological field), we may find ourselves paying more and more for less and less, all because we are fascinated and somewhat blinded by the term "state of the art."

Most of my readers have grown up with this technological explosion, more incredible and ingenious inventions in film and tape in just these past ten years than during the entire history of the industry. If the invention of sound on film was a milestone, and *The Jazz Singer* was its monument, then we are producing a hundred *Jazz Singer*s every month as "state of the art" technology continues to change rapidly, making equipment purchased for millions just last year suddenly obsolete.

Perhaps the most important point of all is that the mere invention of all this technology

does not eliminate the *personal responsibility* of the producer toward the eventual end product, not only in the area of budget, but in the very important concern of what the film/tape *looks* like. Much of the technology offered to us is so terribly expensive on a per-minute or per-hour basis that we seldom have the time (or take the time) these days to discuss a specific shot or the nuance of an effect. More important, perhaps, is the fact that there may well be *another way* to accomplish what we had visualized in the first place, if only we would stop and think about it. The new technologies that have showered our industry with new terms, and new equipment, may well mean "less work for Mother," but they

The Tyler mount has made helicopter photography steady and effective by smoothing out the bumps and vibrations of the aircraft. But with an open door, the job can be shiveringly cold for the cameraman.

do not relieve us from the thinking and planning that absolutely must go into a successful film project.

Earlier, in discussing his work with me, John Sayles mentioned the fact that his budgets may not allow him the luxury of a "Hollywood" crane shot, and thus he must come up with something else, and something just as effective. Film producers have been faced with this problem as far back as the hand-cranked camera, and will be faced with it long after the language of today has given way to yet another language, when "the standard 3500C accepts RS170 RGB/ TTL input with either separate or composite sync" will take its place with other obsolete terms, like Kodachrome II, the Edsel, and the icebox. But the one constant will be that the *ingenuity* of the producer will continue to be tested and tested again.

Think carefully about what follows in this chapter dedicated to the rapid technological changes in our industry. And remember that as a filmmaker you are responsible for creative productivity, that the budget doesn't end at the terminal of a computer or with a shiny new piece of film equipment. The best stories in film are the ones that tell us how a producer overcame the problems of production, whether because of economy, lack of planning, or, most often, the natural unpredictability of location shooting:

★ For years film crews have needed a dolly when they didn't have one, either because no dolly was available, or because there was no room to carry even the smallest one along with the twenty equipment

Film crews also use balloons as camera platforms, in addition to helicopters, planes, and the Skycam. The Hartwick/Przyborski crew poses in front of their balloon basket before filming a beer spot for Martsteller, Inc., in Nashville, Tennessee.

cases. More often than not, a director is suddenly given a vision from heaven and commands in the middle of a sequence, "Get me a dolly!"

After a consultation and some suggestions (considering that you are shooting in the middle of a Kansas wheatfield or in Belcherville, Texas, where the natives have never even seen *a film crew*, not to mention a Western Dolly), something generally manages to appear.

★ Someone goes quickly to the nearest hospital or clinic or medical/surgical rental store or large industrial plant with an in-house clinic and borrows or rents a wheelchair. The cameraman sits down, and a dolly is born.

★ A nearby factory or office building rents or lends a four-wheel hand truck, sometimes one with large rubber wheels. On the proper surface, film crews can use it with great success. And if the surface is not "proper"? The crew manages to borrow four-by-eight-foot plywood panels from a nearby construction company to make the surface "proper."

★ The nearest convertible car or pickup truck, with tires flattened a bit, has made the dolly platform for hundreds of film crews. We once put a convertible on a running track and used it as a dolly while the jogger slowly collapsed take after take in the hot sun.

★ We have used children's wagons, typewriter tables, and supermarket shopping

Director/cameraman Bill Fertik shoots a "dolly" shot in Rome. Even with the development of ultrasophisticated film equipment, the ordinary wheelchair is often put into service as a quick, reliable, convenient dolly platform.

carts! But the best and most ingenious "dolly" of all was invented on the spot in Manchester, England.

Our location was a cotton mill, and our cameraman, Jon Fauer, was to photograph two executives walking down a long, long hallway. He noticed the frittered light coming through the windows, casting patterns as they walked. Jon turned to me and wistfully said that if we had a dolly, he could do a wonderful shot of their *feet* in close-up, moving through the light patterns.

Of course, we had no dolly. But there, standing in the corner, was a large, soft-textured, combination broom/mop, used to sweep the scraps from the factory floor. Jon placed the SR-16 on the mop, held it with his hand, turned on the switch, and *pushed the mop* along with the feet of the two men as they walked down the corridor! The shot was exquisite. It even got into the film.

But then, we might have used the Steadicam or the Skycam!

Videotape: The Boom Goes On

If I were to summarize the primary question that now plagues the entire communications industry in an era of rapidly changing technology, I might

quote from a statement written by one of the students who attended my lectures at the Global Village in New York. The words are interesting because he is very much a part of this new generation of younger film/tape production people who are generally at home with the computer, and indeed many of them even have a computer at home. He is twenty-six years old and he is a video technician:

"I am concerned about the future of motion pictures. In five to ten years, will they be shot entirely in video with new technology? Will there be a place for film? Will a director need to master all the technical operations and applications? As a video technician, I am slowly grasping the 'high tech' stuff that keeps on changing. With digital audio and recording methods, laser discs, satellite transmissions, I feel bombarded with information that worries me to the point that I feel that I must keep up or it will pass me."

His comments concluded with an interesting observation, considering the fact that he trained in the video field:

"What I like about film is that basically the medium is fixed or standardized, leaving me 'only' with the problem of how to tell a story."

The film/tape discussion has raged for twenty years now, and it certainly shows no signs of abating. In fact, as the tape field grows and more filmmakers begin to work in the medium, the "battle" intensifies. For one who was

brought up in the early days of live television and entered the film industry in 1956, I am particularly fascinated with the discussion, since I now produce in both film and tape; yet I have both prejudices and some high regard that date back to editing two-inch tape with a razor blade and strips of metallic tape! Even with the advent of the Chyron, Vidifont, the Ampex Digital Optics, and the Mirage, Dubner, and Ultimatte, many of my earlier prejudices remain, some have been further strengthened, and my high regard grows in some areas, along with a continuing awe at the scope of this vast revolution.

Most of all, much of my writing and my seminars have been in the area of career opportunities in our field, and my thrust has always been to encourage the younger filmmaker to continue his or her efforts to get ahead in an industry that has no other role model in our society. Thus, the growth of a *new* area is of particular interest to me, for it creates a most fertile field of new job potential for this generation of computer-educated people. I feel that this should be the prime factor in considering whether or not tape will replace film or live side by side with it for eternity. There is no doubt that tape is one of the greatest growth areas since the publication of *Getting into Film*. Along with cable, computer graphics, videoconferencing, and the expanding area of interactive video, the tape industry has experienced an almost geometric surge.

In New York City alone there is a listing of over two hundred videotape service companies and individuals who provide production facilities, studios, dealerships, repair and maintenance,

National Video Center's editing suite "G" as the state of the art constantly changes. Producer Scott Webb, editor Ivan Anhalt, and National Video Center engineer Norm Powers at National's Grass Valley switcher, Ampex ADO, Datatron Vanguard editing system, ADM Technology audio board, Conrac and Techtronics video monitors, BEI CG 3000, Urei sound monitors, and the backup VPR 3s and VPR 2Bs. Ten years back it was all a foreign language.

recording and editing facilities (off line and on line), and mobile equipment. For each facility that opens, there is a need for technicians, video engineers, scenic designers, studio crews, transfer and color experts, drivers, construction people, and all the adjunct services that are required for production of even a ten-second spot, not to mention programs, training tapes, music video, and the booming market of video-cassettes.

As the field expands, however, the same problems and myths arise that plague the introduction of any new development. We are too quick to call it a panacea, we discount too quickly the history that has gone before and the ability of other parts of our industry to adapt to change. Just a year or two after the introduction of videotape, the doomsayers were already burying the film industry. Too many beginners enter our field, rushing into videotape without the solid background that the earlier film technicians required as part of their learning process.

If you are to straddle both fields, if you are to follow a career path that may well move from film to tape and back again to film, you would do well to get to know *both* technologies, and to understand some of the advantages and disadvantages that film and tape can offer you, not only in a creative sense but in the job potentials that will determine your eventual career goals.

After a most remarkable and rapid growth, the videotape industry is currently going through what has become a standard and continuing procedure for small film production companies—a flattening out and a shaking out of its ranks. "Boom" doesn't always equate with "success," and many small facilities, started on a shoestring and trying to keep up with the expense of a changing technology, have already fallen out of competition. Back in 1983, for example, the cable industry faltered and television commercials dried out for a time; in describing the situation, videotape consultant Geoffrey Kelley remarked, "The summer was a lox!" At the same time, the larger conglomerates, seeing tape (correctly) as the next big boom, began to enter the field, backed by almost limitless amounts of capital. The small tape houses began to see the shadows of Gannett Industries and Warner Brothers outside their doors.

The summer chill of 1983 created a price war, facilities were going begging, and it took several months for the top people in the tape field to predict that it had finally begun to stabilize somewhat. The reality suddenly appeared: entering the videotape field and *staying in it successfully* can be an incredibly expensive undertaking:

★ Equipment is now terribly expensive, and it is no longer possible to pay it off long term.

★ The technology changes almost every day, and a million dollars' worth of sophisticated, computer-generated equipment is obsolete or noncompetitive.

★ As technicians and engineers have become more experienced and the industry has begun to develop its editing "stars," these people have been asking for and getting premium salaries. The industry is out of its learning stage.

★ The cost of building an editing room has almost doubled in the past two or three years.

★ The price cutting that now goes on plays to the advantage of the larger houses, pushing small producers into a very thin line of survival.

For the producer in the communications industry, all of this has had one very telling effect. As the videotape industry has expanded, as it has become more and more of a "business" with all of the problems that accompany an established industry, it has also begun to be a more expensive production route than it was thought to be at first.

In those early days, it was always said that tape was less expensive than film, and in specific situations it was indeed. In certain situations, even today, it is also the wise budget choice for specific jobs, such as hidden-camera commercials or taping sporting events with multiple cameras. But for a great part of our world, the myth goes on, in spite of the changes that have taken place. In fact, there are times when tape is now *much more* expensive than film, and as a result there has been a return to the film medium by producers who have become disenchanted with the new technology. Both because of budget and because we have discovered the limitations of videotape (a good sign), we are beginning to find that film is not really dead at all, and my best advice to the young man who wrote the letter at the beginning of this section is to get to know them both!

As late as the middle of 1984, film continued to be the standard for much of network television. Nearly *80 percent* of the prime-time network television in the United States in the previous year was produced on film! And if we look carefully at the job market, it might be wise to realize that many of us who produce both in tape and in film generally choose *only* film-trained people for our tape jobs, for many of the reasons that will follow shortly. Almost every film person I know has made it a point to train in tape technology. We bring to our tape work years of training in concept, color, design, and continuity, while accepting the things that tape can now add to our creative armory. On the other hand, tape has had such a sudden growth, and schools have been turning out technicians and would-be tape producers in such great numbers, that I generally find the opposite is not the case: tape people generally know very little or nothing at all about film, its philosophy, and its technology.

To be fair, I must discuss the other side of the coin. There are film people who have fallen madly in love with the newer medium and have reveled in the terminology and immediacy of some tape production. For the most part, I find that this has occurred in the advertising agency world, where at least twelve people are involved with the creative overview of each ten-second spot. This is said without sarcasm, I assure you, for even my agency friends have admitted that instantaneous playback of tape has been a boon to agency copywriters, producers, casting directors, account supervisors, and all the others who work with a production company toward the final product. In addition, the mounting costs of which

I spoke are of little matter in a ten-second spot when compared with a one-hour documentary.

Much of what I write here will no doubt be assailed by the videotape industry and by the students who are studying their craft in schools around the country, for too often the balance of film/tape is never discussed. Yet it must be if we are to understand. I am merely asking for a reasonable evaluation of tape as a medium and as a job market for those of us who work in communications, so that we may better choose our own options and guide our clients and those who support our efforts financially, be it the foundations or the networks.

Through a great many discussions with film friends and tape friends, I have compiled a list, which I've broken down into two categories:

★ The Blessings of Videotape
★ The Realities of Videotape

Note that I have not listed them as *advantages* and *disadvantages,* for depending upon the project you are producing, an advantage one day may turn into a disadvantage the next—and vice versa. You may well want to add your own comments to the lists:

THE BLESSINGS

INSTANT REPLAY. One of the problems of film, with which we have learned to live, is the fact that some distant location is filmed in a situation that cannot be repeated (such as a festival or a one-time speech or any special event), and we have to get the film back to the

Flying Tiger tape crew in Washington, D.C., for the WQED special Puppets. *Kay Armstrong, sound; Ned Hallick, gaffer; Bud Mikhatarian, recordist; Tony Foresta, camera.*

United States and into a laboratory. For days we sweat out the results, and heaven forbid the phone should ring and we hear, "Mel, this is Phil Sodano at Du Art. . . ." Our hearts drop to our boots and we wait, not breathing, to hear if the negative might have been scratched. The most remarkable thing about tape is that we know if we have it or we don't have it right there, at the moment. We play it back. We find that the actors (if any) can observe their performances, discuss their roles with the director, and make a decision, either "we have it" or "let's do it again."

Francis Ford Coppola has taken the instantaneous aspect of tape one step further. Though his final efforts are on motion picture film, he sits in an electronically equipped trailer and, facing an array of television monitors, sets up another shot by remote control, taping each scene simultaneously as the film camera rolls.

Coppola's theory is that it facilitates the editing process and allows him to watch an instantaneous playback of the framing as well as hear the delivery of the actors' line readings. (I should comment here that I will also discuss the Coppola system in the section that I have dubbed "The Realities," for with every advantage, there seems to be a concomitant problem.)

Interestingly enough, the technique of combining film with video is not new. Back in 1951, when I was a director at what was then the DuMont Television Network (now Metromedia), there was some intense experimentation with a technology called the Electronicam. At that time there was no tape, and if we wanted to record a show that was transmitted live—either to save it for the record or to send it to another station for replay—we used the kinescope system. Unfortunately, this was merely the recording of a show on film taken directly from an image orthicon screen, not the best of images, to put it mildly.

The Electronicam was designed to work by connecting a motion picture camera to the television camera, to simultaneously film the show, as it was transmitted over the air live. I remember an old friend, the late Barry Shear, another director at DuMont, explaining the system to me, and I remember the awe with which I looked at the first color screens in that same studio. *The Honeymooners,* Jackie Gleason's popular show, and other DuMont Network shows were transmitted live and filmed through the Electronicam, reedited on film, and then distributed through the country for syndication. Today, of course, tape has replaced all of that and has done it well.

OPTICAL EFFECTS. There is a vast range of optical effects available through the new tape systems and their electronic alphabet. Dissolves, complicated mattes, zooms and inserts, title production, color correction, slow motion, freeze frames, explosions, crawls, and a thousand other adjustments and innovations are all there in the final editing of the tape project. Certainly it is not cheap, and it sometimes takes hours to accomplish, but when it's done, it's done, and there's no wait for the lab work, no sweating out the complicated film optical to see if it has worked. If it works, you know it right then and there. In a sense, the availability of these technological marvels enables us to add production value to a product—if we learn not to overuse it.

However, one of the production areas most adversely affected by the growth of tape has been the film optical house, formerly our only source for titles, effects, and all the complex graphics from split screen to explosions. For the people who work in film opticals, this has been a time of severe change, and in the early days of tape editing, the industry was beginning to call the film optical a dinosaur. Here's a comment from an old friend of mine, Dick Rauh, of The Optical House Inc. in New York (which has done the title and special effects work for *Reds, Altered States,* and *Tender Mercies,* as well as for hundreds of documentaries and possibly thousands of commercials):

"The advantage of video is immediate. Agency people and art directors can finally make decisions that affect the finished product, and they can do it at once. It's instant gratification in its purest form."

Dick feels that the expertise of the film editor and the optical expert is no longer here, that the aesthetic decisions are being left to the art director, the client, and the producer. In addition:

"People used to want starry skies. Now they want a metallic look, neon kinds of letters. I've received a number of requests to simulate computer games effects. No one wants a simple title anymore!"

But, as so often happens, the eulogy was given before the patient was dead. The film optical houses, fighting for survival, have gone even further into features, special effects, business films, and foreign markets that still demand the craftsmanship and attention to detail that optical experts can offer. In addition, the computer is not new to the film optical world. Dick says:

"I took a computer course thirty years ago, and I thought the film world as I knew it was going to completely disappear."

Instead, the computer was utilized not only for tape edits, but also for the machines that had become the standbys of the film optical world: the Oxbury optical stands, the mechanical concept stands, and the optical printers.

Though the ratio of finishing on tape (after shooting on film) began to creep close to 90 percent in favor of tape, especially for commercials, that ratio is slowly inching back for a reason that didn't enter into our decisions in the beginning: *cost.* The burgeoning costs of tape editing have begun to bring producers and agencies back to film, because, as Dick puts it:

"Video designs a ten-million-dollar machine that can only do one thing—possibly a flip and nothing else. So video is constantly an ongoing engineering process, and since the problems are never the same in this business, equipment is constantly being redesigned to meet the new problems."

Tom Newsom at the EFX Oxberry optical printer. Recent developments in computerization have created a new competitive environment in the field of film opticals.

Up until recently, the ratio of finishing in tape versus in film has been approximately 90 percent/10 percent; optical house executives now report the ratio is closer to 80 percent/20 percent. As editing costs increase even more in the next few years, the proportion will probably almost equal out. And with the increase in feature work, documentary production, and special effects, what seemed to be a dying job market for the young filmmaker has begun to renew itself. Thus, not only is *tape* a viable career path for the artist or the graphic designer, but the *film* optical seems to be holding its own in a severely competitive market. In addition, there's one other bright light on the horizon:

"In our industry, there's no problem in joining the Screen Cartoonists Union. If you have a job, you're in the union. We also use a lot of young people from the local art schools to fill our summer jobs."

COMPLETION AND DUPLICATION. Though the editing may take as long as or longer than film—and might be just as expensive—the beauty of tape is that it eliminates the long film process of completion and duplication (for release prints) once the job is "locked up." When the on-line editing is completed on a tape project, the job is done, it can be screened, and it can be duplicated in hundreds of copies in just a few short days. For projects that run on deadline, there is no substitute for tape, while film requires the matching of the negative, the production of an acceptable answer print, and the making of a color reversal internegative (or other printing strand) and a check print. All this, followed by a week or ten more days in which the prints are turned out for distribution. In that area, I have found tape to be an extreme pleasure, and when I leave the postproduction facility after the on-line edit, the job is quite finished. It is a good feeling.

MORE EFFECTIVE AND MORE ECONOMICAL WHEN PROPERLY USED. The key words are "when properly used." A good example might be the use of tape in hidden-camera commercials or other productions where you keep rolling for hours or even for a full day. The cost of film in this case would be an almost unbearable burden. As Nat Eisenberg, one of the best-known directors of this technique, says:

"When it comes to hidden-camera shoots, both for cost and ease of operation, the nod must go to videotape. You have only to take two or three cameras turning all day during five- to fifteen-minute interviews and figure the cost of purchasing, developing, and printing the film equivalent. Reloading the tape and cassette machines happens much less frequently. Even with the videotape/feed attached to a film camera, you really don't see it all as it's really happening."

One of the prime considerations in the use of videotape, aside from tight schedules and air dates, is the eventual use of the finished product. If it is to be viewed entirely on television screens, this may well be a factor in your choice.

Even here, however, many of us have shot on film and eventually transferred to tape for distribution.

The complexity of the job is yet another factor. There are some productions that cry out for videotape, while others are better produced on film. There are no rules here—just as there are no obvious rules anywhere in our industry. Go over the shooting problems carefully, the preproduction necessary to start the project, the equipment and how it will be transported, above all the editing needs and their costs. Then, as the most important aspect of your choice, figure out the *budget* in minute detail. There are times when you will no doubt be surprised.

Recently I was awarded a job that was to be produced in videotape. With a sharp pencil and an unlimited supply of accounting paper, I went at the budget for several hours—film or tape? When I was finished, I looked at the results and laughed. In dealing with almost one hundred thousand dollars in the production of the series, *the costs were ten dollars apart*! (Film was more expensive, unless I saved one dinner for the crew.) The production time needed, oddly enough, was almost equal. I chose tape because of only one factor: the final distribution of prints to the cities across the country had to be done rather quickly after completion, and tape could do it faster.

EASE OF SCREENINGS. Most of us in the field have to show our samples, whether to a new client or when we screen for potential employers. Finding film screening facilities can be difficult and expensive. Many small production companies don't even have film screening rooms—or even a projector. Today, with the proliferation of videotape records and playback systems, I have found a new freedom in letting potential clients see my work. This has also been true for camera people, writers, producers, and animators. As an accidental blessing, I have found that the Fast Forward and the Search buttons make my life easier. When the sample is terribly dull, I can rapidly move the tape to another section to see if the story improves. I realize, of course, that my new clients can also do the same thing when they screen *my* work.

A NEW AREA OF EXPERIMENTATION. The advent of tape has given rise to a new generation of independents and experimental videotape producers, and this can only be good for the eventual growth of the industry and the development of new ideas. It is very much where film was back in the late fifties and early sixties, with groups such as Cinema 16, a film club that screened some of the experimental works of filmmakers around the world. It was where I first saw a film by Len Lye, work by Norman McLaren, and, of course, some of the most awfully boring (and sometimes bloody) short films ever conceived.

Today, the videotape world has spawned its own group of experimental artists, and some of their work is now being released in retail sales for the home market.

Nam June Paik is probably one of the best known of these new explorers, but new names crop up over and over again in the newspapers

Some directors have made their mark in hidden camera production. The technique requires detailed preproduction planning plus the security of the control room as critical to the success of the shoot. Releases are gotten immediately after the subject is filmed. Here, Nat Eisenberg directs a Tide commercial in Canada.

and magazines now devoted to reporting and criticizing videotape as "art": Mary Lucier, Dara Birnbaum, John Dorr, Jamie Walters, John Canaly, and a host of new entrants each year, all of whom have grown up with television, the video screen, and the complexities of the computer. Only time will tell whether they will provide the innovative artistry that will make their names as well known as their counterparts in independent film, whether they will move television out of its mediocre rut, or whether they are just reinventing the wheel.

Earlier in this book, I mentioned the "filmbabble" that has blossomed in our world. Unfortunately, the video experimenters and their critics seem to be falling into exactly the same trap, and though they frequently claim to be *improving* the TV world, much of their work is as bad as or worse, as well as more boring, than some of the mundane shows that are born at the networks.

The five-channel presentations at the museums and the festivals of video art have begun to develop their own "videobabble" just as we have in film. Critical descriptions abound with words such as "steamy blur," "repetitive fast-paced visual orchestration," and the awesome visual effect of a young woman "demonstrating the virtues of a Wang word processor." It is almost as though the 1960s are being reinvented just for the convenience of the new technology.

But with it all, I can only quote something that I overheard some time ago, when a friend made a heated defense of the new technology: "Sure, there's lousy tape being produced today. But you have to admit that there's just as much bad film. . . ."

True, how very true.

THE REALITIES

As I mentioned previously, the subject of tape is a very personal one. Were a videotape-trained producer to compile this list, many of the statements might well go into the "Blessings" category instead of being tagged "Realities." Keep in mind, however, that I am a *film-trained* producer who works in both categories. So, too, do my film crews, and among them I see a gradual return to the film medium in many areas of production. Obviously there must be a reason. In the midst of a videotape boom, in a field that is growing and here to stay, possibly there is as much of a "shaking out" in our philosophy about film/tape as there is in the steady leveling of the number of companies that offer videotape services. We have been at it long enough now to see its potential and its beauty. But we have also lived with it long enough, just as in long-term relationships among people, to begin to see how ordinary it looks when it "gets up in the morning."

So the following "realities" are observations by many of us, and you may well add your own or feel free to disagree. All I ask is that you listen:

INSTANT REPLAY. Note that this aspect was included in the "blessings" category as well. The reason I have listed it here is that we now have the most collaborative medium ever invented, because now *everyone* can watch and comment and complain and discuss and change. In film, the advantage of the eyepiece of the camera is that only the cinematographer and the director can discuss a shot, possibly letting a third person look through the viewfinder. The film goes to the lab, and a couple of days later the dailies are screened by a selected few.

Now, certainly instant playback will tell us whether the scene was perfect or nearly perfect or unacceptable, but on an actual location, everyone ends up looking at the screen. This is especially true during the shooting of commercials, when almost every agency person has a comment or criticism of the shot just completed. Thus, the suggestion of doing it over "just for safety" or a comment about how an actor read a line, is fair game for interference on every level. I find, in my own videotape productions, that I move away from the set and the actors and inch closer and closer to the video monitor. Soon I am "directing" off the monitor, just as I did in the early days of live television—and my contact with the set is lost.

On the Francis Ford Coppola production of *The Cotton Club*, a friend of mine worked with the crew and was a close observer of the technique of shooting film and tape simultaneously, with the director confined to the control room. Certainly it is one person's opinion, but he told me, "I think it's a waste when you get right down to it. It has nothing to do with the way a shot looks on film—in fact, you can't tell a damned thing about the color or the quality of detail. It has a lot to do with the framing, and for the actor you can get line readings. But it's slow—*and everyone gets involved, everyone is looking at the monitor!*"

With the expansion of videotape, editing facilities have become available all over the country. This is the editing suite at the Palace Production Center in South Norwalk, Connecticut.

THE LIMITATION AND EXPENSE OF EDITING. When tape was known as "quick and dirty," this was not a problem. Many times we shot with three cameras and did our switching right in the control room. Thus, a finished tape was ready in "real time," when we walked out of the control room after looking at the final cut. Today the advent of new equipment and new technologies has made the editing of videotape a more refined area of production, but it has also made it tedious and expensive. As one film/tape editor friend puts it, "Editing tape is like pulling a locomotive!"

In film editing, the entire process is a continual discussion between editor and director, conferences over the smallest of cuts, decisions that hinge on one or two frames, or the nuance of a voice on the track. In the final stages, especially at the "interlock," changes are fairly simple in most cases, and client input can be accepted and acted upon. Tape editing, however instantaneous it is supposed to be, is a time-consuming ballet for each and every decision:

★ You find the edit.
★ You program the edit.
★ You rehearse the edit.
★ You perform the edit.
★ You review the edit.

In addition, there is no way today that a complex audio track can be put together as effectively as in film, though we are promised that it will soon change. Most tape editors are not trained to think in terms of multiple tracks that are mixed before finalizing the production.

And if the edit requires a complex series of track cuts, most editors are now producing the track on film and transferring to videotape. The same goes for elaborate and sophisticated picture cuts. As a result, trying to get a "film look" on tape—which is what all of us trained in the medium try to do—becomes a tedious and, more important, a very expensive job. Again, this makes very little difference in a twenty-*second* spot, but just try to figure your budget for a twenty-*minute* film!

By the time you complete your off-line editing, get an approval, and then proceed to on-line editing, along with the computer-generated equipment that now exists, such as the ADO and the Chyron, your costs skyrocket. Recently I did an on-line edit at a favorite postproduction tape house, and it took two days and three hours (with about three hours of overtime included). Luckily I have a strong heart and I was well prepared. The bill for the time—two days and three hours plus three hours of overtime—was *30 percent higher* than the cost of editing a film of the same length over an eight-week period! And I did not even include the costs of the off-line edit in my figures.

But the most frustrating part of the editing procedure is that there is no time to think, no time to discuss, no time to mull over an edit or an optical effect. It's just too darned expensive to take the time, and film producers suffer eternal frustration in the semidark, complex editing room, watching computer figures appear while the picture seems to take second place.

The solution to all this, I am told, is to be well prepared, come ready with charts and logs and time code information, and then do your edit. But all this—however true—still begs the question: What happens to editing creativity during the process?

TRAINING. Since videotape is a young and booming field, most of the good technicians have been trained only in the areas of the computer, rather than having gone through a long period of training, learning, and appreciation of the larger picture. Although some editors have been (justly) accused of being "button pushers," many are now beginning to take an interest in the way a production should *look,* the feel of the subject, and the composition of the pictures on the screen. As a result, these new technicians are becoming more valuable to film-trained tape people.

For the person just moving up in the field, I can only repeat that it would be wise to train in *both* mediums. The filmmaker thinks differently from the videotape-trained producer, and whether we are right or wrong about our thinking, *we* are still a part of the market in job potential. For me and for many of my film friends the *picture* married to a *track* is really what counts. How we get there is of secondary importance, and if videotape not only will make our lives easier but will make the picture *better,* then we are as enthusiastic as anyone. But if we feel that we are getting less quality for the same amount of money, then we draw back and look again. Which brings me to my next point.

QUALITY OF IMAGE. If a project is produced on videotape and is to be transmitted via television to appear on the average home screen, be it through cable or the airwaves, and the average home screen is tuned as badly as it normally is, the color quality and the sound quality of the final product are generally acceptable. However, in addition to the problems with track and the inability to get the nuances that film can give, videotape presents to most filmmakers a mechanical, inaccurate, and less-than-acceptable picture. Whether it is through our training or our expectations of superb color in the new 35 mm and 16 mm color film stocks, we find that tape leaves much to be desired.

When artist Bob Blechman was producing his animated film *The Soldier's Tale,* presented over public television, he commented that he was trying to get a feeling of the blue that Maxfield Parrish had made famous, a luminous color that would give Blechman's film a look of the 1920s. He was not successful, and in the transfer from film to videotape, "I lost it."

Filmmakers and even videotape producers are beginning to find that for productions that require exquisite detail and accurate color quality, film performs the job more effectively for them. Optical effects are more accurate on film, however time-consuming they are. And when Home Box Office was producing "Linda Rondstadt in Concert" as a part of its *Standing Room Only* series, they completely broke with tradition and produced it on film instead of on videotape. Bridget Potter, a senior vice-president at HBO, explained in an interview that they wanted to give the show a "lusher, richer, juicier quality," so they chose 35 mm film rather than tape. She also preferred the dreamlike, gauzy look of film to the sharpness and raw immediacy of tape.

This subject is one of constant discussion and disagreement between the "experts" of tape and film. However, my own personal view closely coincides with a comment made to me in a letter by Ed Howell, vice-president of corporate communications for Eastman Kodak (admittedly a biased observer): "The tendency to be swept up in electronic euphoria seems to be a matter of faith with our industrial society. It is a marvel to me that such a 'high-tech' product as motion picture film can be so easily ignored. It has been said that if videotape had been invented first, we would still be looking for the ultimate imaging product, film."

I have also found that the final quality of tape depends a great deal upon the compatibility of the equipment upon which it is screened. On a recent job, I screened the final tapes with my client and was horrified to see the wavering, off-color quality of the presentation. The combination they were using consisted of a JVC playback with a Sony screen. The titles jumped, the color went from yellow to orange, and the producer (me) was terribly upset. I suggested that we move to a Sony/Sony combination, which we did, and a brand-new tape appeared before our very eyes. That, too, leads me to yet another "reality."

INCOMPATIBILITY. Be very careful when you enter the tape field as a producer. There are traps for the unwary that the industry is loath to speak of. Much of the equipment that is available today—whether for coding, recording, rerecording, or optical production—is *totally incompatible* with other equipment now on the market. From the very beginning, it is wise to check compatibility, for just as the home equipment Beta and VHS are incompatible, and the laser disc and the tape modes are incompatible, much professional equipment is also mismatched. The videotape industry is going through a replay (no pun intended) of the conflict that plagued the recording industry with the 45 rpm/33rpm battle many years ago.

To confuse things even further, Eastman Kodak is moving into the home video recorder market by producing an entirely new video camera-recorder (camcorder) system that they compare with 8 mm film—and "Kodavision" will be totally *incompatible with every other system on the market!*

In a sense, this new 8 mm system is not so bad, since it will open up new vistas for young, beginning tape producers by providing a reasonable way of making their projects a reality. Eventually more cable slots will probably open up to these new video producers. Some of us can also see using Kodavision for location scouting, testing of commercials, auditions, and even some in-house corporate training. The fact that the unit weighs only five and a half pounds will also open up production possibilities for younger people who want to try their hand at production.

There is always a however, however. Those of us who complain about interference, and the fact that every production is now a complete conference shot by shot, can also foresee Eastman Kodak and Sony's Betamovie creating still more over-the-shoulder producers on each and every project we work on. A recent ad for Betamovie shouted: "Be a movie star: produce, direct, and star in your own home video movies!" Of course, the new machine has everything we professionals have, including a power zoom, filter selecter, earphones, folding handgrip, an eyepiece correction lens adjustment, and a built-in microphone! For those of us (all of us) concerned with independence in a field built on collaboration, this innovation may be yet another encroachment upon our domain.

THE FUTURE: FANTASY OR REALITY. Videotape is still a growing adolescent. When we consider that photography is only a bit over 150 years old, and that only twenty-five years ago a video camera and recorder might cost about one hundred thousand dollars or more, we begin to put the technology into some sort of perspective. The marriage between the older technology and the new upstart is barely past its honeymoon stage, yet we are already promised scanning techniques that will improve the image of poorly exposed film, the storage of motion picture images through electronic media, and the use of ultrahigh-density magnetic or optical discs. In the realistic world of marketing, there have already been both surprises and advances that have created new business and thus new job opportunities for those of you who are entering or making your way through the industry:

★ Cable, whatever its problems, still offers a market for "paying your dues" or having your own production televised as a sample of your work.

★ The home videocassette has been a boom and a boon for Hollywood and the producers of independent features. For a long time the moguls were convinced that video would eat into the profits of the motion picture industry. What actually happened, however, was that a new and highly lucrative market was created *within* the industry.

The average payment for just the rights of the Hollywood output was running about $500,000 per film in 1984. Motion pictures like *Silkwood* and *Santa Claus—The Movie* were purchased for close to $2 million. With a projection of forty to sixty million home videocassette recorders by 1990, the industry has suddenly begun to welcome videotape, and films like *Raiders of the Lost Ark* were offered in cassette by Paramount for $39.95 each—and by mid-1984, 600,000 copies had been sold!

★ Video has also created some cult movies that originally failed in theatrical release but have done exceedingly well both here and in Europe. Michael Cimino's *Heaven's Gate,* a thirty six-million-dollar flop here in the United States, has collected a vast number of fans in England, where it was released on videocassette.

Given a new technology, new uses for that technology are springing up, providing still more potential for jobs and training.

★ Our court system is beginning to accept videotaped testimony, for example, as well

Corporations are now utilizing tape as well as film for their training and communications programs. Here, producer/director Nat Eisenberg sets a shot for Preparing for a Deposition in a Business Case, *winner of the Monitor Award. Seated are Larry Stevens, production manager, and Shelly Zeitz of Matthew Bender & Co., Inc.*

as demonstrations for juries on everything from the scene of the crime to how a hydraulic lift operates and might well crush the leg of the plaintiff embroiled in a litigation. In 1980, for example, lawyer Fred Heller set up his own company for just that purpose—to produce tapes exclusively for use as legal tools in court.

★ Interactive video, which I mentioned briefly in passing, will probably grow in the areas of self-instruction, in colleges, and at places where the consumer wants to "talk back" to a computer. At the time of this writing, an interactive video system called VideoSpond was beginning to move into point-of-sale areas. And if we can respond to the video screen, think of the need for corporate programs, the production facilities and people for a constant stream of materials from trained film and videotape producers.

Not only have film festivals begun to make room for videotape productions, but screening opportunities have suddenly cropped up especially geared to the tape producer, both professional and amateur or student. In addition to festivals such as the one held by Global Village in New York, there is now a National Video Festival Student Competition and a nationwide contest for half-inch Beta and VHS video recordings, administered by the American Film Institute and sponsored by the Sony Corporation. In the latter festival, all categories, including fiction, nonfiction, and experimental, are included.

Of course, not all of the developments in the field of videotape have meant instant riches for the young person in the field. There is still a great amount of work being done for very little money in cable, in the new technology of LPTV (low power TV), where new TV stations can broadcast within local and very prescribed limits, and even in some parts of the music video world. There is also a constant argument about who gets the royalties and the residuals in some of the new distribution areas. The unions and guilds are in negotiation with the producers at any given moment, in order to determine whether you have sold your services forever in the production of a film or are going to share a "piece of the pie" if it goes to video and becomes a blockbuster.

Through it all, I suppose that I bring myself back to earth with the realities that appear constantly, even in the midst of a technological explosion. It happened with film and it happens in videotape. When I think of film technology and how far it has come, I must think past the fact that film has been here so many years that we now have our single standards and that all projectors in 16 mm or 35 mm play films in 16 mm or 35 mm, and however our modern automatic projection equipment tears up sprocket holes, the standard is there and we are comfortable with it. If I screen my film in a public school in New York City or in Ollantaytambo, my 16 mm machine will show my 16 mm film. Nevertheless, we got here on a crooked and accidental path.

In the late 1800s Eastman worked closely with Thomas Edison to develop the motion pic-

ture. Edison wanted to expand the scope of his phonograph by finding a way to reproduce motion as well as sound, while Eastman was working on the development of transparent film. In their discussions about how to go about this development, Eastman asked Edison how wide he thought this film should be. The story goes that Edison held up his hand, extended thumb and forefinger, and answered, "This wide." And with that gesture, 35 mm film was born!

As in film, so in videotape are we brought back to reality by the everyday occurrences that remind us how often it takes ingenuity and responsibility to solve production problems—even with over a million dollars' worth of equipment surrounding us.

On a tape job, we needed a small white circle on the screen through which would appear the first picture of our star. On videotape, as compared with film, this should be quite simple. The on-line editor disappeared into the next room, placed an object under the camera, returned, and voilà: a white circle right in the middle of the screen.

"Great!" I exclaimed. "How did you do that?"

"Oh," he answered, "we used a white yo-yo."

Startled, and not quite ready to believe him, I asked hesitantly, "And what do you use to make a dark circle?"

"A Frisbee!" he retorted.

Later that night, after putting in our three hours of overtime, dead tired and unable to see another code number clearly, we had but one shot before we could all go home, leaving the dirty coffee cups and the close quarters of the room. Right before the last shot, the entire battery of equipment went out. Black. Blank. Not a picture or a hum. Not a visible sign that it was still alive. The senior editor went over to the mainframe—and he kicked it! He kicked it and it went back on. We finished the shot and went home.

So much for basics!

Computer Graphics: Movie Magic With Microchips

I am a sucker for computer-generated graphics and animation. I can sit for most of the afternoon in the screening rooms of friends while they show me their latest productions, with accompanying shouts of, "Wait until you see this one!" And we all laugh aloud as a man is lifted in his chair and flown through an infinity of music notes and space objects until he disappears into blackness.

I loved the uncut version of *2001: A Space Odyssey,* and I saw all four hours of it three times in three different countries in order to relive the trip to Jupiter. I only got to see *Star Wars* twice,

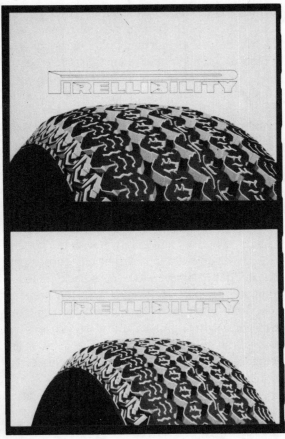

"Key frames" from a Pirelli commercial. The computer animation takes us from inside the tire tread and moves backward to reveal the entire top edges of the tire.

and I was convinced (wrongly) that *TRON* would be the next great box office hit in the feature field.

There is no doubt in my mind that if sound on film was the blockbuster of the twenties, and color film stock the commercial phenomenon of the thirties, then certainly the blossoming of computer graphics and animation must be the most striking development of this generation. Concomitant with the development in microelectronics, which has increased the storage capacity of magnetic recordings *twenty thousand times* in only thirty years with *sixty times the speed,* new generations of engineers and computer-trained graduates have begun to make their marks on both the film and tape industries. This, combined with the fact that many of these younger people have also discovered the marriage between art and graphics with the computer, has made for a job market and career path that did not exist even ten years back. This is a computer-trained, television-oriented generation, with many new filmmakers owning their own personal computers and word processors, both at home and at school. The results are being seen everywhere in the film industry today.

Judson Rosebush was one of the founders (along with Jeff Kleiser and Donald Leich) of Digital Effects in New York and Hollywood. He has now formed his own independent company and is one of the best people to explain computers to someone of my generation and have him leave the studio thinking that he finally understands it all. Judson was raised on a farm in Ohio, did well in school in math and science, but then focused on art history at college, plus speech, radio, and television, graduated with a masters in video, and became interested in computers as a way to do animation.

"Mathematics have been tied with art through the ages. It's not a new development. Da Vinci was a master mathematician. . . ."

Judson feels that we have begun to see a blurring between the media—film, television, videotape, and projected light. Production methods are becoming similar—computer graphics actually combines film and tape—and the role of the computer in all of this is central.

"The computer has begun to change the way we think of information management systems generally. We are already taking most of our cultural facts and relics and consigning them to programs—all the material about Marilyn Monroe, for example. Who shot the stills, who did the movies. We put into our banks of information the films like *Potemkin*—number of frames per cut, number of shooting days, and other information breakdowns. All the tools of film production are going into the computer—just like rolling steel. We take steel and roll it. When the computer senses that it has gotten to one end and has been compressed, it sends it back for the next run. The same with film and the entertainment industry. We have casting data bases, actors and actresses whose credits and background and vital statistics can be called up on a computer. . . ."

Judson is right. At Zoetrope, Coppola used computers for everything, including the technology described earlier—for scripting, cost management, and storyboarding. Other production companies are now using them for financial systems, scheduling crews, technical information, budgets, production materials, editing (especially on videotape), and even for control of the cameras.

"Then there's the *backward* process of the computers. We can operate a camera by hand while the computer *records* and notes the movements and then is programmed to repeat that process whenever and wherever we want to use it. We can also put all that actor/actress information into a computer and then have it call up a composite of all the things we're looking for: musical comedy, five feet two inches tall, blond, twenty-five to thirty years of age, comes from Nebraska, and speaks fluent Farsi. Our machines have become storehouses of knowledge, where we used to use books, pencils, and erasers."

Indeed, we have come a long way, and an industry has evolved where none existed before. The earliest of computer-animated films were developed by struggling independents as far back as the 1930s. There was very little market for the end product, and people like the late Mary Ellen Bute took out personal bank loans in order to finance films like *Rhythm in Light* (1934), which she produced in collaboration with Ted Nemeth, who was later to become her husband.

In the 1950s she worked with Dr. Ralph Potter of Bell Labs to produce experimental films that utilized oscilloscopes and moving electronic images on a cathode-ray screen. And as if just trying to get the new forms accepted was not quite enough, she was also a woman working in a world dominated almost entirely by men!

Today, in contrast to the people who struggled very much alone in trying to find the key to electronics and film, a vast number of young people have entered the film field trained both in computers and in art. One is an old friend of mine, Jeff Kleiser, who at the age of thirty is president of Digital Effects and has already had *seven years' experience* in the computer graphics field. He was a math major at college, took courses in computer generation and music, went to Syracuse for a work/study program for IBM, and there he met an instructor who became his mentor—Judson Rosebush!

"I saw a short film that Judson had made and a light bulb went on! I realized suddenly that you could actually mix film with a computer."

His first job was at Dolphin Productions, where he worked for about a year and a half as an animator on a video synthesizer; then he spent three months on holography, which he felt was a dead end (and it was). During that time, Judson Rosebush began to do his optical printing, and Jeff met him once again. Together, along with four other partners, they started Digital Effects in 1978.

The entire staff of Digital Effects in New York. Average age: twenty-five. The president, at age thirty, is Jeff Kleiser, back center, in the suit jacket and tie.

"I began at no pay and held another full-time job downstairs in the same building at a special effects film house, where I learned more about optical effects. Then I would go upstairs at night to Digital and help design and build the business. My first client was a cousin who worked for an ad agency."

Jeff joined Digital full time in 1980. As with all new technologies, the reception to this "new-fangled" art form was cool at first, to say the least.

"People didn't know what the new industry was all about. They didn't know what we were talking about. Now, of course, they're waiting on line and frothing at the mouth!"

As the computer graphics industry expands, the job market expands along with it. I've noticed that most people who work in the field are young—generally in their midtwenties or early thirties:

"At one time—in the early days—there was no need for credentials. No one even had them. There was no pool of experience. Today you probably need a masters degree in computer graphics, and we all want to see a film sample of your work."

Colleges are also changing their curricula to reflect industry demands for *both* computer training and a solid grounding in graphics, design, composition, and color. Jeff comments:

"In a sense this is not too different from the needs of a film director—an understanding of design and composition, much of which can be gotten from an art background or museums. I think it's an area that is often overlooked in the quest for quick and easy gratification in becoming a filmmaker."

But because the computer is so much a part of our society today, misconceptions have begun to surface. Judson claims that it is widely perceived to be much easier than it really is:

"It's not just wiggling a joystick à la Pac-Man. You have to separate the toys from the tools. The complexity of production is also misunderstood. *Labor* is the major component of the work, not the computer. When the computer becomes the major component, it is no longer creative. Certainly the machine is stimulating to work with—but it's a sculptural, claylike device. You can add, you can take away. You can mold."

Because the industry has begun to make its own guidelines and now serves a very critical function in the production of today's motion pictures, the career paths themselves have begun to be more easily defined, in contrast to the haphazard structure in the early days. According to people like Jeff Kleiser and Judson Rosebush, someone interested in computer graphics:

★ must have a computer background in a university or corporation

★ must speak several computer languages
★ must know the internal structures of computers (according to Jeff, the university computer center is really "boot camp")
★ must have training in art, graphics, and design

A typical move up the ladder in the field might look something like this:

OPERATOR: Does everything, including taking the film to the laboratory, picking it up, assisting as lowest member of the totem pole.
ANIMATOR: Writes programs and generates the graphics that specifically apply to a job. This is the step on the ladder where the person must have a background in animation, art, or graphics.
SOFTWARE SPECIALIST: Works on the design of the graphics and develops new kinds of images that will, in turn, be taken by the animator and used for the specific project.
DIRECTOR: Deals with clients, tells the animator how to proceed with the job, solves the problems, deals with postproduction, handles client approvals. This job is very much like the director in every other part of our industry.

In getting the job, the subject of a sample comes up over and over again, just as it does in the area of live production. It can be the single most important factor in convincing a potential employer that computer graphics are really your chosen field. Judson says that he not only asks for a sample, but wants one that looks like nothing he's ever seen before, something that might be developed for further use.

Jeff is even stronger in his advice regarding a sample film:

"Try to cajole, beg, or borrow (but not steal) time on a high-tech piece of equipment and make a sample."

Mark Lindquist, now twenty-six years old, came to Digital with a background in computers. But he was also trained as an artist using oil paint on canvas. In 1981, he saw the video palette system at Digital—allowing the artist to paint on a computer screen—and he was enthralled. At that time Digital had only used the palette system for small, individual jobs, never for an entire film. Mark talked them into letting him use the system at night, after everyone had quit for the day, and he worked from midnight until three A.M. and on weekends. His final production in computer graphics, using the palette system, was a three-minute film called *The Subway*. He was hired by Digital as an operator—and is now managing their production!

There is always the question, Is it a fad? Or will it stay with us as long as the other technologies that have become the basis for much of the film work produced over the past fifty years? Television screens are filled with flying objects in space, "new" looks that bore us too quickly as everyone jumps into the production circus and begins to copy. Yet, as Judson tells me:

"Certainly there are styles that come and go—the neon look or three-dimensional ob-

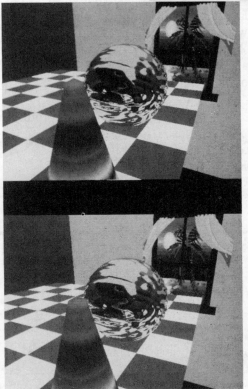

Computer graphics have changed the look of the film world, opening up a new field for young filmmakers. These are some samples from Digital Effects.

jects flying through space. But fads also come and go in live film, especially in commercials and in features. . . ."

He is quite right. At the time of this writing, every feature in movie houses across the country seems to begin in black with voices coming out of the screen and into the audience (*Broadway Danny Rose* and *Terms of Endearment,* to mention only two). Earlier, every film seemed to start with animated titles, and there were *Pink Panther* fans all across our land.

"Computer graphics will become a part of the aggregate vocabulary of film production. There are still surprises waiting for us . . . many things waiting to be done—while some of the other things get beaten to death!"

Judson Rosebush, Jeff Kleiser, and all the other artists are quick to project the future, not only in terms of the way we will all think about information management systems generally, but even in the way we collect things, in the way we see things, and in the way we make others see them. Judson predicts that people will no longer collect miniature trains, but videotapes of trains; not stamps, but tapes of the stamps from all over the world.

In some areas, the changes are already upon us. Computer animation is being used to detail the complex functions of the human body with extraordinary accuracy. Small companies are designing network program introductions, commercials, and special effects for the film industry with new computer-generated, three-dimensional, solid-shaded raster graphics.

In the field of business, the use of computer-generated graphics is growing at a rate of nearly 50 percent a year, according to market research. In sales and sales presentations as well as in training, computer-generated slides are becoming more widely used.

Judson Rosebush has even greater visions:

"When they have completely developed a solid-state screen, you could cover the walls with the materials, and your images would be inherent *right in the screens,* like a digital watch, and with superb photographic quality. Why, just imagine—you could cover *rooms* and *entire auditoriums* with screen images, all of them controlled by computers. . . ."

When he completes his first prototype, I hope that Judson Rosebush invites me to his screening room for an afternoon of demonstrations.

The Music Video Mania

Japan has always had a special place in my filmmaker heart—it is a country where everyone seems to carry a camera. As a result, the introduction of a film crew to a festival or even to the busiest marketplace is taken with equanimity and with an offer of the greatest cooperation. It is also the country where I discovered music video.

A few years back I returned to Tokyo to produce the Japanese track for the film we had just made for Sunkist Growers of California. It was the first time in many trips I had been there without a film crew or the logistical problems that are part of the job. Each day I would return to my hotel room, luxuriate in a long, hot bath, and lie on the bed in my yukata, the long Japanese robe, to watch television programs.

One was a show called *Music Tomato,* or *Mutama* to the Japanese. *Mutama* was rock video in its purest form, and the imagination inherent in each day's programming would leave me breathless and wondering where all this had been taking place and why I had not been informed.

I first saw Michael Jackson's *Beat It!* on *Music Tomato,* and frankly, never having been exposed to the attendant publicity, I was not quite as impressed as the Grammy Award judges.

I was enchanted with imaginative productions like *Electric Avenue* and the whimsical *It's Raining Men* and in trying to figure out whether Boy George of Culture Club was a boy or a girl. I loved the camera work, the editing, and the sheer visual concept of many of them. It was also my first exposure to the movie *Flashdance,* and I, as millions of others, finally paid an admission to see the entire film because of the music video excerpt that I had seen in Tokyo. I discovered much later on that this was, indeed, the first time that a motion picture had become successful because of the intense promotion through the medium of music video.

Well, it may be my generation that is at fault or the fact that I watch very little television. *It* has certainly been here. It is *I* who have not!

In the space of a few short years, this new video phenomenon has opened up an entirely new industry, with a growing potential for filmmakers to expand and flex their creative muscles. Directors are not the only beneficiaries of music video production; everyone in the multiple-production categories of film and tape has benefited: musicians and music directors, choreographers, scenic designers and special effects, production crews, and small independent companies.

Where they did not exist before, production companies have begun to list themselves as "music video facilities" all across the country. And the expansion has not been limited to New York and Los Angeles, though these two cities have become the major areas of production.

The idea of putting music on film is not new. The "illustrated song" can be traced back to every musical ever produced by Hollywood. If we culled the archives as far back as the early thirties, we could probably excerpt enough ten-minute musical segments to fill a thirteen-week series of half-hour television shows. My favorite as a youngster was a music sequence from the film *Flying Down to Rio,* in which a long line of chorus girls danced on the wings of a plane in flight (quite a trick, easily the equal of *Star Wars).* Even before that, a young singer named

Bing Crosby appeared in a series of Mack Sennett comedies, all of them titled after the crooner's current hits: *Blue of the Night, I Surrender, Dear,* and *Just One More Chance.* In each and every case, Bing acted out a vague storyline, just like the music video stars today—Blondie, Billy Joel, The Police, or Duran Duran.

The early musicals and films, like *Ziegfeld Follies* or the original *Forty-Second Street* (now back on Broadway as a "new" musical), were nothing more than a series of short, illustrated musical numbers with thin, high-school-level storylines, featuring stars like Ruby Keeler, Lena Horne, Fred Astaire, Gene Kelly, and Kathryn Grayson. For Dorothy Lamour, practically every line delivered by Bob Hope in the Road series was a music cue, followed by an illustrated song.

In the field of classical music, Walt Disney's *Fantasia* (1940) used animated storylines to fill the movie houses for Bach, Beethoven, and Moussorgsky. I remember being taken with Stravinsky's *Rite of Spring* when I first saw the film, and I ran right out to buy the recording (which is what we are supposed to do today when we see a memorable music video!), and when I got home and played its discordant music on my phonograph with sharpened cactus needles, I was terribly disappointed. The music—without the pictures of the dinosaurs and the explosive beginnings of the formation of the Earth—no longer held an interest for me!

In a more recent time, I was struck again by the use of "illustrated music," but with an even more contemporary visual concept, when I saw the cult film *The Rocky Horror Picture Show,*

starring a very young Susan Sarandon. All the musical productions that take place in the eerie castle—the thunder and lightning, and the introduction of a motorcycle rider in the midst of the maelstrom—are nothing more than pure, unadulterated precursors of rock video.

But the beginning of music video as it appears today has no real genesis, no matter how we try to pinpoint where it all started. For the early "illustrated music" you had to pay ten cents (!) to enter the movie house. In the early days of television, the sound systems were so awful that today's sophisticated music tracks would disappear in the process of transmission and reception. The crackling, tinny speaker, generally about five inches in size, was just not up to reproducing sophisticated sound. In addition, audiences were small by comparison with today's vast numbers, and almost everything was televised live.

As the technology improved, and as the demand for more and more "filler" materials increased, short music films were sometimes used to supply the ravenous appetite of television programming. At the same time, families began to own not one television set, but many—generally one for each room, including the bathroom and the nursery. Where formerly parents selected one "family" program to be seen by all, now each member of the group could choose his or her *own* program, be it rock or sitcom.

At the same time, an interesting thing occurred in Ohio, when Warner-Amex was experimenting with its interactive video system, QUBE (where the viewer could finally "talk back" to the TV set). As in all television systems, there were many schedule gaps to be filled, and as an experiment the company tried to fill them with European music tapes that had been produced originally to promote specific recordings. They found, much to their surprise, that these music recordings were far more popular than many of their regular programs, and their next step was to explore the idea of a cable channel that would be devoted entirely to this new concept of "illustrated music."

There was one other early attempt, and I was reminded of it again in reading an article by Leonard Maltin in *Film Fan Monthly*. Back in the forties the ubiquitous jukebox occupied a space in every diner, restaurant, and bar in America. There was even a film and a song, as I recall, entitled "Juke Box Saturday Night," which shows everyone just how we spent our weekends!

We listened to Frank Sinatra and Glenn Miller and Benny Goodman. One of my first jobs was writing continuity scripts for a show hosted by the popular Tommy Dorsey, and I was quite proud to hear his recordings almost everywhere I went.

Well, about this time, one of the largest manufacturers of jukeboxes came up with the idea of providing "soundies"—a combination of popular music along with 16 mm film. The machine was designed to be seven feet high, with a screen that measured sixteen by twenty inches, and a complex system of mirrors would project the picture while the sound played on. Maltin reports that many of the stars of the era jumped into soundies—Stan Kenton, Spike Jones, Cab Calloway, Mel Tormé, Count Basie. But the system, however commercial its concept, suffered breakdowns such as the binding of film and the "Russian roulette" of never knowing whether or not the song you selected would really be the one to come up. Today we have sophisticated computers that can disrupt the system in exactly the same way, but now we call it "accessing." And if you think we have solved the problems of film projection, just look at the record of the airlines' in-flight motion pictures and the number of times the screen suddenly goes dark or the picture triples its image.

However, if you think that the idea of "soundies" has come and gone, think again. An article in the newspaper the other day alerted me to the fact that a company in Tarzana, California, was moving into record stores in major markets with a "new" system of *video jukeboxes*. They'll be playing music videos free, while interspersing them with commercials and a one-hour program to be repeated throughout the day.

Today, of course, the field of music video has begun to solidify. With cable channels and network and independent programming beginning to feature a flood of new productions, and shows like *Hot* and *Solid Gold Hits* joining the MTV channels in showing them, we have begun to see an increasing flow of film talent moving into the music video realm. Commercial director Bob Giraldi has become one of the early stars with his production of Michael Jackson's *Beat It!* Feature directors Bob Rafelson (*Five Easy Pieces* and *The Postman Always Rings Twice)* and Tobe Hooper (*Poltergeist* and *The Texas Chainsaw Massacre)* have entered the industry and have thoroughly enjoyed the transition.

Commercial producers have begun to establish separate music houses that will concentrate only on music video productions. The computer graphics industry has joined the competition by developing productions that combine both live and graphic effects as an integral part of the story.

One of the most interesting developments in this growth, however, has been a production that is borrowed directly from the film industry. For years we have been doing films called *The Making of . . .*, and some years back I even made one myself, *The Making of the Savage Bees,* for an NBC promotion, located in New Orleans with a cast of ten million honeybees! (I remember with some black humor that the only one who got stung was the keeper of the bees. The crew came through unscathed.)

There have been hundreds of other documentary productions on how a feature film gets made. Les Blank did one for Werner Herzog's *Fitzcarraldo,* and some wags have commented that *The Making of Fitzcarraldo* was more interesting than the original film.

Well, the first of the big music video *The Making of . . .* was produced for release as a home videocassette. Directed by Hollywood's John Landis (*An American Werewolf in London*), it's called *Making the Thriller Video* and it stars, of course, Michael Jackson. Anticipating a booming market, its initial order was for one hundred thousand copies, each one to sell for $29.95! The cost of production—depending upon which magazine or newspaper you read—ranged from $500,000 up to a figure that has been quoted at $1.1 million! When you consider that John Sayles produced *The Brother from Another Planet* for somewhere around $340,000, you begin to see just where the higher end of the music video field is heading.

This brings me to a strong warning for the new filmmaker who looks with anticipation at this growing phenomenon. The figures you've been reading about in your local film magazine or in the newspapers are unfortunately the "stars" of the field. Bob Giraldi's $150,000 budget for *Beat It!* (not to mention Landis's blockbuster budget), the $60,000 spent by Steve Barron for *Billie Jean,* and all the other Hollywood-type stories about elaborate productions are unfortunately not the norm for music video. They are beginning to become part of the new hype that a growing industry must create with the public if it is to continue to thrive.

Tom Buckholtz of New Orleans (see page 30) refuses to call music video "work," not because it's so much fun but because it pays so little! Buckholtz says:

"You can find enough of these things to shoot every day of the year. They're getting a lot of new directors to shoot the things inexpensively, and those directors are building reels out of them. That's fine and dandy. But you can't make a living that way!"

Anthony Payne, the producer of GASP! Productions, Bob Giraldi's music video arm, was quoted as saying, "For anyone who says there's no money in rock video, I'd have to agree with them."

The budgets for most of these short pre-

COURTESY COLUMBIA RECORDS

One of the most unusual of the music videos is Bob Dylan's Jokerman, *the lyrics setting off the haunting imagery of the world's great art, sculpture, pop culture iconography, and headline photography. The works used in the video include Durer, Michelangelo, Goya, Picasso, and even DC Comics, and the blend was created by art director George Lois.*

sentations remains small. Though Jackson and Elton John can afford the amount of money it takes to mount a complex production, the latest budget estimates for music video will typically run between $10,000 and $25,000 apiece. Some are budgeted in an average range of $30,000, and even this figure is but a mere fraction of the cost for a ten- or twenty-second commercial produced for viewing on network television. Payne continues, "If there are people who make TV commercials . . . who want to become filmmakers, rock videos offer a wonderful avenue for them. If their primary objective is to make money, I suggest they continue to do what they're doing."

There is yet another realistic observation about this young segment of our industry, and it is something to keep in mind as you pursue this particular production path. There has been so much product in just a few short years, so much demand, that we have begun to see a repetition of themes and techniques, to the point where many of them have begun to pall. Paul Flattery has called them "video wallpaper."

On the one hand, music video is enough of a phenomenon for *Time* magazine to have featured it as the cover story of its last issue for 1983. And it has indeed been the salvation of a record industry that seemed to be drying up, was forced to cut back its staffs severely, and was wondering where all that young money was going.

On the other hand, because of the growing need for product, the expansion of the number of outlets almost to the point of saturation, the repetitious onslaught of hyperactive editing, and

the symbolism of nuns, children, motorcycle freaks, badly choreographed dancers, and hostile guitarists, music video has begun to create its own library of visual clichés, in very much the same way television has fallen into the mire of mediocrity. As a result, critics have begun to predict a backlash, a shaking out of an industry that is still in its adolescence. Comment continues to be made about the blatant stealing from feature film ideas, the limited number of camera angles available to even the most creative cinematographer or director, and the fact that the surrealism is so rampant in music videos that it is becoming almost laughable.

In a field that is having its normal, albeit rapid, growth pains, the criticism can only be good. For at first the cynics said that music video would never be popular, would die out quickly as another American fad, and suddenly they were proven wrong when MTV became a phenomenal success. Today there are still the doubters, especially among producers who see music videos as underbudgeted and sloppily produced in too many instances.

For the beginner in film, the very fact that music video is being rejected as low budget by too many professionals with years of experience makes it a remarkable opportunity to gain experience and to collect samples of your work. It is also a field that is crying out for new ideas, and I have always believed that budget doesn't necessarily equal creativity. Hollywood is the best example of big budgets gone wrong: *King of Comedy, Heaven's Gate, Zelig,* and *The Right Stuff,* with new lists to remind us each and every season of all the "sure things" that plunge

quickly into obscurity. The same is happening in music video. Though we hear of the Michael Jacksons ad nauseam, there are music videos being produced on budgets that are a fraction of the cost of large-scale productions, many of them more genuinely clever only *because* of a lack of production dollars.

More and more I am beginning to see samples of this kind of production. Music videos are perfect for an editor or young director or production manager who wants to show his or her work to a prospective employer. Since they are comparatively short, while still showing more production value than a brief ten-second commercial, they are just right to present as a work sample. I love watching them and then discussing the production problems with the person who brings them to me.

Where will it all go? I do not have a crystal ball, and by the time that *Son of Making It in Film* is published, it may all be over, indeed a quick fad, or it may have grown still further. As of now, though, it is a vital, viable, growing part of the film/tape field, and it has opened up many more job opportunities for the younger members of the film industry who might still be working for lower salaries and who have not yet found their niche in a guild or union.

Just the other day a new name entered the music video market. He did a spot for Off-Track Betting, and he sang an oldie for the appearance, *My Old Kentucky Home.* It was not Boy George. It was not even Billy Joel. It was, of all people, New York's Mayor Edward Koch! Though it really was a network commercial produced as a music video, I will not quibble. The mere fact that His Honor thought enough of music video to try one somehow gives me enough faith in its future.

I do think music video will muddle through all the problems that affect any growing industry. And I do think it will be around for a long, long time.

MAKING IT ON PAPER

The Writer in Film and Television

It happened during the first years of the fifties. Television was produced live, with all the problems and hilarious incidents that were to become the "war stories" of later years. The medium at that time also had a sense of vitality and innovation that would somehow disappear with the advent of new technologies, most specifically the prerecording of programs on tape and film. The pictures we transmitted were glorious black and white, while in the back rooms engineers struggled with a viable and practical method of transmitting color.

Those of us who were trying to make our marks in this new and exciting technology, in whatever jobs we might be able to talk our way into, were constantly complaining that:

★ it was impossible to break in
★ no one would ever give you a break
★ there was too much competition for the few jobs
★ everyone exploited you and expected you to work for nothing

My own background at that time, at least in terms of writing experience, was limited. I had cowritten (with Nat Eisenberg) several network quiz shows on radio and television for a rather successful packager, and during that time I learned the answers to thousands of questions, none of which would ever help me again in my struggle through television and film or in my quest for fame as a writer. In addition, I had also cowritten (with David Hill) the Skitch Henderson morning program on NBC, which was on the air so early that I did not have a chance to even hear what I had written until several months had passed and I decided to get up at dawn one morning to listen to the broadcast of my introductions to soothing morning music!

I don't know what made me think that I wanted to be a writer. To say the least, the response to my written words up to that time had been less than enthusiastic. From college and through World War II and even into my first jobs in radio, I had amassed a huge collection of rejection slips, all of them displayed like a graphic arts collection in a red-covered scrapbook. (I still have it!) I had rejection slips from *The New Yorker, Esquire, Saturday Evening Post, Liberty* magazine, and smaller journals from as far away as Bean Station, Tennessee, and Ten Sleep, Wyoming. Why I didn't give up, I will never know.

It was at that time that I desperately longed for some recognition as a writer of dramatic plays for television. It was also at that time that my cowriter, David Hill, commented that he had heard that the DuMont Television Network was desperately looking for scripts. I called the story editor, Charles Mann, for an appointment and saw him early in the morning on a Friday.

He described the show, called *Hands of Destiny,* and gave me a sheet with the specifications for each script that they might consider:

★ There were to be no more than five characters.
★ There were to be no more than four sets.
★ Each script had to revolve around some incident dealing with hands.
★ It was to be half an hour long.

If they accepted a script, they would pay the writer a fee of $300!

"Do you have anything that might fit those specs?" he asked.

"And how!" I answered (or words to that effect). "I've got just the story for the show."

"Fine. When can I see it?"

"Monday."

Did I really have a script to fit the show? Well, no. Did I even have an idea of what I might write? Well, actually not really. I had been mulling over an idea for some time, but nothing was on paper. Nevertheless, we smiled and shook hands and I told Charlie that the finished script would be in his office on Monday. And I left, not realizing what I had done. It was Friday. There was Saturday and there was Sunday. And between those days and Monday there was a typewriter and forty blank sheets of paper!

We went away that weekend, a group of us, to a closed-for-the-winter summer camp. While the others rested and walked in the barren woods, I went to a bunkhouse on the outskirts of the camp, wearing my warmest clothing and carrying my paper and a battered old manual Smith-Corona typewriter. For two days I wrote a story. I blocked it, wrote it, and rewrote it. It was the story of two people, both of them classmates at college, one who was to become a brain surgeon (remember the hands?) because of his delicate touch, the other who was to become a boxer (different hands!). The boxer, always taunting the more delicate friend because of his slender, almost effeminate fingers, was always developing his muscles by squeezing a rubber ball. (Are you still with me?) I called the story "Lady Fingers."

Put simply, the boxer is badly hurt in the ring and is brought to the operating table of the brain surgeon, who now has a most remarkable chance to "get even" with the man who had taunted him throughout college and had made his life a living hell for four years. Finally the surgeon had the bully in his power. He could easily kill him. Or, knowing full well the workings of the brain, he could paralyze his victim for life during the operation, making the use of his hands impossible. And no one would ever know the truth.

I don't remember how I ended it! I really don't. And it is not really a necessary part of this story. All I do know is that I found out much later (this past year, in fact) that the summer camp at which I wrote that first dramatic script of mine was *the same place* where Herbert Brodkin got his start, doing scenery for camp shows at the age of twelve and then becoming dramatics counselor, where he was paid $250 for the entire season! (See page 120.)

And what about "Lady Fingers"? On Monday morning, a snowy, blustery winter day in New York, my wife trudged downtown to deliver the script to Charlie Mann (a journey for which she has never forgiven me), and I went back to my career as a starving sometimes writer and a teacher of radio to young veterans who complained that no one ever gave them a break, that there was too much competition, ad infinitum. My bank account was down to about eight dollars, and even the evening dinners at the Horn & Hardart Automat were now a combination vegetable plate (bread was free) at five cents per vegetable. Two weeks went by. The call finally came. "We're buying your script!"

I was euphoric. The break was finally here. I was going to be a writer of dramatic shows. No more quiz shows. No more questions and answers and quiz show contestants over network radio and local television. No more disenchanted veterans. I was so elated that I barely heard the next words from Charlie Mann: "We'd like to see you. There are a few changes that we'd like made." Sure. Sure. I'll be there in fifteen minutes—sooner if I can outrun the subway!

It is probably at this point that the story really begins. For if I'd had more experience writing in the field of television and film, I might have anticipated what was yet to come. My lovely story, my simple, psychological conflict between two different people, was to undergo its own surgical procedure, a series of indelicate operations that would teach me a lot about independence, freedom, and artistic integrity—or the lack thereof. Rather than writing yet another entire book about this one play, let me outline the sequence of events from that day on.

★ First off, they "loved" the script. Did I have any more at home? I did, of course. Well, there were a few changes they wanted. In the time I had written the script, the title of the program had been changed from *Hands of Destiny* to *Hands of Murder*! Could I take it home and "put a murder into it"?

I was a bit startled. This was a simple little psychological drama. To "put a murder into it" would change the entire thrust plus the characterizations. After all, my gentle, sensitive doctor wasn't a murderer. But I took it home and I rewrote it. I was, after all, a starving writer. What's a little murder after all? I put a murder into it. My hero doctor killed the boxer. And I brought it back to Charlie Mann.

★ I was called again. Come on down. We have a little problem. I met with the network again. The problem? They loved the script. It was dynamite (or whatever word was used in the fifties to describe television hype). But—but—continuity acceptance and the lawyers just couldn't have a *doctor* be a murderer. What would the American Medical Association say?

Feeling the critical $300 slip slowly away, I struck a bargain. If I could get the New York Medical Society to agree that it was a harmless script, would the network buy it? Good idea. Go to it. I did.

★ I met with the head of the New York Medical Society, and while he sipped tea and looked sternly at me, I slowly told the story, feeling sillier and sillier as I progressed. Here was the head of the entire New York Medical Society listening to me tell a story about a doctor who was a murderer—a mere television play! Limply I finished and waited for his reaction.

"Well, sir," I asked, "what do you think?"
"I wouldn't give a damn if the doctor had three penises," he muttered. "We've had doctors who were murderers before!"
"Great!" I almost shouted. "Would you put your approval in writing?"
No, he would not! There well might be objections from doctors around the country, and he would not put himself in the position of approving the script. That was that. He sipped his tea. I called the network. The deal was off. The script was rejected. The $300 only a dream.

Was I depressed? *Of course* I was depressed. I went downtown and sat in the waiting room at a friend's office while I told my tale of woe to his receptionist. She shook her head and laughed. "Idiot! Why don't you set the story in *Europe*? The *American* Medical Association could never touch it?"

★ The network agreed! Great idea! Rewrite the script. I did. The doctor was still a brain surgeon. The boxer was now a wrestler (more European, of course), and any mention of dollars was now changed to Swiss francs.

★ The program manager of the network called. Could I go down to Washington with him—travel on the train and talk? He had some ideas. I made the trip. Six hours down with him and six hours back alone to mull over his suggestions. He wanted to change Europe to Russia—to make it a spy story. I stopped listening at Trenton, New Jersey. I firmly disagreed. There was a limit, even to my starvation!

Finally the air date was chosen. My family and friends were all notified about my first dramatic television story. The show went on the air (live), and the title came on the screen, *but it was not mine*! I realized suddenly that they had also changed the title from "Lady Fingers" to "The Rubber Ball"! It was my script—well, at least it was partly my script, for I had not anticipated that the director was also there to make his own changes in my precious first play.

"Somewhere in Europe" became "Vienna,"

only because the director had found this marvelous photograph of St. Stephan's Cathedral over which to superimpose the title. The mention of Swiss francs became meaningless in Vienna, as did the whole storyline, for the most important speech of exposition at the end of Act I, where all the reasoning and the action was explained for Act II, *had been cut by the director because of time limitations*!

Nevertheless, even if no one really understood "The Rubber Ball" (including the writer), it was my debut. My first television play. And I wrote many, many more—for series dealing with newspapermen, detectives, and just plain folks, for specials for the United Nations, and for holidays such as Christmas. Many of them underwent the same metamorphosis and changes, the same struggle as the first venture. But what credits I had when I finally left television to go into film!

Possibly the most interesting thing about that long story (aside from the superb plot!) is that not very much has changed for writers in our field, be it television or film. Yet if you were to poll producers and other executives in the industry—from live theater to documentary films—you would probably hear that what our industry needs most is good writers and fresh, new ideas!

In a sense this is true. Most producers and executives in the film business can't write. And when I make that statement, I am speaking in the broadest sense, down to and including a simple, articulate, pointed business letter! Too many of us, especially those who are at the beginning of the climb up the ladder, have a

tendency to think of "writing" as a synonym for "screenplay." Certainly that is a part of the field. But the kind of writing that is desperately needed in film/tape/television requires the talent to write other things as well:

★ research reports
★ treatments for documentaries, business films, educational films, training films and tapes
★ proposals for funding your project
★ sales proposals and competitive projects (where you are out to prove that you are a better filmmaker than the other guy)
★ even letters, contracts, and requests for an interview
★ copywriting at advertising agencies

When Charles Guggenheim, the documentary producer, stands in front of a seminar group, as he has done many times, he generally voices the constant complaint of film producers around the country: "What this field needs desperately is writers!"

I have heard him deliver that comment at several American Film Institute seminars, and we have talked extensively about it afterward. The problem seems to be that many younger filmmakers who can really write have a tendency to narrow their potential by writing just *one* screenplay, then expending all their efforts in the sale of that document to the exclusion of the other needs of the field.

My feeling is that if you can write—*write*! I know someone who became a very successful writer of network soap operas. Since he was a

serious writer to begin with, he constantly made excuses for the way he earned his rather substantial income. However, during the eight years in which he churned out "plots" for television's wasteland, he managed to sit in his large, elegant brownstone house (which he had purchased with income from the soaps) and write two books and many plays—some of which were produced in Europe and off Broadway in New York! In spite of his complaints about his major source of revenue, he had successfully found a way to use his talents for writing to do both things—earn a living and write with freedom.

Throughout the film industry there is a desperate need for people who can write *visually*. Since most of the people to whom we sell our ideas, or with whom we try to communicate about what our film is going to "look like," are nonvisual (a fact agreed upon by most film writers), if you can transmit your picture images onto paper and, in turn, be able to "paint" that picture through your words, the *sale* of your project becomes that much easier.

In the documentary, for example, we can never write a script or a screenplay, since we never know exactly what it is we will find on location when the actual shooting takes place. Thus, we deliver a *treatment* to the client, the foundation, or whoever is going to fund the project. But it is more than just a catalog of shots that we write—it is a *selling* document, a narrative description of our film that outlines in broad visual strokes just what the finished film will look like (even if it changes as we progress). I must admit that a good treatment is sometimes much better than the finished motion picture! Few documentary producers are able to accomplish the feat.

There is still another point that most successful writers will make when questioned about their craft. Having written only one thing is not generally considered "writing." In one way or another, they generally advise the young writer to "sit your butt down and put your fingers on the typewriter keys!" Interestingly enough, just by practicing the craft of writing, you find that you begin to get better and better at it. You become more disciplined. To the writer there is nothing like the seduction of the outside—the sea nearby, the movie you wanted to see, the walk through a shopping center you would like to take. But all of us find that we need to determine our own schedule and stick to it. I love to work early in the morning, for by afternoon I am a nonproductive zombie. Others work late at night when everyone else is asleep. But all writers write, even though facing the blank page is a trauma to most of us.

All of this holds true whether you are writing a novel, a screenplay, a documentary treatment or a "thank you" note to someone who has taken the time to listen to your story of why you can't seem to sell your screenplay!

There is just one more thing—and this is a question that crops up over and over again in film classes and in discussions with young filmmakers. None of your writing will ever be done in total and complete freedom, at least at the beginning of your career and possibly through your lifetime. The field of film/tape/television is one of compromise and collaboration, and people who can't write love nothing more than to criticize

and make changes in the work done by people who can! If this depresses you terribly, you will have to learn, through training and experience, how to make those changes while maintaining the integrity of your work. It isn't easy, but it can be done.

One of my favorite stories concerns the early preproduction phases of the ABC television special *The Day After,* dealing with postholocaust results in Kansas. Naively thinking that they might get support and approval from the Department of Defense, ABC set up a series of meetings, at which the DOD and the Federal Emergency Management Agency (FEMA) began a process of what I like to call *re*-creation, taking someone else's creation and making it conform to what you might have written—if you could write.

The FEMA called them *"script mending sessions,"* a euphemism closely akin to calling a nuclear weapon "the peacekeeper"! Reports from the participants indicate that this quest for DOD-FEMA approval and cooperation eventually turned into an unmitigated creative disaster. The subject was too depressing, they thought. It did not meet DOD specifications of what nuclear war would "really" be like. It unfairly portrayed our NATO alliance. They made some legitimate comments about correct uniforms, but they also were distressed about some characterizations and asked that they be changed because they did not reflect kindly on the DOD's image:

★ A diplomat in the film makes an undiplomatic statement. The "script menders" suggested that the comment be made in-

stead by an American academic—possibly a young college professor who sported a beard and wore a tweed jacket!

Somehow, as I read all of this, my mind flew back to "Lady Fingers": add a murder, change it to a Russian spy story, you can't have a doctor commit homicide. But don't get us wrong. We *love* the story!

It is a reality that absolutely must be faced if you are to write for the film/tape/television world, for in one form or another you will have to collaborate with people who will have some input, and many of the sessions can be frustrating and difficult. As the writer, you must learn where you can give and where you must hold firm, even at the risk of losing the assignment:

★ In copywriting for commercials, the original idea is put through the Cuisinart of as many as twenty people, including account supervisors, agency producers, the client, and the production house.

★ The business film can have as few as one or two client levels or, heaven forbid, a committee. One of my best clients awarded me a plaque after a film that was completed in spite of a committee of twenty-seven! It now hangs on my wall, and it reads: *God so loved the world that He did not send a committee.*

★ Foundation grants are seldom given with complete freedom to the filmmaker. The subject matter must be "right," and the selling document goes through a process that makes even a committee look like a one-person approval.

★ The screenplay also goes through a grinding process, and too often the original creator of the story is not even listed on the final credits of the film. This is a classic case of where business people generally have the final say.

★ Television is probably the worst offender in keeping an eye on the writer to make certain that he doesn't stray too far from the middle level of the current "party line." However, if rape is in or bubonic plague is currently the chic disease, you may be certain that you will be asked to include one or both in your next project.

If, at this point, you complain, "Why is he telling us this?" I can only say that I think all writers have to understand that writing, just like everything else in this business, is a process. It takes time and it takes energy. It is a series of collaborative efforts that must be understood *before* you get too far into the field. Experience teaches you that when someone says, "I want something that's different," he or she really means, "Not too different!"

Perhaps most important to your writing career, you must understand that there are *many* paths that may open to you, and they might not be the ones that you originally thought would lead you to your first large screen credit on a feature film. (In any case, the audience stands up during the display of credits at a feature, so no one will see your name anyway!) The trick is not to become discouraged—and to

keep writing. Interestingly enough, the statement I made at the beginning of this long dissertation is valid—the field needs writers.

As in every other part of this industry, while you grow and gain experience, the people who are moving up alongside you will eventually be in the position to buy the screenplay or hire you for the documentary treatment. Most important of all, as you keep writing, your file of samples grows, and as John Sayles says in the next part of this chapter, you'd better have more than one thing to sell!

Everyone Has a Screenplay: Some Advice from John Sayles and Dave Ketchum

The film screenplay is a most unusual form of writing. The French screenwriter Jean-Claude Carrière, who has worked with Luis Buñuel, Peter Brook, and Milos Forman, describes it as "a strange object. It is written, typed but not published. Only about sixty people read it! And everyone reads it for different reasons." In a

charming interview with the *New York Times*, Carrière's list of "reasons" was one of the most instructive lessons for any potential screenwriter to keep in mind during the long, hungry periods of frustration.

★ The producer reads a screenplay to see if it has commercial value.
★ The actors read it to see what their roles are like.
★ The lighting director thinks of domes and twilights.
★ The executive producer is counting the number of costumes, locations, and sets, the numbers of extras, and the number of days and nights of shooting.
★ The director reads it for all the above reasons and some of his own—and then makes his own changes.

These may be some of the best reasons why having only one screenplay can turn out to be a dead end, for anywhere along the line there is the possibility of rejection. As I mentioned earlier, John Sayles began his career as a novelist; writing as a craft was a part of his life-style, even if you keep in mind his comment, "When I wrote my first novel, I was on food stamps and I worked in factories. . . ." He is a determined advocate of the theory that you need more than one sample of your writing:

"Essentially, having many screenplays is important because of the *timing* of a subject, something they might just be looking for at the moment, a story of a thirty-five-year-old Columbus, Ohio, divorcée. It's sort of like playing the quinella at jai alai. And I also ask: Should you really want to be a director or a writer in this business if you only have *one* movie to sell?"

He suggests that screenwriters have a range of work to show—a thriller, a cop show, a period piece, a western, sci-fi—instead of one New York City domestic comedy and nothing more. John Sayles was also an actor, so he is a natural storyteller.

"The people you meet in this field (who buy the material) are usually not visual. They don't make pictures in their heads when they read a script. If they haven't read your screenplay, you have to be prepared to tell the story in ten minutes—to make it exciting and to make it visual. If you can't tell it well in ten minutes, and if they seem to be drifting while you tell the story—maybe it's not the way you tell it. Maybe the screenplay is no good!"

He also comments that when you start out, you'll be meeting the lower-level, junior story editors, and the trick is to get them interested. When he was living in Santa Barbara, California, in the early days, he'd make his appointments in Los Angeles and drive down to the city, taking the one or two hours ("depending upon traffic") to rehearse.

"I'd go over the story in my head until I could tell the whole plot in ten minutes. Then, when I'd see their eyes blank over because the last thing they wanted that day was a black western, I'd shift at once to another story I was working on. So I'd always have a ten- or fifteen-minute version of *each* screenplay ready to tell, whether the meeting was a courtesy to a new writer or they were really listening. I know one executive out in Hollywood who has a five-minute attention span!"

Hooray for Hollywood! I have an old friend out there who writes quite successfully for television films and the world of the sitcom. He and his partner, Tony Di Marco, have written for *Laverne & Shirley, Mork & Mindy, Fantasy Island,* and *Happy Days.* His name is Dave Ketchum, and I wish I could say that we originally met one another through our involvement with the industry. Actually, we met because both of us are bread bakers, and in addition to being one of the West Coast's busiest writers, he makes the best jelly-stuffed bran muffins in California! Much of what he says is the same advice John Sayles gives, and it's well worth listening to if you've written that one great screenplay:

THE GRATING FINALLY POPS OUT AND LAVERNE BRINGS IT INSIDE THE VENT. SHE POPS HER HEAD OUT AND LOOKS AROUND. CARMINE MANAGES TO DO THE SAME, EVEN THOUGH IT'S A TIGHT SQUEEZE.

LAVERNE

It's all clear, Shirl.

SHIRLEY SQUEEZES BETWEEN LAVERNE AND CARMINE, SO NOW THREE HEADS ARE STICKING OUT OF THE VENT.

SHIRLEY

Great. I'll go down first.

THEY ALL START TO MOVE, BUT EVERYONE IS STUCK. THEY STRUGGLE TO BREAK FREE TO NO AVAIL.

CARMINE

Shirl, you suck in everything you can, and I'll give Laverne a push. Ready, go!

SHIRLEY TAKES A DEEP BREATH AND MOVES BACK INTO THE VENT AS LAVERNE SCOOTS FORWARD. CARMINE GRABS HER LEGS AS SHE BEGINS DROPPING DOWN HEADFIRST TO THE FILE CABINET BELOW. LAVERNE ENDS UP DOING A HANDSTAND ON THE CABINET.

LAVERNE

I wonder if the Girl from U.N.C.L.E. started like this.

LAVERNE MANAGES TO RIGHT HERSELF ON THE FILE CABINET, AND CARMINE AND LAVERNE HELP SHIRLEY DOWN.

LAVERNE (Cont'd)

Alright, now we're cooking. (POINTING) Hatrack! Careful, Shirl, don't let it hit the floor.

SHIRLEY PICKS IT UP AND HANDS THE HATRACK TO LAVERNE, WHO STARTS TO LAY IT FROM THE FILE CABINET TO THE SOFA THE WAY THEY DID IT IN THE FANTASY. ONLY THIS TIME THE HATRACK IS TOO SHORT.

A page sample of a three-camera script format from Laverne & Shirley *("The Bardwell Caper"), written by Dave Ketchum and Tony DiMarco.*

"You know what usually happens with new writers? They write a spec script, give it to an agent, and maybe he gets a nibble on it. The agent wants another script of a different type to give to someone else. The writer won't write it. Suddenly he or she gets on the high horse and says, 'Let 'em read the first one!' Believe me, the readers are not that imaginative. If you've written a comedy, they'll never figure you can also write drama. They have to read it."

At one point Dave had had a regular role as an actor on an NBC show called *Camp Runamuck,* and his contract would not allow him to do any acting anywhere else, including commercials. So a friend of his, Garry Marshall, suggested that he write, beginning with a spec script.

"At the time, it was 'fashionable' to write comedy with a partner, so I picked a friend of mine who was in advertising. We went through a *TV Guide* and picked out a show that we thought we could do a good job for, and we wrote. Our plan was to write five spec scripts and then, if nothing happened, we'd hang it up for a while and reappraise our chances. The show we picked was *F Troop.*

Garry Marshall took the script to his agent, and the agent told Dave and Tony that it was "great":

"I hadn't heard 'great' that much until I got into show business!"

The agent got it to the folks at *Petticoat Junction,* who asked them to do a few scripts for them, and they were "off and running in the writing world." Nothing became of the *F Troop* script.

Certainly neither Dave nor I intend to make it sound easy. He feels that even feature screenplay potential is better than television, because there are basically only three television networks to which you can go. He echoes John Sayles in this area.

"I would say that the biggest problem selling *anything* is to get it to the person who has the final say about buying it. All the companies seem to have people working for them who, for the most part, have never written, produced, directed, or acted. *They,* strangely enough, are the ones that seem to pass judgment on what is salable or not. I never understood that. And selling a script or television idea is tough, because no matter how good it may be, the networks seem to buy from established producers. After all, if you were working for a network, would you risk your job by buying from an unknown, or from an Aaron Spelling or Norman Lear or Garry Marshall? I would say that the best thing to do is to get an agent!"

Get an agent! The film classes and the constant questioning by new writers generally brings the subject up in one of two ways—or both:

★ Do I need an agent?
★ Is it possible for an unknown to get an agent?

For the first question, the answer is probably "yes." Though many of my friends who work in the business, both as writers and actors, do not have an agent or have had one in the past only to find that they do much better without them, you have to look carefully at the advantages and disadvantages for the beginning writer:

★ Agents can open doors, there is no doubt in my mind. Most production companies will not look at unsolicited manuscripts, and this is also a policy of the networks. The agent generally has contacts who know them and who trust them (for the most part).
★ The problems of writing *and* trying to make calls, do the contact work, make the first interviews, and build a reputation can be almost overwhelming. Ideally writers like to write and agents can do all the rest. (Though the world is not always ideal, as we shall soon find out.)
★ The agent also acts as a buffer between writer and buyer in the areas of business negotiations, residuals, rights, and the monies you will receive for the sale of your work. Most writers (artists and actors) get stomach knots when they even think of doing business.
★ A good agent can generally be the best first critic of your work even before it is submitted to the buyer. He or she generally knows what is timely, what is the "hot" subject, which producers are looking for material.

On the other hand:

★ If an agent has a stable of very successful writers, there is a good chance that the beginner will drift into the background or wither away without a sale.

★ The agent is *not always* the best first critic. I have had scripts of mine turned down by my agent in past years and have gone across the street (!) and sold two of them to a producer who was just leaving for a series in Italy! On the other hand, I have had an agent tell me, "Baby, you write a hundred scripts like this, and I can sell a hundred," and then end up never even selling *one*!

★ Believe it or not, many producers and publishers actually *hate* agents. They know that they have to deal with them, but they don't really like to. Your first big break might well lie with a producer who feels just that way. One word of warning: Be careful when they hand you the first contract. The agent may well be able to read "the fine print" and you may not.

For the second question, the answer is also a qualified "yes." It *is* possible to find an agent, even if you are unknown, though it may not be the easiest chore in the world. John Sayles feels that you should have an agent, and he has some good suggestions:

"The biggest campaign is to get an agent—a good one. How? You see a good flick, you get the name of the screenwriters, and you call the Writers Guild of America, find out who reps the writer who did the film. Call the agent, ask if he or she wants to see:

★ all of your screenplays
★ *one* of your screenplays
★ *ten pages* of one of your screenplays"

John also cautions that once you get an agent, don't expect him or her to do the work. Don't sit on that one screenplay. If producers don't like it, and you have nothing else to show, that's it. It's also true that some well-known agents are just not interested in beginning writers, as I have said. Dave Ketchum adds:

"There are two theories about that. One is to try to go with a big agent because they have all the contacts. The other is to go with a hardworking small agent because there's more personal contact and they'll work harder for you. I've been with both. My vote would be for the smaller, hardworking one. If, years later, he or she goes out of business, and by that time you're making a few million a year, why, then you can go with any agent you want!"

I suppose it's easy to write that the most important thing of all is not to become discouraged. Finding an agent can sometimes be as frustrating as writing that first script and then trying to peddle it yourself—door to door at the office of every producer and television network in the country. And, having found an agent, it is almost as frustrating to learn that you have the wrong one! The chemistry is bad. You really don't like one another. You can't get to him or her when you call. Worst of all, nothing seems to be selling. (But there are promises. "They love it! *It's great!*")

For some years, in the early days of television, I was signed with a rather well-known agent. I wrote variety material and was quite successful at it (though it took little writing ability). But I was frustrated. I wanted desperately to write dramatic material. I wanted to do shows with actors, stories, sets, glamour, credits my mother could tell her neighbors about.

"Relax," my agent counseled me, "you're a variety writer and you're doing rather well."

So I continued on, going door to door *myself*, and finally I began to sell my dramatic scripts without her help. In a few years, having written for about ten different dramatic series, I found out that my beloved agent had heard about a top-paying variety show on television and had given it away to *another writer* in her stable. Furiously I stormed into her office, asking the reason that *I* was not given a chance at a show that paid $1,000 a week (in 1952 dollars)!

"Relax," she said, "you're a *dramatic* writer!"

Dave Ketchum tells a story that is typical in this weird business:

"I was told by a producer that I was a nice guy but that I should get out of the business because I didn't have it. Two years later, I sold the same producer a new pilot script!"

As with everything else in the industry, there are no rules that apply in the writing and the selling of a screenplay.

★ For some, like the sale of *Under the Volcano,* written by Guy Gallo, it was a series of lucky contacts, a director who had wanted to do the story for decades and a serendipitous meeting of the two. It all happened very quickly.

★ For others, like Buzz Hirsch and Larry Cano, the trip from idea to screen for *Silkwood* was long (from *1974 to 1979*) and tortuous—interminable problems with options, family executors of the estate, disinterest, rejection, and a time of potential surrender on the entire project—until they discovered that Meryl Streep was interested in doing the role of Karen Silkwood. Suddenly the dream became a reality!

The interest of a star may be the important selling point for a screenplay. If producers are looking for "commercial" potential, what better encouragement than the interest of a Meryl Streep, a Susan Sarandon, or a Robert Redford? Your job then becomes one of getting it past *their* agents and managers in order to have the star read your screenplay!

The timeliness of a screenplay can also play a role, as the newspapers so often show. If a *Saturday Night Fever, Flashdance, Rocky,* or *Star Wars* becomes the box office bonanza of a particular time, you may be sure that Hollywood will offer us clones as quickly as new screenplays can be ground out of the word processors. It might well be your story of a Vietnamese divorcée in Scarsdale who gives birth to quintuplets that becomes the next great vehicle for Shirley MacLaine! It is not at all impossible, for in the past few years, screenplays adapted from major news stories have been sold almost at once to the studios—the American medical students in Grenada, for example, or the two young spies who sold secrets to the Russians. Sequels to successful box office films are also popular. Ours is an industry where imitation is often equated with creativity. It may end up as your open door.

Will there be freedom in all this? Probably not. Even if you should sell your screenplay, there is a good chance that you will have sold only the idea and one rewrite. Somewhere along the line "they" may take it away from you and have another battery of writers redo the film as "they" see it!

The industry is filled with stories of writers who have had their names removed from a film, of others who were pushed out to make way for people who could deliver the "commercial" message as perceived by the executives who control production. Your first screenplay contract (if you can finally achieve it), will probably allow you the first rewrite—and only the first one at that—after which the producers can use their discretion and turn the project over to another writer or team of writers if you can't deliver a script that meets their needs. Can they do it? Yes. Of course they can.

"Most writers never have the opportunity to see their work filmed *as they wrote it. . . .*" This was a comment made by Richard Levinson, who, with his partner, William Link, was the creator of *Columbo,* the film *The Execution of Private Slovik,* and other well-known television series and movies. The only way to have total creative control, he feels, is to write a novel or produce your own work—which, of course, is what some people are trying to do. (One excellent example in addition to the John Sayles story might well be the successful first film of the Coen Brothers, *Blood Simple).* Levinson adds, "Write for nothing and trade it for control. If it's a success, then you make your money."

New Programs, New Ideas: An Interview with Herbert Brodkin

In his book *Inside Prime Time* (Pantheon), Todd Gitlin offers a statistic that is probably valid for almost every part of our industry: In a typical year, the networks receive about three thousand ideas, from which one hundred scripts are eventually culled, and of that number about twenty-five pilots are developed. Five or ten end up in the program schedule, and only *one* or *two* will go on to survive the first season!

In the area of new and original screenplays submitted to the established production companies, to independents, and to the networks for made-for-television features or miniseries, the statistics are equally grim.

As a result, I am always fascinated (as are my students) by the stories of the people who not only have managed to climb through this almost impenetrable morass, but also have surfaced as the very few who have maintained their integrity while making an indelible mark on the industry. Possibly the most important thing that I can think of in terms of the career of Herbert Brodkin is that he has managed to bring important and intelligent programming to the networks, frequently at the cost of severe conflict with the executives and the censors. Through his early years in live television *(Alcoa Hour, The Defenders, Playhouse 90,* and *Studio One* among others), up to and including the more recently acclaimed *Holocaust, Skokie, The Missiles of October,* and *Sakharov,* he has refused to lower his standards of taste and quality. For many young people just entering our field, this is a critical area of consideration, for it so seldom happens in film, in tape, and especially in television programming.

Herb is an old Fire Island friend, a sometimes fishing companion (who also excels in the sport as he does as a producer), and a man who—by accident—started his own career at the summer camp where I first wrote "Lady Fingers" that cold winter weekend.

"Keep in mind—I didn't become a producer until I was thirty-nine! That's a long time since I began doing it all at summer camp when I was twelve. . . ."

Herbert Brodkin.

His path led to a few years as a dramatics counselor at the same camp, followed by the University of Michigan, where he majored in engineering (!) and later switched to drama.

"During World War Two, I was a training films director at the Astoria Studios in New York. I did about forty-five training films ranging from *Double Apron Barbed-Wire Fence* to *Infantry Stream Crossing Expedients!* I was a captain at the time, got into an argument with a colonel, and was transferred to Special Services where I supervised the production of over one thousand USO camp shows—including four hundred legitimate plays over a period of five years. . . ."

His first professional job out of the army was designing scenery for an industrial show/film company called Jam Handy, and eventually he directed a live musical/dancing/acting extravaganza called *Round the World with Coca-Cola.* (In it, by the way, was a newcomer—an actor named John Forsythe. The industrial show world was, in fact, a place where many actors and actresses were to begin their careers—and still do.)

He designed scenery for the New York City Center, where José Ferrer was directing, was hired by the New York City Opera, and in 1952 went to CBS to do scenic design for *Charlie Wild, Private Detective.*

"When I finally went into TV, I had had training in collegiate dramatics, physical production, stock companies, and five years in the army.

On the set of Sakharov. *Jason Robards and Glenda Jackson with Jack Gold, the director, and Tony Imi, the cinematographer (far left).*

With all that training, it wasn't even that I knew so much. It was that the others knew nothing!"

Six weeks after joining CBS, the job of producer opened up and he was selected to fill the spot. (Timing?)

"Remember, it took me thirteen years to get into the scenic designers union. There's nothing easy about all this. I don't think anyone makes it without talent—but the ones who refuse to be defeated are the ones who make it."

As most of my readers know only too well, for I have a propensity for repeating anything and everything that I feel must be learned, I have always believed that the greatest trap a young filmmaker can fall into is to ignore the fact that ours is a business first and foremost. The schools ignore it, we don't like to think of it when we are trying to sell our screenplay or our talents, and yet it surfaces over and over again if we are honest about it. Herbert Brodkin feels the same way:

"If you want to be successful, I'd suggest that you go to law school or business administration school. The guys running the industry are all lawyers or accountants. The great majority of people running production—the ones I meet in the development of my shows—are all lawyers, statisticians, businessmen, accountants, or research experts. I seldom meet people who know drama or who have a back-

Glenda Jackson, costar of Sakharov, *gives cinematographer Tony Imi a hand on the set of Ylena Bonner's apartment.*

ground in it. I'm currently dealing with the production of six features for a major cable network—and none of the people are drama people. *All of them are business people!"*

In a sense, his comments are not much different from those of John Sayles and Dave Ketchum and all the others in our field who keep reminding us that we specialize in being visual while dealing with buyers who are generally *nonvisual.* It is one of the reasons I continually mention that even our writing becomes a *selling tool* in trying to get ahead.

"It doesn't start right at the networks, though. There are other ways that writers can become known. . . ."

Each year, Herbert Brodkin and Robert Berger, who work together at their Titus Productions, help select the winning script from the previous season at the Eugene O'Neill Theatre in Connecticut. The winner, in turn, is produced by their company for network television release over ABC.

There are also programs all over the country, playwriting contests, people who will produce the works of unknowns. Marsha Norman's prize-winning play, *'night, Mother,* first saw the lights of a theater in Louisville, Kentucky, before coming to Broadway to great acclaim. There are also over one hundred regional theaters that showcase new playwrights, many of them local writers, and every major college has a program devoted to the production of new plays.

In addition, I have already mentioned the American Film Institute programs for new writers and new directors and the unusual approach at Sundance in Provo Canyon, Utah. At Sundance the student offers his or her completed screenplay, accompanied by a budget, a suggested shooting schedule, and a summary of how the scenes would be shot; the would-be filmmaker is even given the opportunity to direct a few sequences on videotape to visualize the finished material.

The writer or would-be writer for film/tape/television needs to search for new avenues in which to practice the craft, even if the only goal is to sell a screenplay for production as the great American feature. The stone wall of the major production companies and the networks should not discourage you. Somehow, the first doors that are stormed by the new film school graduate or filmmaker with too few credits are those awesomely difficult places:

"The networks are even more rigid today than they have ever been," Herb Brodkin says, "in what they want, in what they expect, in what they accept. The self-censorship is more prevalent than ever before. . . ."

So if the film industry itself is one of collaboration and compromise, you may have to find another path at the beginning in which to flex your writing muscles while you continue to churn out screenplays and television script ideas. But don't make excuses for the writing that you have to do—each day at the typewriter in the process of putting words on blank pieces of paper only helps to make you a better writer. Dave Ketchum adds:

"The best tip is to write! If you want to be a writer . . . write! Hanging in there is the answer. Of course, it's good to know what the market is. And it's good to write what you feel. But the most important thing is to keep at it. Writing isn't easy. There are a lot of strange rules and even stranger people that you'll meet. Your job is not to fight it . . . it's to beat them at their own game!"

Herbert Brodkin has certainly found a way to play the game and to win. And although he has managed to develop a reputation over the years of not compromising in major situations—and, in fact, turned down the presidency of Paramount Pictures because he would have to do things "I didn't want to do"—he is above all a pragmatist when it comes to the path that must be taken by the beginner:

"The art of politics is compromise. And the film business is also total compromise. If you're going to be successful, you'll have to accept a certain amount of it—a certain amount of give and take."

As with all careers, it takes a certain amount of time, a long period of "paying your dues," of writing or directing or producing a vast amount of material, before you can command the position of turning down over one hundred shows because you could not get them into production in exactly the way you wanted to see them—as Herb Brodkin has done.

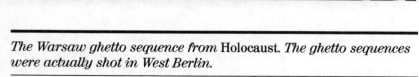

The Warsaw ghetto sequence from Holocaust. *The ghetto sequences were actually shot in West Berlin.*

The railroad sequence of Holocaust. Fritz Weaver (Dr. Weiss) meeting his wife, who is joining him in the Warsaw ghetto.

The crew sets up one of the most moving sequences in the film Holocaust, the mass execution at Babi Yar.

The crew sets up for the sequence in which Fritz Weaver joins his wife at the station.

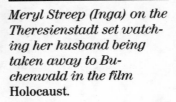

Meryl Streep (Inga) on the Theresienstadt set watching her husband being taken away to Buchenwald in the film Holocaust.

I realize that a great number of would-be filmmakers have a commitment to "do something important" with their films—to help change or communicate an important message to the world. In the world of the documentary, I certainly understand that credo, and people such as Frederick Wiseman, Alan and Susan Raymond, and Pam Yates have managed to achieve those goals. In the world of the screenplay and the dramatic film, there is no doubt that Herb Brodkin is a perfect role model, for he *has* managed to devote himself to bringing to a mass audience the social subject matter that the media had been afraid to tackle: nuclear war, racial bigotry, Nazism, alcoholism, drug abuse, medical malpractice.

It's probably an inherent character trait, a sense of determination, and a talent that have allowed him to move to top rank in the field. These are probably the qualities that make Herb Brodkin such a darned good fisherman, too!

The Young Writer: If They Could Do It, So Could We!

There is one more story that I would like to relate before I close this section of the book. I have concerned myself and my readers with the stories and advice of the well known—Herbert Brodkin, John Sayles, Don Taffner, Dave Ketchum, and all the others who were kind enough to speak with me and, in turn, to offer their advice to the young filmmaker. The reasons are obvious, for all of us are interested in how *they* made it. It helps us, too, because we begin to realize that all of us in the field, veteran and beginner alike, manage to find our way through paths that no one else seems to duplicate. I suppose we get from all of this a feeling that whatever we are currently doing to further our own careers, even if it seems at the time to be a diversion, is probably okay—for now.

If we look at the new writers, the new directors, the people who will eventually be our top producers (or who may even *leave* the film field to take a job at Dad's booming manufacturing corporation), it is interesting to note that a great many crooked paths are being trod in exactly the same way the old hands have described. Here, too, as in every other part of our field, there is no *one* story that will serve to illuminate *all* the serpentine paths being taken.

David Yazbek is a young acquaintance of mine who is twenty-four years old at the time of this writing. Though I had known him only as a fishing enthusiast out at Fire Island, I did not realize that he was also very much a part of our industry. Quite by accident, someone mentioned that David was one of the writers on the NBC Network's *Late Night with David Letterman*, that one of his shows had won an Emmy, that he had written a screenplay, and that he had produced a very successful stage production of *Hair* up in Boston. All this at twenty-four!

"I've always admired John Sayles, because he believes as I do . . . if you want to express yourself, don't send it off to someone. Do it yourself!"

An English major at Brown University, he wrote some humor columns for the newspapers on campus, met a man who was to become his writing partner, Ted Greenberg, who was then attending Harvard, and had the usual doubts about his future.

"For all of us, the period after college is one of crisis. What am I going to do in the real world? Do I want to be a little fish in a big pond? Actually, my first love is music, so I became a page turner in a musical comedy orchestra!"

With a borrowed $2,000, he decided that he would produce and direct a production of *Hair* in Boston.

"That's all we could borrow at first. Everyone told us that we were crazy, that we needed at least $50,000 to produce the show. We figured we'd go ahead anyway, and if they were right and we were wrong, we had the rest of our lives to pay it off!"

They were not wrong. The Boston production of *Hair* was a huge success, giving them a pile of good reviews to show their future backers. Following the show, David and Ted worked on a screenplay together and at the same time heard from a friend who was a researcher on *Late Night with David Letterman* that some of their writers were leaving and that they were looking for new talent.

"We had friends who were working in comedy writing, including two guys right out of college who were writing on *Saturday Night Live*. We figured if they could do it, so could we!"

Ted was working on Wall Street at the time. He and David took three days of a long weekend, locked themselves in a room, and wrote comedy material together. Finally they had seven pages of written and rewritten and rewritten comedy material with which they were satisfied, and they sent it off to the head writer of the show.

When David told me the story, I smiled, for once again—for the second time—I relived that cold weekend at the summer camp where I wrote my first dramatic script. It was also a replay of Dave Ketchum and Tony DiMarco and *their* first script. Now, once again, I was hearing a story of a team of writers who locked themselves in and wrote the material that they thought the market would buy. And then?

Then? Silence. For two months they waited to hear from the show. Nothing. No word.

"I went fishing with my friend Jeff out at Montauk. I was depressed about the silence. I was even more depressed when Jeff caught a thirty-one-pound striped bass and I got seasick. That night, feeling miserable, I went up to my room and there was a knock on the door. The hotel manager told me that Ted was calling from New York."

They had an appointment with Letterman the next day! The material was "great," and they worked on the show for seven months, at the same time rewriting their screenplay. Did they have an agent?

"Yes, we had an agent at first, but we didn't like him. But now, with the David Letterman credits, we can get into *any* agent's office!"

As of this writing, the screenplay is being considered by several major studios and some independent producers, and David's dream is not only to cowrite it but to do the music for the film as well. They are also toying with the idea of going the "John Sayles route" by trying to raise $150,000 themselves, using a director they used to know at Harvard, and producing it independently.

Remembering the experience with *Hair*, David is confident, and somehow so am I:

"Being young is a good thing in this business. You can afford to take all the chances you want. *You have no reputation to lose!*"

MAKING IT THROUGH LUNCH

Film Is One Continuing Horror: The Never-Never Land of Production

I have heard that Francis Ford Coppola was the first one to describe the motion picture process as "one continuing horror," but I can certainly attest to the fact that *anyone* in film who has ever been closely tied to the production of a project would mutter a firm and heartfelt "amen" to that statement.

It is the pragmatic and stomach-knotting part of film, and art and creativity be damned! It is getting a film started, through production, and out of the laboratory with a minimum number of "war stories" to be recounted later. It is the part of film that is never taught in film schools because *no one* can teach it! There are problems that appear in the production of a film that have never happened before, might never happen again, and, no matter how forewarned you may be, will still take you completely by surprise when they do occur. It is the bursting of the budget at the least expected moment, because not spending the money at that instant will stop everything dead in its tracks. It is taking a chance during the shooting in order to meet a deadline and finding that it works beautifully ninety-nine times—and is a complete disaster on the one hundredth time that you attempt the short cut.

We learn how to expose the film properly, how to make a perfect edit, how to deliver the film to the lab, and how to ask for what we want (though no one has ever really learned the difference between an "A Wind" and a "B Wind"!). *But no one ever tells us how to get a crew of eight people into a typical American Midwest restaurant during lunch hour, feed them all, and get them out in one hour so that you can go back to work and take advantage of the sun* (which is forecast to disappear in late afternoon).

Well, if you learn nothing else from this chapter, I will at least give you the solution to that particular problem later on. Meanwhile, think about it. You may one day be required to solve the problem.

Be aware that there is much more to producing a film than director's chairs and screen credits and the "glamour" and "excitement" of seeing your product on the screen.

You must also realize that what I am about to recount doesn't happen only to *other people*. It happens to everyone, and it will happen to you!

Some time back, I was delivering a guest lecture to a continuing education class at New York University. It was their last week in an intensive course, during which time they had produced their class film projects, all in the space of five hard weeks. I had facetiously titled my lecture "Film Is One Continuing Horror," and we were all laughing together at my "war stories" from around the globe. The door burst open and a harassed, wildly excited young man ran into the room and went from student to student, whispering as he progressed around the group. Horror passed across the faces of the men and women, who quickly got up, grabbed their coats and books, and hurried from the classroom. Startled, I stopped my stories. The professor stood up and explained: The class project was in the lab, and they had just received notification that all the splices were coming apart

during the printing of the answer print! I looked up at the title of the lecture, emblazoned across the blackboard. I didn't know whether to laugh or cry for them all.

Everyone who has ever been in production can add his or her own tales and cautionary rules. As you progress, you in turn will tell your own, many of which will probably top mine. If it makes you wary, if you learn that the best of production people (be they production assistants, production managers, directors, or producers) are efficient, suspicious, paranoid worriers, then I will have done my job well.

Come with me, then, into the never-never land of production.

NEVER MISS A CALL UNLESS YOU'RE DEAD

The phrase has been attributed to director of photography Freddie Young, and it's probably the best first advice I can offer you in the area of production. Every member of any efficient film crew is always there on time! I notice that in film classes and seminars there is a constant stream of latecomers, something that would not be tolerated on any professional film crew. Whatever the time of the "call," producers expect their crew to be there, and to be there on time.

If one member of the crew is late, everyone waits. The production slows down. The next day a second person is late and the movement slows down even further. Thus, being on time is almost a compulsion with producers like me.

Two small stories will suffice. We were shooting for Eastern Airlines in Puerto Rico, one

of those jobs when the only scenery you get to see is the airport runway. The call, downstairs "having had" (meaning that all have had breakfast), was at eight A.M., and everyone was indeed there and waiting—except the sound man. We waited five minutes—ten—and called up to his room, but the phone was busy. I went up in the elevator and knocked loudly on his door. "Oh, yeah," he called. "I'll be down as soon as the *Today Show* is over!" Needless to say, he never worked for me again.

On the other hand, most film people are on time almost to the second, and you can probably set your watch by their arrival downstairs at the hotel desk. A few years back I knew just such a person, a cameraman who would walk into the dining room at 7:33 A.M., order juice, two eggs, bacon, and coffee, and be out by 7:58, get his gear, and be downstairs again at 8:00 A.M. sharp.

One job that we had required that we meet at 4:30 A.M. (!) to make an early plane from Albuquerque to Vancouver (an impossible connection). Since I had the room next to the cameraman, I went out my door at 4:28 and knocked on his door, just letting him know that I was on my way downstairs. He flung his door open angrily, still dressed only in his jockey shorts. He shouted at me, "I have *two minutes*," slammed the door, and went back to his room.

Two minutes later he was downstairs, fully dressed, helping to load the van for the trip to the airport.

NEVER TRUST A HOTEL WAKE-UP CALL

Every filmmaker carries his or her alarm clock,

and some of us (like me) carry *two*. Hotels are notorious for forgetting wake-up calls and then blaming you for having been asleep when they called. In addition, we sometimes make arrangements to have whoever wakes up first call the others.

In spite of this (remember the "horror"?) a hotel in Havana, Cuba, forgot my wake-up call, and *both* of my clocks broke during the night! I managed to use my internal alarm clock and awakened in just enough time to catch the plane out.

NEVER LET A CLIENT OR LOCATION CONTACT MAKE YOUR HOTEL RESERVATION

Certainly you want to check with the people out on the location to get their suggestions. And, many times, when you're working in Transylvania, North Carolina, or Crab Orchard, Nebraska, there may only be *one* motel in the community. But I have found over the years that clients and contacts tend to put you in the closest motel to the location, rather than understanding that you probably will have a van or some other transportation and that a ten- or fifteen-minute ride from a more comfortable accommodation will not make very much difference (especially since there's nothing to do at night and the entire crew will probably retire at eight P.M. in order to get more than enough sleep before traveling to the location).

Do your own research. Question. Make calls. And as I said, use your contacts to give

you some advice, but then make up your own mind.

NEVER LET YOUR LOCAL GUIDE GUIDE YOU

Again, it pays to have someone on location who knows the area, speaks the language, can help you get around easily or get through foreign customs clearance. But after a while you begin to learn that *your* cultural background and *his or her* cultural background are as different as videotape and film stock. What is exciting and filmable to you might well be too common to even consider for your guide.

Let me illustrate with three short tales:

—AFRICA. We are deep in the interior in Nigeria for the production of a travel film for Alitalia Airlines. The road is long and winding, and the government has insisted that we film a large hydroelectric project of which they are justly proud. I, in turn, am on the lookout for the serendipitous sequences that make for an effective and interesting travel film.

(Incidentally, this is always the case. The governments of countries, especially developing nations, will always insist that you see the steel plant or the factories, while you are looking desperately for "people" sequences that will convince tourists to spend a thousand dollars or more in air fares to visit that country.)

The car rounds a bend and suddenly I see the most incredible market right alongside the road. Filled with colorful people who are all wearing native dress, women with dangling earrings with lobes pierced and stretched widely,

men and women who have traveled long distances carrying produce and products on their heads, it is enough to make my mouth taste of the expectation of a great travel sequence.

"What is that?" I ask our Nigerian guide.

"Oh, that's only the local market," he sleepily answers, his eyes still on the road.

"Stop!" I shout. "Stop. I want to film it."

A look of disbelief comes into his face. "Film it?" To him the market is an everyday occurrence. He does not see it through my eyes, of course. To him it is his A&P, his chain of supermarkets. And *I* want to film it.

—CAMBODIA. It is right before the war destroyed much of Southeast Asia and we were still making films of Siem Reap and Angkor Wat and trying to induce the traveler to stop thinking of Europe and let the mind wander to the Pacific.

Again, along a winding road, we suddenly see a crowd outside a small village. There are drums and fire and flaming hoops through which two dogs are jumping.

I practically turn my head out of its socket at the sight, the smell of smoke, the beating drum, the crowd gathered around a man who is chanting some kind of sales pitch. The guide keeps driving right past the crowd.

"What is that?" I ask our Cambodian guide through our Thai interpreter.

"Oh, that's only the local medicine man," he sleepily answers, his eyes still on the road.

"Stop!" I shout. "Stop. I want to film it."

A look of disbelief comes into his face. "Film it?" To him the medicine man is an everyday occurrence. He does not see it through my eyes, of course. To him it is his druggist, the place he fills his prescriptions. And *I* want to film it.

—CHILE. We are on the Pan American highway north of Santiago and we are looking into the Andes desperately for something that gives a sign of life, that might be the makings of a sequence on South America. Suddenly, up on the top of a high mountain, I see what looks like a cloud of yellow dust rising to the sky and billowing wildly in the air.

"What is that?" I ask my Chilean guide.

"Oh, that's only the farmers threshing wheat. That's the chaff in the air," he sleepily answers, his eyes still on the road.

"How do they thresh the wheat?"

"Oh, they use wild horses to run on it."

"Stop!" I shout. "Stop. I want to film it."

A look of disbelief comes into his face. "Film it?" To him the threshing of wheat with wild horses is an everyday occurrence. He does not see it through my eyes, of course. To him it is his ordinary agricultural process. And *I* want to film it.

This last story has a postscript, for I can never let a good story end. The crew got out of the car, and along with my guide, we began our trudge up the mountainside. There was no road, no path to follow, and all the while the guide kept trying to dissuade me from proceeding. He told me that the *huasos* (farmers) were quite hostile to outsiders, that their *fundos* (farms) were isolated, and that they got quite drunk when they harvested the wheat. I went on ahead, little hearing what he was saying. It was a perfect sequence for the film. I would just smile a lot if they were hostile.

I was the first over the crest of the hill. Before me was a filmmaker's dream. A large, round corral had been built, and in it were about twenty wild horses being driven around the circle by two *huasos* with wide-brimmed hats and flowing, colorful serapes. They drove the horses around in the circle by shouting loudly and waving their arms. And rising from the center was a large, yellow cloud of wheat chaff, backlit by the sun in a blue, clear sky.

Then they saw me. And they stopped. There were about eight of them, and they were, to say the least, quite curious. I smiled.

They rode over just as the rest of the crew topped the hill, and my guide came up and began to explain what it was we wanted. Finally one of them nodded and looked at the others. He went to one of the horses and took the rein in his hand and led the horse over to me, putting the leather into my fingers and popping a hat on my head. Somehow I stopped smiling and turned to my guide.

"I told you they were not very friendly," he said. "They'll do what you want—if you ride the horse in there."

I gulped. "In there? In the corral?"

He nodded.

"Behind the wild horses."

He nodded.

"But if I fall, the horses will run over me."

He nodded.

I summoned up my entire background and experience. In my younger days, my father had owned a dude ranch in the Northeast and I had owned a remarkably wild and spirited horse

named Flame. I went back all those years, took a deep breath, and got on the horse. With one of the *huasos* I entered the corral. I looked at him and yelled a loud, high-pitched whoop and started off behind the herd of wild horses, holding on for dear life, all the while knowing that this was going to make the best sequence of the film—if I lived to direct it.

I don't know how many times we went around. When I finally wheeled the horse out of the corral, the *huasos* whooped and yelled and did just about anything we wanted. In addition, I had become so much of a "gringo hero" to them that they went up to the *fundo* and came back with their women, after which they performed a Chilean folk dance, the *cueca*, on horseback for our cameras!

I smiled.

Essentially, especially in the documentary, one must take advantage of timing, of the serendipity of travel, of the incident that happens only at that moment and will never be repeated again. It is the festival you suddenly come upon, and which was never publicized, the common and the ordinary that will make up a memorable sequence in your film, only because you were aware enough to take advantage of the situation as it happened. It need not be a foreign story. It happens here in the United States all the time. But, should it happen in some distant country, there is one more word of warning that I must give.

NEVER TRUST YOUR TRANSLATOR

I have noticed time and time again that I might

say something in English that takes about twenty or thirty seconds to describe. My translator, in turn, does the trick in five seconds. At the time, I wonder at the conciseness and the brevity of his or her language, until I learn at some point that what I am asking is not being translated accurately at all! This is a most difficult situation, generally caused by a difference in culture and, frequently, a request that would be impolite or cannot be exactly translated into the language of the country. It is sometimes even more complex, as it was in Cambodia, where each sentence was filtered through two languages (plus English) and three diverse cultures!

NEVER TRUST THE WEATHERMAN, THE WEATHERWOMAN, OR PEOPLE WHO LIVE IN THE AREA

All of us, when we are planning exterior locations, will (or should) generally make inquiries about the weather conditions in an area. It makes sense, since much of your budget can be blown by a bad week of weather. Thus, when you're planning the shoot, I can only tell you that there are two groups you absolutely *cannot* trust to give an accurate weather forecast:

★ professional meteorologists
★ people who live in the area

The first group, of course, is notorious for being wrong a great part of the time, in spite of the fact that weather forecasting is now considered a "science." Somehow, after thirty-five

The author, after his macho ride in the Andes with the Chilean cowboys.

years in the film business, I would rather trust my luck to Atlantic City or Las Vegas than predict my shooting schedule on the forecasts for an area.

Remember, too, that the people who live there are not filmmakers; a "nice" day to an ordinary citizen may well be an overcast day for a professional film crew, or at best a day in which large, puffy clouds keep crossing the sun and making any take longer than five seconds an impossibility. As a result, the people who live in that community will generally tell a film crew one of several things:

★ You should have been here last week.
★ You should have come here next week.
★ I can't understand it. We generally get such nice weather at this time of the year.

This also works the opposite way. You arrive in Urubamba to film the rain dance only to find that the worst drought in the history of the country has parched the area. Here, too, you should have been here last week, next week, or last year when they had a lot of rain!

We are too frequently the victims of weather hype in the film business, and it's something to be wary of. In February of 1983, the middle of the winter doldrums on the northeast coast and in the Midwest, filmmakers trooped by the planeload to California, only to be greeted by one of the worst series of storms ever to hit the West Coast. Oceanfront homes were washed away, the Santa Monica pier was destroyed almost completely, and mudslides closed the Pacific Coast Highway. Nevertheless:

Never underestimate timing. Nat Eisenberg shot a commercial with Hank Aaron at the end of spring training in West Palm Beach. The commercial was released the same season that Aaron broke the record with 715 home runs!

★ One production company was en route to the Santa Monica pier to shoot a shoe commercial, only to find the pier had collapsed into the Pacific. The site was declared hazardous and cordoned off by the police.
★ A commercial for a coffee product was canceled after Dock Wyler Beach turned into a quagmire.
★ Another production company had paid high location fees to a private golf course in order to do a golf ball commercial, the shooting of which was canceled because of the downpour.
★ A Playboy Fashions shoot was canceled when the Venice Beach location washed out and yet another location—a house on the Pacific Coast Highway—had been washed out to sea!

One positive story did come out of the deluge. One production house was ecstatic, since their storyboard called for a jogging scene in the rain!

Before the entire state of California throws rocks at me, and my friends (ex-friends) out there take issue, as they always do, I must quickly say that this can happen anywhere and to anyone—and it usually does. I have had the most exquisite weather luck in places like Utah during the winter, while striking out in states where I was supposed to be "guaranteed" good shooting weather.

I did an NBC fashion show in Rome one midwinter, during February, and we had nothing but sun for ten days. The next year, a member of our crew, knowing what marvelous weather we had had on that first shoot, scheduled a bathing suit film during that same time. He had ten days of rain! As did I during a ten-day shoot in Rome during October, noted as the most beautiful weather month in that city!

Is there a solution? If I can tell nothing but horror stories about the weather, can I at least give some advice about how to avoid it? No. The best that any of us can do is to have as many "weather days" as possible before setting out to the exterior locations. Whatever can be shot indoors can fill the gaps when the rain hits the windows or the clouds make shooting impossible. There are times, too, when you will cleverly decide that a sequence planned for the outside could well be reslated for an interior, if you make some small changes. My friend who did the bathing suit film finally hired a large, lovely trattoria, rented lights in Rome, and filmed the entire job indoors!

This next "never" from never-never land has two parts, and each contradicts the other, showing once again that there are no rules in the film business.

NEVER FILM ON LOCATION WITHOUT GETTING PERMISSION OR A PERMIT TO FILM

NEVER BELIEVE ANYONE WHO TELLS YOU THAT YOU CAN'T SHOOT THAT DAY

No matter what your location—whether in the United States or (especially) in a foreign country—it's a good idea to find out in advance if you'll need a permit to film. It's like entering an impenetrable jungle without a compass, for every city, every state, every country, every national monument, every event in sports, every festival, every airport, building, street, and river seems to have its own rules and regulations for the professional filmmaker. Some permit requirements are simple, others are so complex that they bend the mind of even the most experienced and patient production people.

A small town will generally have no permit requirements (at least in the United States), and in places like Koshkonong, Missouri, and Alligator, Mississippi, the townfolk and the police will probably greet you with smiles and even a vocal greeting from the loudspeaker above the patrol car as it makes its rounds. This is generally true—unless:

★ you are there to cover a violent strike
★ you are there to film something that will put the town into a not-too-complimentary light
★ they are suspicious of you because of a previously bad experience with a film crew (which happens more often than we care to admit)

In those cases, you'll just have to do a lot of talking and a lot of smiling.

My own experience has taught me to check in advance, and I take nothing for granted, whether I am filming in Cairo, Egypt, or Cairo, Illinois—in Lima, Peru, or Lima, Ohio—in Tokyo, Japan, or Tokio, Arkansas.

Washington, D.C., for example, can offer the most complex system of red tape to any film crew trying to produce even a small travel documentary. There are overlapping jurisdictions and restrictions that only a government could invent! For example, the architect of the Capitol has jurisdiction over the Capitol grounds. The National Park Service has the final say on almost every historic monument in the city, while the government of the District of Columbia and the city police are in charge of filming permits everywhere else in the city. A long time ago we did a travel documentary in Washington for American Airlines, and there were parts of the area that required *four separate permits* for each location!

Situations, of course, also change rapidly from time to time. What may be the case one day may alter radically the next. During the Olympic Games in Los Angeles, for example, the cities of Beverly Hills, Long Beach, Pasadena, and Arcadia all rescinded filming permits for the duration of the games. In any case, every smart producer across the country had already canceled location filming for Los Angeles and had moved to other sections of the country.

In many cities and states there are specific and simple rules for getting a permit. And the great boon to filmmakers over the past few years has been the formation of film commissions in almost every state in the Union. Florida advertises itself as having "Hollywood weather without Hollywood overhead" (but it rains there, too), and Texas is now "the third coast." Colorado, Kentucky, Louisiana, and New Mexico are just a few of the states that have begun to woo filmmakers through advertising in trade maga-

All fifty states now offer some kind of assistance to motion picture crews—finding locations, crowd control, issuance of permits, and lists of postproduction facilities. They generally will help not only feature crews but also documentary units and commercial producers.

zines and intense promotion. Take advantage of it. My own production jobs have changed radically in recent years because of this help and because I can also find help, production facilities, and talented people all across the country and around the world. Thus, I now staff my crew with key people out of my own city, adding an assistant cameraman or sound person or lighting technician and occasionally some postproduction work (though *never* the use of laboratories out of New York or California).

In addition, on overseas trips, I try to get a North American who speaks the language, either as assistant cameraman or production assistant, and I also try to contact the overseas location and get a crew member who lives in the area. It is almost a necessity, for the local film person generally knows the city or the country well enough to cut corners, to find lights or another camera where you are certain that none exists.

If you are working in the United States or overseas, contacts with client representatives, ad agency executives who work in the area, and occasionally another filmmaker who is based there can help clear the way. Strangely, I have found that the tourist offices or foreign consulates in the United States are friendly, generally encouraging, and *totally useless* in setting up overseas shooting. In over thirty-five years, they have been the least helpful in my foreign work. Others may have had better experience.

If you are going to contact an advertising agency to help out with planning and preproduction, have the client representative do it. Ad agencies jump when the client speaks but can be

State film commissions can be of invaluable help to the film production crew. Warner Brothers' feature National Lampoon's Vacation used the Durango area of Colorado as their outdoor set.

terribly lethargic or even hostile to favors asked by filmmakers.

Well, then, it all looks easy. No? No. And the reason for this long dissertation on permits is to get us all to the second part of my advice, the part when you hear:

★ No, we don't give permits for this place.
★ Yes, we know you have a permit to shoot, but we've changed our minds.
★ Oh, is today the day? You can't shoot *today!*

Film crew after film crew can tell stories about permit problems, especially overseas. And these same film crews, pressed for details that become funny after they get back home, will generally tell a hair-raising tale of how they managed to overcome the refusal or the problem. There is a sinking, hollow feeling that comes over a filmmaker when he or she arrives at a location after having traveled hundreds or thousands of miles, the equipment weighing down the jeep or station wagon, and is met with a refusal that seems—at the moment—to be insurmountable.

Years ago, when we were shooting in Rome, my local production manager taught me a trick that we have used successfully again and again. There is a law in Rome that if you set a professional tripod down on the street, you must have a film permit. The same holds true if you are going to film actors. However, if you hand-hold the camera, it's okay to film. But the marvelous Italian mind has come up with an even more ingenious technique: *That same camera mounted on the rear floor of an open convertible car is also considered off the streets and can be used with impunity!*

The use of local production people can be of invaluable help to filmmakers, even if they do translate incorrectly or inaccurately. Having been through the mill of experience with their own film crews, they can generally ease the way for your production unit. Thus, having learned that a camera in a convertible is not really a camera, it then becomes a fairly simple matter to brief your actors to play the role of "tourists" as they walk down the Spanish Steps while you film the sequence from your red Fiat Spider!

Expect to do a lot of talking and a great amount of explaining, and to use as much charm as you can muster to convince a steely-eyed guardian that you really *can* film the location that day without causing the fall of the government or the dissolution of society.

The most important thing to remember, though, is that even when you have permission, other things manage to crop up at the most inconvenient times:

★ A hand is suddenly put over your camera lens, stopping the filming instantly. The first reaction is to lash out and push the intruder away, but unfortunately it happens to be a plainclothes officer (in Turkey or France or Portugal or any other country where film crews are suspect), and you smile and show the permit (and mentally punch him in the nose).
★ You are filming in the recovery room or the cardiac arrest clinic of a hospital when the chief surgeon bursts through the door to

Sight your sets in *Ely, Nevada*

BRISTLECONE FILM COMMITTEE
P.O. BOX 343   702-289-4531
ELY, NEVADA 89301

One of the more unusual film committees is that of Ely, Nevada. With an unemployment rate of 25 percent in the town, the Bristlecone Film Committee was formed to lure film crews to the area. Note the promise of "No Permits" and "No Hassles."

stop you. There is no way he's going to let you film "his patients." You smile (!) and you talk to him. Some of the most hostile doctors have turned into the biggest hams alive.

★ You have permission. The location is lit and set to go. A harried person comes in to tell you that someone (probably that executive) has forgotten to clear it with the chief honcho and you'll have to come back to Soda Springs, California (from New York), "some other day."

★ You are filming. All is well. A harried person comes through the door. You tell that person about having gotten permission. He or she draws up to full height and notifies you in no uncertain terms that you might have gotten permission from *him,* but *"I'm the one in charge here and no one bothered to contact me!"* Smile. He's probably as big a ham as the doctor.

★ The fountains (fill in any specific location here that you like) are not working today. They tell you you'll have to come back (to Rome) tomorrow; but you're leaving for Paris that night, so you'll no doubt find the minor executive who can turn them on for you (even if he's off that day, too).

When it comes to permits, however, there is one thing I can say with some certainty. Except for the few instances where police officers are suspicious, once you have a permit in your possession, no one will ask for it! Somehow film crews in possession of permits manage to

exude an air of confidence that must make itself felt by the people who oversee the location.

A few weeks ago we were filming in New York on one of the busiest corners of the city, 57th Street and Fifth Avenue, right in the middle of the noon rush hour. We had a permit. I was smug. I looked around waiting for someone to ask me for it. On the corner were two mounted police officers who watched our filming with interest, but who barely acknowledged the fact that there was even a film crew tying up the lunchtime traffic.

I waited for them to ask for the permit. They sat there atop their horses, immobile. Finally I strode over, looked up (smiled), and said, "Aren't you going to ask me for my permit?" They both laughed. They never asked. I walked away thinking that if we hadn't had one, they would have been off their horses in a minute!

The problems of production—any production—are a constant geyser of the unexpected, the unthinkable, the unpremeditated, the ungodly, and the unwanted! You learn to be an ambassador, salesperson, prophet, mind reader, diplomat, counselor, and original thinker. The moment you relax, a problem surfaces that no one has ever met before, and the solution to that problem is also something that no one had ever conceived before:

★ The location has been scouted. The crew has set up outdoors. You suddenly find that the nearest city is having a thunderstorm and that *your* location is the holding area for the jets that are circling every thousand

feet while waiting to land! You cannot possibly record sound.

★ You learn (as did the crew on Farrah Fawcett's film *Burning Bed*) that the next door neighbors at the location keep ten peacocks in their backyard and the squawking of the birds interferes with the sound recording. (They spiked the peacocks' feed with alcohol, and the birds dozed off!)

★ You have a brilliant idea for a sequence in a film about energy that will put a lone man dressed in a magician's costume on an oil platform out in the middle of the Gulf of Mexico. (Yes, Virginia, this is a true story.) You get him there by helicopter and then return for the rest of the film crew. On the way out again, *the pilot promptly gets lost* and your actor is out there in 100 degrees of heat, dressed in white tie and tails—alone—for almost five hours while you search desperately for where you left him, a dot in the water! (Yes, Virginia, we finally found him.)

In the deep recesses of my mind, I see a submarine putting up its periscope, and in response to the captain's query, the sailor looking through it says, "All I can see, sir, is a man in white tie and tails standing on an oil platform!"

NEVER THINK THERE'S ONLY ONE WAY TO DO IT

Director Rick Schmidt, who made his ninety-minute, 16 mm color feature *Emerald Cities* (1983) for $21,000, also teaches a college course called Feature Filmmaking at Used-Car Prices. Schmidt and other independents in the film field, as well as directors of small-crew documentaries, business films, and commercials, have learned to ignore the sophisticated and expensive Hollywood production techniques by using canny inspiration to achieve film effects at minimal cost. Friends and acquaintances have been pressed into service, actors have provided their own clothes for "costuming," and sympathetic lab owners like Irwin Young of DuArt in New York have been terribly supportive to new filmmakers working on less than a shoestring.

I have touched on this in my discussions with John Sayles (page 55), but you will find that most of us in the field become used to working with budgets that, as someone once wrote, "are less for a feature film than what Hollywood would spend on coffee breaks!" Shooting ratios are kept at a minimum—sometimes as little as three to one. If Hitchcock could do it, so can the young filmmaker. There are always friends who want to write music for films. The chronic lack of cash in a very expensive industry has not kept independent filmmakers and low-budget documentarians from turning out superb and professional work.

This has also been true for those of us who have worked professionally in the documentary for many years. Our crews are "short," our money generally limited. Where the average Hollywood feature now costs $11 million, we have found that our average film budget is well under $100,000—frequently much lower than that. Yet we use excellent crews, stay in the best of hotels, and sometimes turn out notable

On location at the St. Regis Mohawk Indian Reservation on the St. Lawrence River for a commercial shot for Mazola Oil. Jim Reilly, assistant cameraman; Bill Fertik, director/ cameraman; Jim Gruebel, grip; and part of the cast.

work. My own Academy Award nominee, *To Live Again,* was made for a budget of $25,000 in glorious black and white back in 1963. Today it probably would cost about three times that amount.

Professional cameramen like Jon Fauer have learned that renting a Tyler mount for helicopter shooting (including the shipping to Thonotosassa, Florida) can be a terribly expensive investment for a small crew. Some years back, Jon—a mountain climber and skier—invented his own helicopter rig, made of shock cords and caribiners, and screwed firmly into the fuselage of the craft, it can give him as steady a mount as the more sophisticated Tyler. His helicopter photography is about 85 percent usable, an incredible ratio even for ground photography shot on a tripod!

Every crew has its stories about how they managed the shot—cameras hoisted up flagpoles, moving shots from supermarket shopping carts, even the lighting of an Aztec dance one night in Mexico by the headlights of eight borrowed automobiles. In Rio one carnival year we arrived with a crew of three—no lights (they were too heavy) and determined to film every dance, every festival, every street corner samba, every ball in town. We learned that the grand balls held at night were the highlights of the carnival, but there was no way we could possibly shoot with our slow stock. We asked around and found out that a *feature crew* was filming that night at the Metropolitan Ball—and we got our permits to film inside. It was simple, and we mingled with the crowd. And each time that the feature crew turned on their powerful arc lights for their sequences, *we also shot our footage.* It worked out beautifully.

NEVER CHOOSE A FILM CREW WITHOUT CONSIDERING COMPATIBILITY

When people ask how I choose my crews, I generally answer that I weigh talent with compatibility, the ability to get along with me (for I am the boss) and with the people we are going to meet on our job. Film crews not only work together, they *live* together on location, and in some places you can't get away from one another for breakfast, lunch, or dinner.

Given a choice between talent and compatibility, I would choose the latter. Not only am *I* subjected to the whims and vagaries of the person or persons with whom I am thrown together professionally, so is everyone we meet on the job. If my cameraman can't make friends with the people we are to film, if the sound person is obnoxious and communicates this trait to the people who live in the area, our filming becomes that much more difficult.

If the crew member who drinks a little too much or goes out too late the night before doesn't show up on time for a call (remember "Never Miss a Call Unless You're Dead"?), then both the crew and the job suffer. I once worked with a cameraman who wouldn't start the day unless he had his H-O Oats for breakfast, and if we were in Minkcreek, Idaho, and he couldn't get H-O Oats, he sulked the entire day. There are crew members who are hostile to authority—police, customs officials, secret agents, or undercover people of foreign governments—and to everyone in general. How would you like to spend two weeks or two months with those people—twenty-four hours a day?

Interestingly enough, there are some crew members who are great workers and lovely people here in the United States, but who turn into monsters once they get overseas, unable to handle language change, money, tipping, or foreign cultures. Twice I have sent people home from an overseas location because their work was affecting the entire crew. (And me!)

Especially on a small crew documentary, it is remarkable to see the chemistry that takes place when the crew is compatible and the members are at ease with the people they meet. My very first trip around the world in 1961 with Bernie Hirschenson taught me a great deal about the relationships of crew to populace, for he was probably the most outstanding example of the perfect "people" cameraman. Since that time I have always chosen my crew with care, for people like Joe Longo, Jon Fauer, Cheryl Groff, Michael Barry, Don Matthews, and Peter Henning (and many more whom I have left out) make *my* job easier, and they make all of us look good.

So when you are looking at the sample footage of potential crew members or listening to the reasons why they want desperately to work with you on your film, take particular note of their personality, their values, their charisma. And ask them if they *must* have H-O Oats for breakfast!

NEVER EXPECT THE CAMERA TO GIVE YOU THE "REAL THING"

There is one thing that can be said about the film (or tape) camera. It *intrudes* on life, rather than recording it. All of us in the documentary field, and those of us who are trying to do "real life" commercials, expect to go out into the world and become invisible, recording all that goes on around us. Cinema verité proclaimed that just such a result was its purpose and its achievement. Pure baloney!

The very presence of the camera changes life. The awareness that people have just of your being there, of the expectations they are led to develop through constant exposure to television and motion picture fan club stories, are enough to make it almost impossible to film real life as it is happening (without a hidden camera in a closed van). In an interview, Dustin Hoffman commented that film crews expect to go to New York "to get the 'real life' of the city." However, he correctly observed that the minute you rope off a street or block a crowd, you change it. "Movies tend to take out life," he said, "and then put back a substitute for it."

Back in 1974 there was a series of programs that received a great amount of publicity, in that it was hailed as the "real life" account of a family, chronicling their lives and the breakup of a marriage. It was called *An American Family,* and it dealt with the Loud family out in California. In her book, *A Woman's Story,* Pat Loud stated that "a miserable marriage can wobble along for years until something comes along and pushes one of the people over the brink. . . . For

A much younger Bernie Hirschenson on his first world film trip with the author in 1961. His relationship with the people, as with this youngster in India, had much to do with his success as a documentary cameraman.

me, it was a whole production staff and camera crew."

The remarkable thing is that not only the producers but also the subjects felt that they could put an entire crew into a private situation and then record it as it might have happened had the crew never been there! My only wonder is *why* the Louds let a film crew into their home in the first place.

In a more recent example, the presence of cameras took on an even more questionable role. The rape trial in Fall River, Massachusetts, held after a young woman was assaulted in a tavern while onlookers cheered, was one in which the cameras were allowed. The biggest question was not whether they *should* have been allowed in the courtroom, but whether *their very presence* altered the proceedings and thus made them a part of the process.

On one of our documentaries, done to raise funds for a hospital, we wanted desperately to get the real life interaction of doctors, nurses, and their critically ill patients. We knew that once the cameras rolled we would alter their attitudes, their words, their emotions. Thus, we filmed for a while, then turned off the cameras and talked to the people we had filmed. We then used a wireless microphone and I walked up to them and complimented them on the job they had done. Relieved that the filming was over—for most people are nervous with cameras around—they spurted out their feelings, what they "really wanted to say," and without their knowledge, the cameras rolled, the sound turned, and we got just what we had wanted to get. *Then we told them we had filmed it,* ex-

Cheryl Groff, associate producer and sound person, on location in Haryana, India, for Dadi's Family, *as the heroine, Dadi, listens to a sound take played back to her. The film was later broadcast over PBS.*

plained the reasons, and got them to sign the release. Unfortunately, this cannot always be the case.

My comments here have much to do with the previous discussion on compatibility and the ability to get along with people on location. If you are filming a documentary, keep in mind the effect the camera has on the entire process, no matter what you would *like* it to be. You and your film crew and your cameras are intrusive, and thus the results you will achieve are far from the "real life" you originally set out to capture on film.

NEVER SHOOT WITHOUT INSURANCE

First of all, there are some places that will not even admit a film crew unless they can prove they have insurance that covers everyone and everything. Certainly you can shoot without coverage, but it would be foolhardy even to try. Without going too deeply into the subject, for any good entertainment insurance agent can give you the facts and the figures, there are two insurance policies you should have for your project:

★ *Negative Insurance,* which covers all mishaps that might occur during and after filming, thus providing you with funds to reshoot if necessary. This would include a lost or damaged original, lab foul-ups, or other "horrors."
★ *General Liability Insurance,* generally for a minimum of $300,000—to cover damage to property, injury to your crew or cast or the

people who live there, coverage of vehicles used for crew or equipment, and other risks inherent in society once you leave for location shooting.

As I've mentioned, you can do without it. But in any location—including a factory, shopping mall, street corner, or other private enclave—you will be asked for the policy.

A few years back I also learned that most domestic policies don't cover foreign shooting, and I nearly learned it the hard way. We were in France, ready to film the Tour de France, the most grueling bicycle race across the country, ending in Paris after about thirty days. Since coverage of the race by a crew of three, without network clout and money, would be most difficult, we decided to ask the government for a helicopter! It wasn't easy. Using contacts with the police, the tourist bureau, and executives from our client's company, a major soft drink manufacturer, we finally got through all the red tape (or whatever it's called in French) and were ushered into a meeting with a captain from the French air force.

We told him what it was that we wanted, and our friend in the Paris police smiled with us and jovially made friends with the captain—and finally, with a handshake, the agreement was made. We would be given an army helicopter to take us down to where the tour was currently making its way up the roads toward Paris. However . . . however, there was one little matter. The insurance. Did our film crew have insurance? Certainly, I said, and I whipped out the paper.

As I turned it over to the captain, I noticed something printed in large letters along the bottom of the policy certificate, and it was the first time that I had seen it: *Not valid outside the United States.* But, being a filmmaker, and having the luck that all filmmakers have in such situations, it dawned on me that *the captain could not read English!* However, he looked at the document, and my heart went into my mouth; then he smiled and gave it back. With another flourish, he stamped the permit, and we were off.

Not very smart of us, perhaps, but I mentioned that I am a filmmaker, and possibly that is one of the prerequisites!

NEVER TRUST AIRLINE PERSONNEL, TRAVEL AGENTS, SKYCAPS, PEOPLE WHO GIVE YOU DIRECTIONS

NEVER LET FILM STOCK GO THROUGH AIRPORT X-RAY MACHINES

NEVER LET SOUND STOCK GO THROUGH METAL DETECTORS AT AIRPORTS

NEVER SEND YOUR FILM EQUIPMENT VIA AIR CARGO

NEVER ARRIVE AT AN AIRPORT TOO CLOSE TO THE TIME YOUR PLANE IS LEAVING

On each of the above, I might offer you a lecture.

And for each one there is a "what if," of course. What if the airport insists that you send the film stock through a metal detector? You will have to work it out like all smart film people, for in spite of what they tell you, X-ray machines can damage film (especially high-speed film), and all X-ray exposure is additive, so stock that takes a trip through ten airports will most certainly be ruined. Pack it and send it through as luggage (with identification all over it), and in a foreign country that is hyper about terrorists, smugglers, and hijackers, wrap it in lead foil first.

The reason we never ship film equipment and stock via cargo is that your valuable materials are just not handled properly, there is no guarantee that they will get on the same plane, and most cargo goes through a severe customs process that might keep your equipment in bond for a long, long time.

I know one film crew that listened to me and then sent their equipment to Brazil via cargo while they traveled down to South America on a scheduled aircraft. The equipment arrived almost the same time they did, but Brazilian customs officials, notorious for impounding equipment for no reason at all, held the entire fourteen cases in bond for ten days while the production manager tried desperately to get it out for the location shoot. All equipment and film stock, no matter what anyone says, should be sent as personal baggage and the excess charges paid. It's more expensive, and it's safer. I might add one more note: If your cargo material arrives late Friday night, there's a good chance you won't be able to get it out of customs until Monday morning.

For overseas trips, a marvelous document has been developed that is a boon to all filmmakers. Because film equipment brings a premium price if you resell it overseas, many countries are rightfully concerned about the possible resale of that equipment once you get it inside their borders. For years we used customs brokerage firms who were familiar with the problems of import and export of such things as our film equipment and the film stock that was exposed within the country itself.

Then the Carnet was developed, a simple method of importing and exporting film equipment through the use of a special customs document for temporary imports. For the countries that participate, the Carnet is the same as an open door if the papers are filled out properly. A Carnet holder can generally use the document for one year, can visit as many countries in the system as he or she wishes, and only has to certify that the equipment will be returned to the United States when the job is finished.

There is, of course, a fee and an insurance premium, but compared to what we used to pay for brokerage fees, including the amounts they, in turn, paid in foreign countries as bribes (labeled Miscellaneous), the costs are minimal.

I mention the Carnet specifically because I find that most young filmmakers about to embark on their first foreign trip have never heard of the document. At present it is accepted in almost forty countries from Australia to Yugoslavia—including all the Common Market countries.

For a complete list of countries and a booklet detailing the application and the procedures, write to:

United States Council of the International Chamber of Commerce
1212 Avenue of the Americas
New York, N.Y. 10036

When we look at the list of "nevers," it all comes down to the fact that all of us in the film business are a terribly suspicious bunch of paranoid personalities. This is quite true. We make our living in an industry that has its own particular type of problems, its own special variety of solutions. Somehow I have always tried to teach my own production people that there is only one "never" that is more important than all the "nevers" that I have listed in the pages before this. In one sense it is a "never" that is emblazoned above my office door in flames and indelibly etched in my obsessive filmmaker mind.

NEVER TRUST ANYONE!

And, as I have stated, I am not alone. Speak to anyone who has spent some years in this business. The road to filmmaking success in your own career is filled with the potholes of serendipity and chance. Each production you begin will bring new problems and, interestingly enough, *you* will find a way to solve them.

Production manager Larry Dubin, a veteran of the field for over almost two decades, reflected my feelings only too well when he published a delightful list *(Backstage,* September 30, 1983) of some of the things he thinks about in this field of continuing horrors. I reprint it with his permission:

"MOMENTS THAT STOP A PRODUCTION MANAGER'S HEART

Taped to my wall is a list of important telephone numbers: key agencies, major suppliers, a few crew members . . . and a leading cardiologist! As a production manager for over fifteen years, I've experienced more than my share of palpitations. Here is my list of moments that stop a production manager's heart:

★ when the lab calls me at home while I'm getting dressed for work
★ when my producer calls from location to ask if I can answer a question about our insurance
★ when the union business agent calls on a shoot day
★ when the production assistant asks if our company uses its own accident report form
★ when the messenger service asks if the can we gave the guy on the bike contained print or original negative
★ when the agency producer calls in the middle of the shoot day and asks me to get out a copy of the budget
★ when the assistant director calls from the stage to ask if I can suggest a good dinner caterer
★ when the receptionist I fired two years ago calls to tell me she's now the business manager at a major agency
★ when the driver of the equipment truck

calls collect on the morning of the shoot to clarify his directions to the location
★ when the set designer calls to ask if the job is cost-plus
★ when I spot the assistant cameraman frantically thumbing through the cinematography manual"

And yes, there is but one other thing that I have promised to cover in this chapter, and you have no doubt thought about it, wondering if I would ever give the answer.

NEVER TAKE A FILM CREW OF EIGHT INTO A RESTAURANT AT NOON AND EXPECT TO GET THEM ALL FED IN ONE HOUR, UNLESS . . .

Everyone in America eats at twelve noon. Exactly. Promptly. By "America" I am not speaking of those sophisticated urban cities like New York, San Francisco, or Chicago, where business lunches can extend to three o'clock in the afternoon. Rather, I am speaking of small community America, where the selection of eating places is limited and everyone in town descends as the clock strikes twelve—and disappears just as quickly at one o'clock sharp. No matter what the size of your crew, by the time you add clients, guides, hangers-on, and any others who happen to be around at lunch hour, you will generally end up with eight people. This is not a film rule. It just works that way.

Well, when you get to the restaurant, you find that they have, indeed, been waiting for you; they put you at a table for eight, and while

everyone else is eating rapidly and the noise level ascends, your crew just sits there—waiting. It is next to impossible for a kitchen, it seems, to feed eight all at once.

Feature crews have managed to counteract this slowdown (can you imagine trying to feed 175 crew members?) by catering through the use of professional commissary companies. Many times we order in advance and have it sent to the location so that everyone can sit somewhere and relax for an hour. There are locations where picnic tables are available, and the crew can eat at a lakeside spot.

Too often, however, everyone wants to get away from the location. Lunch is a chance to tell "war stories," to see some of the people of the town, to take the break so necessary to hard work. And many times the client or local contact is genuinely proud of the little restaurant and wants to show it off, as well as to introduce his film crew to the people he knows so well.

So the eight of you arrive just as the rest of the community is walking in. And after all this, the trick is simply to *split up*. Four of you go to one part of the restaurant and four go to the other, where an entirely different waiter or waitress will serve you. A restaurant that cannot serve eight people efficiently can always serve *two tables of four* in half the time!

There now. If you realize that I have been waiting thirty-five years to give that piece of advice, you know full well why I am smiling. I have sent you on your way into the field and upward through your career with an ability to get through lunch and back to work promptly. Which—after all—is what it is all about!

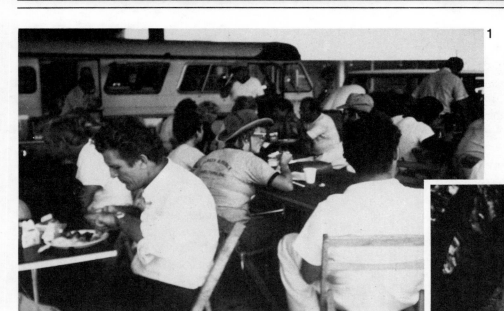

Among the ways to avoid American restaurants that are crowded at noon and still feed a film crew in one hour: (1) a catering company to feed a feature crew; (2) a picnic lunch if the weather is good; and (3) get invited to the Hawaiian picnic appearing in your documentary.

A "HORROR" POSTSCRIPT

It is Sunday.

I have completed the tales of horror and there is a certain satisfaction in knowing that all these things are past. They are all happening now to someone else.

On Tuesday I am to mix the tracks of the new science careers film I have been producing for Duke Power Company over this past year. It is a good film, I think. The clients loved the interlock. I have worked long and hard with Suzanne Jasper as she has edited a brilliantly intelligent story for young people, and she is coming to New York from Bat Cave, North Carolina, tomorrow to be with me at the mix.

The phone rings.

It is Suzanne. Depressed. My stomach knots. After all, it is Sunday. It should be a social call.

The splicing tape that she used on the work print of the picture must have been defective. *Every single splice on the eighteen-minute film has stretched.* And on either side of *every* splice, ten to twenty sprocket holes have been torn as a result of the stretching!

Therefore, not only must she replace *every* splice—front and back—on the work print, she must also repair every sprocket hole that was ripped in the process! It will take at least thirty-six hours, but she will probably "make the mix."

She does.

It goes well.

Tomorrow will bring another horror.

And we will no doubt solve that one, too.

Film crews can have a difficult time if the political climate is not quite right and the "natives" are not too friendly. This sign greeted the author in Australia during the Vietnam War.

The Ethics and the Arrogance of Film

This may be an uncomfortable section of the book for you, for I would like to discuss some subjects that are not often analyzed by film-makers, though there are occasions when the press does take us to task. Let me pose a problem for you.

You have been selected to direct a feature film. Excitedly you read the screenplay that has been delivered to you by special messenger (in a Cadillac limousine). The film has everything to make you famous—action, emotion, character depth, a superb storyline, even a tentative acceptance by two Hollywood stars who will guarantee box office success.

As you reach page 120, you notice with some discomfort that the script calls for you to kill an animal on screen. At first you pass it off as a special effect, but in the margin the producer has noted that this will be "dynamite" because you will actually kill the animal. No special effects for *this* film. The animal might be:

★ a dog
★ a cat
★ a deer (make it a fawn!)

It is not important that you answer the query right this instant. After all, we *know* that as a filmmaker you would never kill a *human*

being on screen. The television crew that let a man burn to death in front of them while they taped the segment for the evening news were just an aberration, weren't they? So let's get back to the animals and go just a bit further.

If you have rejected killing the dog, the cat, the fawn, then let me ask you what you would do if the screenplay called for you to kill something ugly, but alive:

★ a rat
★ a snake
★ an alligator

What I have asked is not as farfetched as it might sound, for time and time again students have asked me what can be done if the subject for a film goes against their deepest emotional and ethical feelings. I can only answer by posing the same question right back at them, for I am not a missionary, nor am I the last of the ethical filmmakers. Professionals who have discussed this with me take completely opposite views, ranging from "I would turn it down cold" to "What can you do when you've got kids to send through college?"

Since very few animals are killed directly on screen (we hope), let me pose the question to those of my readers who will be working in the field of the documentary, the business film, the television report, and the commercial. There are areas of your life about which you feel strongly. Yet you will be either free-lancing or producing films on your own for a number of producers and on a wide range of subjects.

You are approached to meet someone for

breakfast, as I have been, someone you've known for a long time and for whom you've produced several films. This time he asks you to produce *another* film, but the subject is one that makes you stand on a platform and proclaim loudly to the world that you will not budge in your feelings. Possibly the subject is:

★ Abortion. Pro-choice versus right-to-life.
★ The nuclear issue. Not only nuclear proliferation and the freeze, but nuclear power and peacetime uses of the atom.
★ Politics. The candidate for whom you've been asked to do a film is anathema to you. You cannot hear his or her name without turning beet red and sputtering.
★ The environment. Either side about acid rain or the rape of the land or pollution. Suppose you were asked, for example, to make an excuse for Love Canal.
★ Travel. Yes, even travel. There are countries about which you have strong negative feelings. Interestingly, some of them still produce travel documentaries about the lush land, the white sandy beaches, the happy natives, and the warm greeting for the tourist (along with the strong dollar). You can name your own countries—possibly you don't feel that way about any of them—but maybe you do have your "bad guys" and your "good guys" and your "neutrals."
★ War and peace. During the Vietnam era, this was a classic problem for filmmakers who felt strongly about the war (one way or the other) and were asked by the gov-

ernment to do a propaganda documentary, or by the networks to give a "balanced" view.

You must understand that for the most part your film life will never put these ethical roadblocks in front of you. The average feature, documentary, business film, or commercial is harmless in the long run. My own career spans thirty-five years, and I can only think of a few instances where I have had to choose—once about abortion, once about a political candidate, and twice for companies that followed what I considered unethical practices in the Third World. How did I answer the question? I told you that I was not a missionary and it should not be important to you whether or not *I* did them. The question I am asking you is, would *you* produce them? The fine line is yours to determine.

Remember that this industry is quite incestuous, and jobs—for the most part—are hard to get. It might be easy for you to make your decision quickly when you read the questions on paper. But in the "real" world it is going to become more difficult:

★ You have not worked in four months. A job comes up that seems unethical to you. It pays well. What is your price?
★ You have worked rather continuously for the same producer. This time he or she asks you to do a film that is on the "wrong" side of an important question. You stand to lose the entire relationship if you refuse. Or will you lose it if you stand up and explain your feelings?

"He's one of those hyphenates . . . a writer-producer-actor-asshole. . . ."

I ran into a young assistant cameraman the other day. He had just returned from the West Coast and he seemed rather glum and dispirited. We talked a while and he told me that he was terribly unhappy about the job. It was on the "wrong" side of the nuclear question, so far as he was concerned. I asked him why he took the job for one day's work. (Suppose it had been two months' work?)

I stated before that I cannot take issue with my friend who has to send kids through college, nor can I criticize my young associate for being on the wrong side of an issue for one day, but I always recall with some discomfort the question that was posed to me by that long-term client who flew to New York to meet me. When he had finished his proposal for the film (on the "wrong" side of abortion for me), I turned him down; he looked quizzically across the table at me and said, "I just don't understand why you can't separate your filmmaking from your ethics!"

For those of us who still think of filmmaking in terms of our dedication and our love of the visual, there is a twin to this discussion about ethics, and it is again a subject that filmmakers do not like to be reminded of. Either it is passed off or excuses are made, but years in the field have shown me another side of filmmaking that is not very admirable: arrogance.

Certainly the film field is not the only one that breeds arrogance. Tennis has its share of "brats," and John McEnroe is certainly someone I would not look forward to having on my crew on a trek through the jungles of Ecuador! Opera has temperament, big business often has an arrogance unmatched even in film, my short

time in the garment industry when I was in college still brings memories of rudeness and insolence that make me glad I moved into another field.

But we are a high-profile profession. We are seen on the streets, and we enter people's lives for a few hours or a few days and then we are gone again, much like an unfaithful lover who disappears after each intense affair. And the excuse, the battle cry all over this world, is always, "But . . . *we're* a film crew. . . ."

To the people who refuse to let us shoot because of very personal reasons, the hotel or restaurant that loused up our reservations, the public made uncomfortable by the blocking of traffic or the closing of a street, the disregard for rules or the flouting of a country's traditions, the insensitivity to indigenous cultures, the disregard of common courtesies, the answer always is "But . . . *we're* a film crew. . . ."

The feature film *Ragtime* shot one sequence just a few blocks from my apartment in New York. It was a remarkable transformation of a Lower East Side street from present to the turn of the century, and it probably cost a small fortune to achieve. I wandered over one day to watch, wondering as I always do at how a feature ever manages to get made. As someone once wrote to the *New York Times,* "I don't know how many times I've come across a crowd gathered to watch . . . trucks, cameras, dollies, wires, lights . . . but no action. All I ever see is people in work clothes drinking coffee and eating doughnuts. No actors. No actresses. Where are the stars? How do movies ever get made?"

Well, about three in the afternoon they

finally were ready for the shot. Extras in costume. Arc lights filling in the dark shadows. The street really looked great. Suddenly an assistant director spotted a man leaning over his fire escape and watching. He was wearing an undershirt, and he was also standing right in the middle of the master shot. The assistant looked up and shouted, "Hey, you! You! Would you go back inside? We're making a movie!"

The man looked coldly at the young assistant, called down a rather impossible copulative instruction, and said, "I live here!" And he stayed right where he was. The master shot was changed.

John Sayles and I were discussing the problems of arrogance in film. A week or so before, he had been walking through Grand Central Station in New York, where a feature film was being shot. People are curious about film—just watch them stop when a feature crew is on the streets, then drift slowly away when nothing seems to be happening. A man started up the staircase just as the crew was about to shoot. Curious, he stopped for a moment, and the assistant director, now the new owner of Grand Central Terminal, shouted up at him, "Make up your mind! Up or down the stairs!" John comments:

"I tell my crews, 'We're guests here.' At the opening of each film, I get the crew and cast together and we have a long talk. No one orders anyone around. Assistants ask, 'Would you mind . . .' After all, we're the invaders. If you *ask,* people will let you do incredible things. *They'll give you their children!*"

Why am I so incensed with other people's arrogance in our field? There is a simple reason. If it were done in the privacy of a home or in a studio, I frankly couldn't care less. But every time a film crew shows the kind of arrogance that I am writing about, it affects *me*—and it will affect *you* in your film career. Each time a film crew goes to a location or a country and in any way flouts the common courtesies or the customs of the area, chances are that *you* will be met with suspicion or hostility when you arrive to shoot your film.

You might be the most kindly, gentle, caring, courteous (and all the other Boy Scout/Girl Scout attributes) people in the entire film world. But *you* will be vulnerable when a previous film crew has littered the location or the area with bad feelings.

★ There is a well-known hotel in San Francisco that will no longer accept feature film crews (though documentary people are still welcome—so far). I was at the hotel when they finally threw out over a hundred people and told them never to return!

★ The Ritz Hotel in Madrid, one of the finest in the world, will not accept film crews after a disastrous experience with a Hollywood crew and its spoiled stars.

★ A German crew, working at the Acropolis in Greece under a false permit, turned out to be producing a pornographic film—at a national shrine! It only served to block access to every legitimate film crew that was to follow, no matter how innocent.

★ I followed another film crew by about two weeks into Pakistan back in the sixties. Unfortunately for us, the crew had tried to smuggle gold into the country by sealing the metal in Eastman Kodak film cans! You can well imagine *our* customs problems when we arrived, the very next crew, there to do a travel film. We spent eight hours in customs and only prevented them from opening the sealed cans by calling our best client in Karachi and having him come down to speak to the authorities!

The arrogance shown in any country, the impertinence shown because "We're a film crew," directly affects *my* relationships, even my ability to get permission to shoot in an area called for in my treatment. If a film crew enters a country under false pretenses in order to make a political statement harmful to that country, then *my* film crew—arriving to do a harmless travel film—will suffer.

Some years back we were asked to do a travel film in Thailand, one version to be distributed by Paramount as a short subject, another version to be distributed nontheatrically by Eastman Kodak. I had the "brilliant" idea that I might film a sequence of Thai monks in the early morning light of Bangkok as they left the temple to beg, as their religion demanded.

Thailand is a filmmaker's dream in terms of photographic potential, though it is difficult to work in because of heat and an occasional government crackdown on film crews and their equipment. I could see in my mind the misty fog of morning, the sun just coming through the trees, and the monks—begging bowls in hand—walking down the avenues and slowly paddling their boats up the klongs. It would be gorgeous. The only thing left was to get permission.

We flew to Bangkok from Hong Kong in the middle of the monsoon season and went to our appointment with the abbot of Wat Po, a temple at which I had filmed before. However, the greeting was cool and reserved, and for almost eight hours we were questioned about our crew, our origins, our treatment of the subject, the final distribution, and everything up to and including our heritage and where our grandparents had come from. Considering that most of the session was conducted while we sat on the floor cross-legged, you can understand our discomfort and our painful joints!

Finally the abbot smiled and permission was granted. As we got up to leave, bowing and grateful for the acceptance of our project, the abbot gently apologized for the time he had taken and told us the reason he had queried us for so many hours. It seems that just the previous week a film crew had also gotten permission to shoot at the temple under the guise of filming a travel film. The sequence, however, was actually a *comedy pie-throwing* romp through the temple grounds, to be included in a feature film for Europe later on!

I am not exaggerating, nor am I making more of an issue of the subject than it really is. Most filmmakers who return from location have their reasons and their excuses, and most filmmakers might well resent my even writing about the subject in a film book about careers. But it surfaces again and again, frequently with the most experienced crews in our business.

Back in April of 1980, I read a story in *American Film* magazine that once again reminded me that all of us who make films are vulnerable to the insensitivity and arrogance of others in our field. Given the budget, the publicity, the network hype, and the vast audience just waiting for a story of Japan, the twelve-hour miniseries *Shogun,* with a budget of almost $20 million, did indeed achieve the expected ratings. And in terms of production problems, the size of the project, 560 pages of script, over a thousand scenes, more than 2,700 camera setups, and a running time of 656 minutes, it was indeed a giant undertaking, and I'm not sure that any filmmaker alive could have come through the experience unscathed and without a vast array of "war stories" (no pun intended).

However, what struck me strongly was the fact that this seemed to be the classic case of an American film crew expecting a foreign culture to bend to *its* needs and *its* way of working, even though the Americans were the "invaders." I cannot minimize the frustrations of the production crew, for I have spent many years working in Asia and there is no doubt in my mind that "never the twain shall meet." But as I read the article, my mouth dropped open at the descriptions given by the American crew—most of them critical of the Japanese:

★ The producer felt that the Japanese were the most inflexible people with whom he had ever dealt in his life. They have their own way of doing things, he said, and they just won't bend.
★ He added that what we call negotiation and compromise in the United States might be called "blackmail" in Japan.
★ An example of the above is that the film crew sealed off a section of the harbor where Japanese fishermen had to pass in order to do their day's work. The producers could not understand why the fishermen were annoyed and asked for compensation.
★ The crew complained about the food, prepared with the Japanese crew in mind. I am reminded of a famous Hollywood actress who had hotdogs sent to her location in Africa.
★ Language, to say the least, was a problem. The American crew expected everyone to understand instructions in English and were rather put out when they learned that the Japanese spoke Japanese.
★ The cameraman, in spite of Japanese custom, refused to take off his shoes when he worked on the tatami mats in the temple set.

The story was so discouraging to me that I promptly wrote a letter to the magazine, which printed it in a subsequent issue. Then I forgot about it, knowing that I had vented my spleen and realizing that it would do very little good in the future anyway. And one day, sitting in my office, the telephone rang. The call was from Los Angeles and it was a conference call, set up by three members of the crew of *Shogun*. A knot appeared in my stomach, and I felt that they would really take off and let me have it for my insolence (and my own arrogance in writing that letter).

"I have to tell you," one of them began, "that we can't give you our names, but we are three members of the crew that shot the series. We loved your letter. But the story doesn't even *begin* to explain what really happened in Japan. *It was much worse than that!"*

This past year I returned to Japan for the new track of the Sunkist film, and I was discussing the incident with some Japanese film friends. Their response, given the natural reluctance of the Japanese to overstate a case, was that the *Shogun* incident had soured the working relationships of other film crews that had followed the Hollywood group, and that things had still not cleared up almost three years later!

Finally, there is another area of arrogance in our industry—I speak now of our arrogance in the personal area, in our dealings with our own people on the crew, and the demands we make because the only thing that counts is what goes on the screen.

In recent years stunt people have been complaining that directors have demanded they take chances that are life-threatening or even moderately dangerous, and if they refuse, they risk the penalty of not working again. Thus, there have been injuries, and there have even been deaths.

I cannot make an objective judgment of what happened on the set of the movie *Twilight Zone,* but at the time of this writing three people have been ordered to stand trial for manslaughter. During the filming of the movie in 1982, Vic Morrow and two children, Myca Dinh Le, age six, and Renee Shin Chen, seven, were killed by a falling helicopter, while the actors were dodging explosions and gunfire.

As a result, John Landis, the director; Paul Stewart, special effects coordinator; and Dorcey Wingo, the helicopter pilot, were all charged with involuntary manslaughter. The stories will no doubt conflict at the trial, but I can't help wondering just how much of the reason for the accident can be attributed to the incredible drive that comes with any production to get the best possible sequence on the screen, and how much of it might have been caused by even a subconscious arrogance that *this* is a film . . . and anything, *anything* goes, in spite of our better judgment.

And have I, as a filmmaker, ever been accused of that same arrogance, that same drive to get a shot even though someone might suffer for it? Certainly (luckily) not in as serious a way as someone being injured, and I hope that I am never so caught up in the excitement of a situation that I order a member of my crew to take a chance. I am, fortunately, too much of a coward myself to allow it to happen to anyone else. But I have been accused of just such arrogance, and the story again treads the fine line. Why is one thing okay and another to be condemned?

We were filming in the Philippines, doing a fund-raising film for Foster Parents Plan of Canada. The "star" of the story was a five-year-old youngster with the most marvelous face and sad demeanor. She was perfect to make everyone dig into their pockets for a contribution and become foster parents for a small monthly fee.

Interestingly enough, we *hated* one an-

The author has been most successful as a fund-raiser for social agencies, since children automatically cry when he approaches with his film crew. This howler is in Manila.

other. She called me "the big American" and I called her "the brat." Nevertheless we worked together over a period of several weeks, and the film progressed nicely, in spite of our location at the most horrendous slum in Asia, Tondo, some negotiations with the local underworld, and mud, rain, and huge crowds of onlookers. Actually I rather enjoyed it.

The final sequence was to be a long shot of a path that leads to the Manila headquarters of PLAN, a large, gabled white building that was rather impressively set at the end of that path. The iron gate, closed, held back a hundred people including the child. The gate was to open and all were to make their way to the house. Over that shot we would superimpose the titles. Okay? Fine.

Well, when we set the child and the group outside the gate, she began to cry for her mother, bitter, gasping, choking tears. The crew went to comfort her and I called them back. "Leave her alone," I ordered. With the kindly impulses blocked, I asked the cameraman to shoot, told them to open the gate, and instructed that he follow the child, no matter what.

By now my wife was edging closer to me, uncomfortable because the little girl was sobbing and screaming almost uncontrollably and still I would not budge. The gates opened, we held the crowd back, and the child went bounding down the path—alone—her arms flung up in the air, the screams coming from her throat. "Mama! Mama! Mama!"

When the shot was finished, I let her mother go to her—and the child never forgave "the big American," and neither did my wife, the

Tom Buckholtz with one of his "stars." The best filmmakers are people who can work closely with their crews and with the people they meet on the job.

cameraman, the assistant, all the people who watched, and possibly God.

But the end sequence in that film is one of the most powerful we've ever shot—and more important, the film, *I Heard a Child Cry Out,* and the fund-raising spots that were produced from it, have been more successful than any other film produced for these clients!

So . . . was I any less arrogant than the people whose stories I have recounted? If we are to draw a line across which no filmmaker is to venture, where do we draw it?

MAKING IT THROUGH THE INTERVIEW

The "Auteur" Looks For a Job

I suppose that, over all, I have a very positive and encouraging view about working in the film business. On the other hand, I am also a pragmatist, and I know both the odds and the serendipitous paths that can make a career climb both difficult and terribly dependent upon chance and timing in addition to hard work. I am aware of the arrogance that infects our business, and I know that the same arrogance and disdain for the beginning filmmaker can sometimes make the job hunt an ego-damaging ordeal.

But the most interesting thing to me over these years has been the fact that *most* of the people who keep at it with determination *do* manage to make it somehow. I am not a Polly-anna, and this you also know from my comments and cynicism about an industry that has treated me rather well. But remember, my early days were a struggle that included teaching to make a living while directing on early live television for the "glamour" of the business and the cheers of my parents, relatives, and friends.

Those who spend the time at it, those who make it a point to learn and to follow every bit of advice and every lead given in the job hunt, somehow manage not only to survive but to eventually flourish in an industry that is like no other, certainly quite unlike the world of lawyers, accountants, doctors, business executives, teachers, or stockbrokers.

Because I still lecture and conduct film seminars, and since my name is generally published in the production manuals, and certainly because of the first film career guide that I wrote, I manage to receive about one hundred letters or more a year. This is in addition to the normal torrent of unsolicited resumes that come through the U.S. mail. I've been looking at them and I find the file fascinating, for buried within those letters from editors, production assistants, film students, directors, cinematographers, and writers are some wonderful tips that might well help *you* in your search. I have printed certain of these paragraphs here, and as you go through this chapter, read them carefully, for they comment on a great many things:

★ They show that there are others in exactly the same boat, looking, worrying, probing, searching.

★ They show that somehow, someplace, sometime, a little bit of luck or an overheard conversation can make a break for them.

★ They reflect a sudden realization that they are actually *in the field,* working, active, even making a small living out of it.

★ They also show something that I have been shouting about for many years: There are no rules in this business.

★ They tell me—and the reader, perhaps—that if you really love film, you somehow never lose hope.

★ Most of all, they offer good, solid advice to the job hunter. Remember, this is *your* peer group talking.

As many of you know, I have always had an "open door" policy toward young filmmakers, for what you are offering, what you can bring to all of us in new ideas, is terribly important in the furthering of my own career and the look of my own films. In the course of a year, I interview a great many people who have asked for my time and whatever counsel I can give, and there are many times after the interview that I close the door, smiling to myself, wishing them luck, and knowing that if *I* could but have a hundred openings a year, I could easily find the hundred to fill those jobs.

But being a pragmatist, as I've said, I also meet too many who have not taken the time to understand the industry, to do their homework, to understand the role of the *interviewer* and what he or she might be looking for, to write a letter of thanks for the time given, or to be sensitive to the special nuances and requirements in that part of the film field. But then, I suppose that's what experience is all about.

To begin with, any filmmaker must understand that the job hunt in our field is quite different from any other profession, something that may already have occurred to you. A few months after my first film book was published, I was invited to be a part of a career night seminar at Northwestern University, and I accepted the invitation with enthusiasm. In spite of the miserable, snowy Chicago weather that put the entire lakefront under a sheet of ice, the meeting hall was packed with about three hundred communications students, notebooks and pencils in hand, eager to graduate and ready to get the sage words on how to confront the job market out there in all that snow.

I could never understand, however, why the university chose as its seminar leader a recruitment executive from *IBM*! He was a charming man who had had lots of good experience and who came to the seminar with many sound ideas, but all of his advice somehow ignored the realities of *our* world, the world of communications and the young filmmaker who needs that first break to show just how good he or she is. The executive based his entire presentation on the premise that *a recruiter* would one day show up on campus and would interview the new grads, offering them jobs across the country from Hollywood to the burgeoning East Coast. I listened with disbelief, for at that time I had *never* heard of *anyone* being offered a job on a campus by a recruiter—like engineers, computer experts, Silicon Valley technicians, or lawyers! It was only much later that I heard of the

---

"Although I have a driving ambition to enter the field, I have been worried by things I've heard and read concerning the slim chances one has of finding work and the possibility of film dying. It was so encouraging to hear two people who are active in the field paint a hopeful picture. It's great to hear that there are jobs available if one is willing to work at finding them."

—THIRD-YEAR FILM STUDENT
DUBLIN, PENNSYLVANIA

first example when a young woman I met on a plane told me of the recruiter who came to Harvard looking for a financial and business wizard.

Later that evening, when we finally broke up into small seminar groups, I told my eager class that it just wasn't so. They, just like everyone else, were going to have to put on their boots and trudge through the blustery snow outside and *look* for work. It isn't easy. Yet the ratio of success is higher than some of us who are veterans in this business care to admit when we recount to the young filmmaker the appalling odds out there.

If I have described motion picture production as "one continuing horror," what words might I use to define the trials and tribulations of the job hunt in our overcrowded craft, and especially in the major markets of New York and glutted Los Angeles? For many it is not certainly the easiest way to pass the time:

★ The timing might be wrong. "You should have been here last week!" And if the prospective employer doesn't have an opening that day, he or she might well forget you in six months when he does.

★ The chemistry is wrong, or you go away thinking it's wrong. It's what makes good (or bad) personal relationships, and it's what makes good (or bad) interviews, with both of you knowing full well that you would probably like (dislike, hate, murder) one another given two weeks together on location.

★ Your background is wrong. Though you know you can do most anything in the field to help the producer turn out an Academy Award nominee, your strongest credits are in editing and they need a well-trained production manager. Or you have written twenty programs about children, all of which have won awards and have been presented on PBS, but they are looking for someone who has experience with geriatrics! You can substitute any two subjects for the sentences above!

First of all, stop worrying. I have been selling my films to potential clients and foundations for over thirty-five years, and thus, I have been selling myself, just as you are:

★ I have, on first meeting, called a top vice-president of a corporation by the wrong name through an entire interview! We still got the job (though he firmly corrected me about the tenth time).

★ I—the experienced filmmaker from New York—flew to Washington, D.C., for a presentation to a committee of sixteen (!) to show that we were the right people for their job. After a long sales pitch, I turned to put the film on the projector—*and I couldn't get the case open!* It was around the time the new plastic, automatic lock cases had come into being, and one of the committee members laughed and snapped it

---

"Most of the time I never get by the secretary and leave with the uneasy feeling that my resume will be used to warm up the building. . . ."

—PRODUCTION ASSISTANT/EDITOR
BROOKLYN, NEW YORK

"Good news! I've been awarded a NEH grant to produce/direct a twenty-eight-minute film about women in rural Appalachia."

—PRODUCER/DIRECTOR
NEW YORK, NEW YORK

---

open for me. I made some sort of lame joke. After all, I have an Academy Award nomination and I couldn't open a film case. We got the job.

★ Several times I have been confronted with a newfangled, automatic projector, Satan's gift to the film industry, and I have been unable to thread the damned thing!

There are times when you think you did poorly (and you did), and there are other times when whatever you managed to do wrong will make absolutely no difference to those of us who are doing the interviewing—and are also wondering how *we* are coming across to *you*. The most important thing to remember is that you only need *one job*, only *one successful interview*, in order to continue your career climb.

Thus, as I have suggested, read the boxes in this chapter and read them carefully, for buried within each one are the "rules" of the game that has no "rules." Determination, luck, hard work, contacts, courage, and above all, *attitude*. And, added to these, let me just run over some other tips that I have given young filmmakers who have discussed the job hunt with me.

TENACITY. The first complaint we generally hear is, "I can't even get through to him [her]!" No one ever said that film people are nice. Most film people, in fact, are not nice, for whatever reasons they give for being that way. Some of us are nice. But Grandmother never told you that everyone has to be nice! You have to keep after some people. You have to drop others from your

list as unreachable. You have to take advantage of every lead, every contact, moving from one person to the next the moment you hear the name of someone who might help. But you also have to keep from being a good swift pain, balancing the fine line between follow-up and harassment.

ROUTINE. You might as well make up your mind. You will have to devote as much time to the job hunt as you did to your extracurricular activities in school. Keep a "tickler" file. Follow up your notes and your calls, even though each time you pick up the telephone, your heart sinks a little bit more.

MAKING THE CONTACT. If you can reach the person whose name is on your list [especially], if that person has been recommended as a

potential interviewer or employer by someone else, the best approach is to ask him or her for advice. That person may not have a job but may be able to suggest someone else you might call. You only need one "hit."

PREPARATION. It helps to know just what it is the company or the production unit or the producer actually does in the film field. A telephone call to the office or a glance at a production manual will give you the information quickly. I can't tell you how many times I've had job seekers come up to my office and then ask me, "What is it you do here?" A letter followed by a telephone call is generally my best advice, though I do know many people who have gotten their next job by just "dropping in." Frankly, I resent an unannounced call.

"You brought me luck. The day after I met with you, I got a call from a friend working in film, asking if I'd be interested in pursuing a research position working in Europe for a California-based film house."

PRODUCTION ASSISTANT
NEW HAVEN, CONNECTICUT

"This has been and still is a very trying and oftentimes discouraging period for me. The unpredictable nature of the film business, which is both blessing and curse, is proving to be more of the latter at the moment. However, I'm determined to be a part of this business. . . ."

—ASSOCIATE PRODUCER
HONOLULU, HAWAII

THE RESUME. My advice here is probably going to stun a great many people, particularly those who have spent inordinate amounts of money to print their latest list of credits. When I submit a proposal for a film project, I write *each one* individually. There is no standard, printed background either about me or about my company. If the job is for a fund-raising film, I emphasize my background and experience with Foster Parents Plan, Greater New York Fund, St. Barnabas Hospital, and Pan American Health Organization. If the film is about energy, I list first my credits with Duke Power, Southern Company, and Combustion Engineering. If it is about corporate image, I do the same, putting the weight where it will be of most value.

Remember, I am *not* speaking of your *first* resume, when the credits are thin and schooling takes the largest space on the paper. I am speaking of the climb, of the changing background, of the acquiring of experience and the best way to show that experience.

I feel the same way about your job category. If you are a producer/editor, and you are being interviewed for an editorial job, my best advice would be to redo the entire resume, eliminating the producer credits and listing only those for which you were the editor. There are two reasons:

★ It makes your editorial skills appear stronger.
★ There is an innate suspicious jealousy in our field. Producers don't want other producers working for them in other categories. As paranoid as it seems, most pro-

ducers feel that another producer will steal their clients right out from under them!

Your first reaction is that all this takes a lot of work and an inordinate amount of time. Yes, it does. But no one ever promised you that life would be easy! Of course it takes time, but it is a *job* you're looking for, isn't it?

MORE ABOUT YOUR CREDITS. How you list your credits is important, and there is an awful lot of "creative writing" that takes place in the resume and in the personal interview. There is also a thin line about what is a lie and what is merely boasting or a slight inflation. Most of us who read resumes and letters ignore the titles. We *know* you have inflated them. The other day I noticed an item in a trade paper. Someone who had worked for me many years ago as a production manager (and a good one) now listed himself as *producer-in-charge* of the unit at the time he held the job so many years back. I called and chided him—but I did understand.

On the other hand, I have seen a blatant misuse of credits in our field. In my free-lance days, I once walked into an interview to find that the person who had preceded me was using *one of my credits* even though he had never written the show. Remember, this is an incestuous business. One stumble through the misuse or falsification of an important credit, and your reputation might well suffer. Nevertheless, I must admit that this is a recurring flaw in our industry, especially as the experience gets further and further away from the present and there is less chance of checking. But I think it's appalling!

YOUR EXPERIENCE. Frankly, most of us in the interviewing chair are not really interested in the work you did on the philosophy of film. Larry Dubin (page 145) commented to me that perhaps the film schools were wising up, for he is now beginning to see more *driver's licenses* from prospective employees than copies of their theses on the subject of Potemkin!

The fact that you can't drive will often lose a job for you more quickly than any other reason. Thus, when I mention that you should somehow convey your other interests and skills in addition to your film experience, I am merely reconfirming that some jobs I have offered have been based upon fluency with a foreign language, familiarity with a particular country, pursuits such as mountain climbing, camping ability, or even cooking know-how.

Some years back we were putting a crew together for a trek by motor coach through the most desolate part of western Mexico. Thus, not only did we interview prospective film people for their craft and their in fluency Spanish, we also talked about their cooking skills and their ability to drive a large, cumbersome recreational vehicle. We were just not going to begin the trip without making certain that *everyone* could take a turn in the kitchen and could take a shift at driving the elephantine RV across the worst kinds of roads. It is something that is somehow missed in film school!

As a postscript, I might mention that the trip turned out to be a disaster (horror)! The RV broke down in Mexico, but not before one man who had said he could drive turned out to have had no experience past wheeling a Volvo down the Los Angeles freeways! Before the breakdown, the same man put the RV into reverse by accident and smashed the private car of a gas station owner. The assistant cameraman who said he could cook *couldn't.* One night he put frozen beans, plastic bag and all, into a hot frying pan, sending everyone out into the humid, mosquito-ridden air gasping for breath.

We never did fix the RV, and finally we had to rent a house, in which six of us lived miserably until the job was finished two weeks later. How-

---

"I suppose my eventual goal is to produce and direct, and hopefully to become the first black person to win an Academy Award for directing!"

—FILM STUDENT
NEW YORK UNIVERSITY

"No matter how interesting and qualified you are, unless you know someone, 'the only openings we have for you are secretarial'! Would it be different if I were a man? Ah, well, they do not know what they are missing and I have no intention of letting them get me down. I'm afraid I'm addicted!"

PRODUCTION ASSISTANT
N. SCITUATE, MAINE

"I headed for the golden-paved streets of London. Two weeks of nerve-racking footslog seemed to be paying off. I worked on a rock video with a director who kept shouting, 'Cut!' London was the place to be. I came back to Scotland to pack, to say au revoir, when out of the blue BBC Scotland phoned me and offered me a job. . . ."

—RESEARCHER/PRODUCTION ASSISTANT
STIRLINGSHIRE, SCOTLAND

ever, I now tell the story with laughter and good cheer to film students at universities, for out of travel are born the best of "war stories."

Let us, then, return to the job hunt.

THE COVER LETTER. Sending a resume without a cover letter will probably get you the same response as sending a request for funding your film to the President of the United States. Of course, sending a cover letter will not *guarantee* a response and an offer of a job, but the reality is that most of us read cover letters, especially if they are addressed to us, and many of us even answer them. The answer, in turn, might come from someone in the organization other than the person to whom the letter was written, but it *is* a response. When you write the letter, you might keep the following in mind:

★ Keep it concise. Make it eye-catching. No more than one page.

★ Write a letter specifically for each person to whom you are applying. That means typing each and every one separately. Nothing annoys me more than receiving a letter where my name and address have obviously been put atop a letter that everyone gets.

★ Find a way to include your other interests or the contact who first suggested you write to this person. Some of the information, such as your hobbies and other skills, can go into the resume, but a specific mention of just one thing might spark the attention of the reader. For example, a bread baker (my hobby) will get more at-

"The struggle to find a paying job is not so monumental as I had assumed. However, yesterday I had a somewhat disheartening experience. I met with a woman who is a partner in a small production company. She told me I would be wise to change all the credits on my resume to 'editing.' This lack of integrity really disturbs me. To tell people that I have done work which I haven't seems sleazy."

—EDITOR, PRODUCTION ASSISTANT
HOOSICK, NEW YORK

"During my three-week free-lance stint at this small production company, I worked on revising a script for one of their motion pictures, as well as promotional materials and article ideas. At the end of the three weeks, they offered me a full-time position based largely on my writing strengths. I feel especially gratified by this offer since there was really no position available and they created one. My hours are long, my salary better than I'd hoped, and my opportunities are expanding by the second."

—WRITER/PRODUCER
NEW YORK, NEW YORK

tention from me—at least at the beginning—than an Academy Award nomination. (I now expect to get several hundred letters from bread bakers!)

★ Get the person's name! Don't send a letter to a title or to "Dear Prospective Employer." (Yes, after all these years and as many warnings, I still get them!) Letters that are addressed to some vague person are treated with the same disdain as mail addressed to "Occupant, Apartment 7D." A telephone call or a quick check with a

production guide can get you the name of the right person.

★ My grandmother always said, "Go to the head, not to the bottom." (She used more of the vernacular when she said it, though.) Write to the person who might have the final say about hiring. In some companies it might be the production manager. In others it might be the president. If you are looking for a job as an assistant, it might be the editor or the director of photography to whom you write. Think about it carefully before sending the letter and the resume and then following up with a phone call.

THE CHEMISTRY LESSON. You either like one another or you don't. You hit it off or you know you are just wrong. Seldom do you get a second chance to interview, and that might be unfortunate for both of you. That's life. And life can be unfair.

Remember, the person interviewing you has to project how you will get along with her (him) and also think ahead to how she (he) will get along with *you.* It is more of a mutual situation than most job hunters ever realize.

There is the problem of honesty. How honest should (must) you be in asking for your job specifications, in putting your own requirements and feelings to the fore? When I first interviewed my editor (now in Bat Cave), Suzanne Jasper, she told me up front about her need for child care when she worked and that she would not work in Manhattan but would consider only her own home, which at that time was in Brooklyn. It was, in turn, something that I, as the producer, had to consider. How might my clients like going to Brooklyn? (They loved it, especially the noncrowded Arabic lunches on Atlantic Avenue.) Would the child be a problem? (Would I ask the same of a man? my wife taunted.) Would it be as convenient to go to Brooklyn to check the film? (Is it more convenient to go to Bat Cave?) The important thing is that once the ground rules were set, there could never be any doubt in my mind as to just how we had to work

together. And remember, we are not talking of your *first* film job—we are speaking of the time you begin to have credits, when you have something more to offer than a gleam in your eye and a desperation just to break into the field, no matter how.

There is another aspect to this interesting phenomenon of chemistry. As with everything else, there is a fine line. Past that line, we begin to discover some real problems that border on *insensitivity.* Too often the job hunter does not consider the interviewers and just where they are coming from, their backgrounds, and their own little psychological insecurities. Let me give you a case in point.

As I've mentioned before, there is a feeling in our industry (and outside the field, too) that the feature film is the be-all and the end-all, the final achievement of any filmmaking career, and I do understand the reasons. But time and time again, young filmmakers come to see me and make the same mistake, and it bothers me. Possibly it is a good lesson for your own job hunt. A few months back, an editor, a graduate of NYU Film School and only in the field about three years, came to see me. It was, unlike other interviews, not just an exercise, since there was a short-term job opening in my company at that moment. We talked. I asked him what he wanted to be "when he grew up," and he told me that he wanted to edit features. Fine, up to that point, and here is where the line of chemistry and honesty began to blur, to be taken over by the specter of insensitivity.

"Well, until I edit features, I do documentaries and business films," he explained, "just to make money—and until I do what I really want to do!"

How should a producer who has made his career and life-style in the documentary and

---

"Since I last spoke with you, I have done a bit of free-lance camera work and was awarded a contract to produce four thirty-second TV spots on the bald eagle for Washington Fish and Game."

—CAMERAMAN/EDITOR
BELLINGHAM, WASHINGTON

"I miss the challenge of New York, dodging muggers, taxis, and the high prices. They say that variety is the spice of life. The only spice L.A. has is in the Mexican food. . . ."

—ASSOCIATE PRODUCER
LOS ANGELES, CALIFORNIA

"Free-lancing demands talent, self-discipline, the ability to perform on short notice, and a consistent performance level. It also requires some political and personal talents, an attractive personality, survival instinct, willingness to pursue work and perform in less-than-perfect situations (this includes swallowing pride, remaining calm, and knowing when to keep a low profile), and the ability to work well with people in the field, including employers, contractors, and peers. Free-lancing also demands a certain life-style—flexible and odd working hours, willingness to travel, and the ability to cope with low income and periods with little or no work."

—MUSICIAN
NEW YORK, NEW YORK

"My student film, which I produced, directed, and edited, recently won the best dramatic film award at the Academy of Motion Picture Arts and Sciences annual student film competition. It will be screened in the fall on WNET's Independent Focus *program and at the Film Forum in New York, as well as in California and on cable. The film was taken to a fine cut for $2,000, shot in nine days, and completed on a $5,000 finishing grant from the American Film Institute."*

—NYU GRADUATE FILM STUDENT
NEW YORK, NEW YORK

"This production house is quite small (two full-time people), but efficient. I'm learning all about the time and energy needed to produce a thirty- or sixty-second spot. Last week we were on location for twelve hours. Oh, the glamour of film. Is there anything that matches it?"

—PRODUCTION ASSISTANT
CAMBRIDGE, MASSACHUSETTS

business film *feel* about a statement like that? Somehow I put the interview in the same category I did the statement by Scottish director/writer Bill Forsyth (*Gregory's Girl*), who began his career after the National Film School in London (a good school), producing business films. To an interviewer, he commented, "We weren't very good at making these kind of films. It's very hard work, you know, trying to make things like marine engines interesting."

At an interview, the last thing a producer of commercials, television sitcoms, business films, or social documentaries wants to hear is that his or her field is less than *your* final goal! Perhaps after you've made your first feature you can get away with statements like Forsyth's. But to the person dedicated to his or her particular kind of filmmaking outside the feature, the first thing that comes to mind is a hostile reaction and an "*Oh, yeah?* Well, what about business films like *Glass* and *Seaward the Great Ships* and *To Be Alive?* And what about those awful dogs of films made in the name of the feature?" (Fill in your own titles here!)

So again we have the fine line between honesty and sensitivity. And we also have the breakdown of chemistry between job hunter and interviewer in a multitude of other areas:

★ being late, for whatever reason, and not calling ahead to say so
★ not thinking carefully about the dress code for that particular job (this is tricky, since comfortable clothing—not sloppy clothing—has become more acceptable for film people, but not at corporations!)

★ just "dropping in"—even though I must admit that this has worked in countless instances

TIME FOR A PAUSE. . . . I had just completed the first part of this chapter when I received another letter from Larry Dubin, my production manager friend who has spent more than twenty years in the business. (See page 145.) I smiled when I read it, for he could well have written this chapter, and it started me thinking that *I* am not the only one who offers job-hunting advice that at first glance seems harsh and definitive. If what he says seems repetitious in terms of what I have written here, then take heed. Maybe we're *both* not crazy. Possibly there's just something to what we're saying. Let me quote some paragraphs:

"I was always astonished at the widespread lack of preparation that was displayed by many of the job applicants. I was the production manager for one of the country's foremost commercial houses, and many of the people who were being interviewed had no idea of that whatsoever. Some thought we were an ad agency! Can you imagine a graduate of a law school being interviewed at a top law firm and not bothering to find out everything they could about the place?"

He comments further that film school grads often came in very casually and unprepared and left an impression that was bound to work against them.

"Each cover letter that I send is geared for one major purpose: That they notice me! That is why my resume is on nonwhite paper. I draw a colored border on it, and my letter tries to catch them in the first line or two and keep them until I have told them all I can to make them want to meet me. I have nightmares that I should fit into that unimaginative category of the misty gray death of the six-inch-thick file drawer!"

—PRODUCTION ASSISTANT/ARTIST
KEW GARDENS, NEW YORK

"Researching the film industry isn't easy, I'll admit. But I suggest that those who are really interested and committed try to read every trade publication they can get their hands on. Keep track of who does what. Make notes about what you see on the air, and try to track down the company that did it. All the major advertisers have PR departments who will tell you the name of their agency. And a few calls around the agency will generally reveal the name of the production house (if it isn't already listed in the trades or the various festival awards booklets)."

The last suggestions are good ones, and they made me grateful that I had received Larry's letter before the book went to press.

"In addition, it's very flattering to hear, 'I'm really glad to meet you because I loved that commercial you did for XYZ. How did you ever get those football players to dance like that?'"

Larry feels, and so do I, that it helps show that you have an interest and enthusiasm, and it can also distinguish you from the hordes of others knocking on doors. Another area in which we agree is the denigration of other parts of the field outside the feature. Larry comments:

"I spent my career in commercials. I liked doing them, never felt they were some inferior aspect of the film business, and always had a hard time when I interviewed what I called the 'feature freaks.' These are the pseudo-Spielbergs who knocked commercials, and who said they were good income between features. . . . Commercials in New York provide the major income to crew people. Fifty-two weeks a year, spots are produced by companies of all sizes. Yet come spring and it's feature season, and you can't get your regular crew, or a stage, to say nothing of equipment! Then in comes this young person, ostensibly dying for a break, and they announce that they'll 'do' commercials, but they're really trying to get on the new Lumet picture. . . ."

His advice, as mine, is that you never put down the interviewer's craft—ever. Be sensitive to your audience and "play the music that they want to hear. After all, if what they do is objectionable, why did you ask to be interviewed?"

Finally, Larry Dubin comments (I never said his letter was a short one!) that many people just starting out have a strong resistance to exploiting connections. Yet most film professionals will readily admit that their own early careers were launched or aided by a contact, friends, family, or neighbors. (Remember my own dentist's wife's friend?)

"There is no shame in calling friends of parents, neighbors, or other contacts. In fact, not doing so is *stupid*! Once you get the first job, you're on your own. No degree of 'pull' will keep an incompetent on the job long in the film business. . . ."

Having broken into the rules for what I think was very good advice (especially since he agrees completely with the author!), let me go on. There's another thing that you should consider having with you at the interview:

A SAMPLE OF YOUR WORK. If at all possible, and if your job category is one in which a film or tape sample is a practical tool (director, actor, cameraman, writer, editor, graphic artist, animator, and so on), then it can be of great value if you want to impress someone with your talent.

I must admit that the greatest boon to screening samples of young or experienced film-

"Amidst all the new production lingo and video skills I have developed, the most valuable insight I have gleaned is not to let my inexperience limit any of my possibilities."

—WRITER/VIDEO PRODUCER
SILVER SPRING, MARYLAND

"To hear you confirm my conviction that the film industry needs writers has restored my confidence, bolstered my job-hunting stamina, and enabled me to look at a typewriter again without wincing. I am busily researching corporations, ad agencies, and film production companies, gathering a list of execs to get in touch with directly; No more personnel agencies! Now I am relying on my own hard work and serendipity."

—WRITER
NEW YORK, NEW YORK

makers has been the advent of the tape systems. Though I detest what happens to a cameraman's work when it was originally shot on film and then transferred to tape—both in color quality and the fact that the frame is now set for television viewing—I will admit that it has been easier for me to screen samples and to see more of them efficiently and whenever I might find the time. Previously, unless I was working for a large production house, it meant dragging out my vintage World War II Bell & Howell Navy projector (with a jeweled head that does not tear up film like the automatics!), setting up a screen, and projecting the sample late at night. Most other producers have also welcomed the introduction of film to tape transfer for just these reasons.

If you are a writer, have a sample of your writing available. In fact, have several samples of different styles. There are problems for the job hunter when it comes to samples, however:

★ Some people want to keep the sample "for a couple of days." This becomes a problem because they are expensive, the "couple of days" becomes "a couple of months"— after which they somehow get lost.

Try to make some kind of specific arrangement to screen your sample—either at the moment you are sitting there or at a specific time, after which you can pick it up again. I have found that people who do not screen my samples quickly generally *never* get to them at all. This is especially true with advertising agencies, which brings me to another point:

★ Many people ask that you show them "your reel." In the ad agencies, this is practical, for they will be looking at a reel that is composed of several commercials, each one between ten and sixty seconds. In the space of five minutes they can see a sample of your work.

For the documentary producer, however, putting a reel together with bits and pieces of several films is an exercise in futility. You have spent months, even years, producing your film, only to cut segments out and splice them together to make "the reel." All the effort toward continuity, pacing, and rhythm is erased in one moment. If you had wanted the film to be shorter, you would have made it shorter. I would prefer to see *one* good film from a job hunter than to see segments of several films all spliced together. Frankly, I have always refused to show segmented samples, and I insist (nicely) that I would rather show one than parts of many. This is a tricky area, but you have to make up your own mind as to how you want to handle it. The segmented idea may work for a cameraman. For the producer/director or writer of a film, I doubt that it can ever make sense.

★ This is a society of people who are in a hurry. Often, in my screening of my samples, someone has said to me, "I don't have time now—I'll just look at the first part of it." I think it's rude, discourteous, and

arrogant, and I try (nicely) to ask them to find the time to see *all of it*. I will not show a part of a film, and I know that I have lost jobs because of it. But I also know that someone who wants to see part of my film because he or she is in a hurry is probably not going to hire me anyhow.

There is still another problem area for those of us who have to show our work for a job or for the assignment of a film project:

★ Everyone always wants to see a film that is just like the one they want to produce! Though they always protest that you can show them anything, so long as it illustrates your talents, they are really looking for a film that is a duplicate of the one they already have in mind!

This is a frustrating experience, for you may have twenty samples as your career pro-

gresses, and you will *never* know just which one will get you the job. I have had the strangest experiences in this area:

★ For a group of aluminum manufacturers, I showed film after film about steel, about aluminum, about coal, but finally got the job after screening a seven-minute film about *people* around the world!
★ For a large cruise line, the film that finally won the competition was a document, shot over four years, of an architectural project that took place in Georgia!

For the most part, however, the choice will be a subject that is as much like the client's or foundation's or agency's mental image as you possibly can get. The fact that there really is *no* film exactly like the one they are looking for is beside the point. They will still be looking for it. Thus, before you screen your film, the best

---

"Having graduated from the University of Maryland in May, I've found a nice, introductory niche in the film and video world through cable television. I'm selling subscriptions to put gas in the car, and in my spare time, I'm getting involved with the local access and local originating channels. This has to be one of the greatest things to come along for people with an itch to create. Cable access channels are quite eager to air just about anything, good or bad, amateur or professional . . . the only expense is in time and energy, and the cable company provides the cameras, tape, studios, and the necessary crew to complete a project."

—PRODUCER/WRITER
BOWIE, MARYLAND

---

thing you can do to counteract the problem is to explain:

★ the audience for whom it was made
★ the objective of the film—and keep reminding them of that objective, for they are looking for something that explains a product, and you may be showing a fund-raising film
★ some production stories or production problems that you had to overcome, especially if they're funny

THE FOLLOW-UP. Even if it's a short note that will be glanced at and then thrown away, the follow-up is a courtesy and will be welcomed. One of the best sound people with whom I work, Algis Kaupas, always includes a note along with his invoice—a comment about the quality of the job, his interest in screening the finished job, and a short explanation of the figures on the invoice. The fact that he is a superb sound person and a nice guy are the important things—but the note doesn't hurt, does it?

A few weeks ago I received a note of thanks after an interview, and I liked it enough to keep it for my files. In addition to letting me know that he had appreciated the time taken out of my busy schedule, his gratitude for honesty during the interview, and his acknowledgment of some helpful information for his job hunt, he ended the brief note with, "My dream is that someday I will be in a position to help *you*!"

Who knows? In *this* business, I may someday need that offer!

"I am now a vacation relief news photographer at KMGH-TV, the CBS station. It's quite a challenge, and it's a change from the production work I've done. However, it's done wonders for my photography. There is a full-time position opening up in another three to four months, and I'm working on that goal."

—CINEMATOGRAPHER/SOUND
DENVER, COLORADO

Actor Auditions: Charm at the Cattle Call

Although almost all of my own film and tape production deals with the documentary film and thus the use of "real people," I have had some extensive experience in television, in the making of commercials, and in the areas of casting and directing actors. I must say that my deepest reactions over the years have been awe, admiration, and a profound feeling of empathy for the people who choose this most difficult part of our profession.

If those of us in the production area of film can complain about the odds of the job hunt, the rude treatment, the closed doors, the seemingly impossible task of being there at the right time with just the right credentials, what must it be like to be on a *constant* job hunt, with the competition verging on the impossible, to be constantly rejected, and then to go right back, confident that the next step to making a living (forgetting stardom or recognition) may be through the next door to the next casting director.

The figures vary, depending upon where you read them, but most statistics indicate that about *15 percent* of the actors on both coasts account for about *90 percent* of the income for the profession! Certainly this book is not going to change the ratio much, and there are probably a thousand other volumes that tell you how to get the part, how to audition, how to open the doors, how to handle the callback—and still the ratio doesn't change! Added to that, possibly a hundred coaches and schools have flourished for exactly the same reasons—and, in fact, in my early days in television, even *I* conducted classes for actors and models who wanted to learn to read audition copy "cold." (It can be done.)

On the other hand, for those who make it in the field of television, film, tape, and commercials, the rewards can be astounding, especially on the union level, with negotiated residuals that can run for years. In addition, our culture is geared to the publicity given our stars, whether they appear on soap operas or on Broadway, and society devours their photographs, their wise and witty sayings (most of them invented by press agents), and their personal appearances on nighttime television. Given the golden carrot that is dangled in front of us all our lives, and factors of ego, expression, determination, and goal orientation to "make it big," the business continues to see new talent pour into it from all across the country. In fact, I would wager that 95 percent of the talent in acting comes from outside New York and Los Angeles, where almost all eventually end up knocking on doors.

It is not my role to tell actors just how difficult the profession is. If they have been around a while, they already know it. In my own casting sessions over the years, I have tried to reflect my empathy for an already difficult job by scheduling casting far enough apart so that twenty people aren't waiting out in the hallway for an audition that will last but a minute or so.

On the other hand, the people who do the casting do not have the most perfect of all worlds, either, and in spite of their good intentions, *they* run into problems caused by the actors themselves:

★ Late arrival in spite of a specific time given.
★ Telephone calls outside the casting hours. I received one a few months ago at one A.M. on a Sunday. To say the least, I was not pleasant to the caller!
★ Unprofessionalism in the handling of the interview or the audition—deliberately ignoring the specifications for the job. The most common area where this takes place is in the age range required. Most actors feel that they can play anything from seven to seventy!

The problem is compounded by the fact that anyone who sees a hundred people over a period of two days or more is bound to blur the images eventually, not remembering whether they liked or disliked the one with the red hair. It is the reason for "callbacks." On that subject, I have had many discussions both with actors and film-makers about which slot you would choose, given the chance. Would you rather be first and let everyone try to top you—taking the chance that you might blur after a few hours? Or would you rather be last and be so memorable that they breathe a sigh of relief and ask you to take off your glasses and take down your hair, exclaiming: "Why, Ms. Jones—*you're beautiful!*" (For the younger reader, this is a generic line from countless Hollywood potboilers of the thirties.)

I have had experiences where I have chosen the first 2 out of 150; other times I have selected someone from the middle; and occasionally I have hired actors from the very last group. There is no answer, unfortunately. The

---

"One thing quickly learned in this business is the importance of following every lead and every clue no matter how strange. Once, when I was asking my bank manager for a loan, he mentioned to me that someone somewhere was trying to build a film studio on Clydebank, the old shipbuilding area of Glasgow. Fascinated, I rang the local newspaper for any information—none. The local planning office knew little more. As a last shot, I rang the Scottish Development Agency. Yes, they knew about it, had all the addresses, and were willing to give me the information. I visited the man in charge of the project, and if it succeeds, there may be a job for me!"

—PRODUCTION ASSISTANT
GLASGOW, SCOTLAND

"The moment of truth came in 1981, when as a tentative foreign student experiencing "the States," I walked into a local radio station in Pennsylvania: 'Great! Just what we need! An English accent. Can you read the news? Tonight?' "

—ACTRESS/PRODUCTION ASSISTANT
BOSTON, MASSACHUSETTS

---

only thing that seems to remain constant is the odds.

From the other side—the casting director, the director, and the agent—there are bright signs and some good advice for the person who pursues an acting career, not only in the feature but in the field of the commercial and even in the business film. The first encouraging statement comes from Doris Gravert, director of casting for Dancer Fitzgerald Sample:

"Actors have to remember that they are *my* livelihood. If I can't find actors, I can't do *my own job. . . .*"

In terms of the commercial world and the advertising agency, there are many times that the well-trained actor, the qualified professional, is not as successful as the person who thinks commercials are wonderful, would like to try for them, and is trained at the type of school that takes a body, tells it how to move and to walk, and then sends it out into the world to get a job. And many of them do!

"The commercial is a short period in which we have to tell a story. Some people who are the 'right type' may have more success than the trained actor. The true actor may have taken years to construct 'building blocks,' but frequently someone comes along who has 'the look,' an unusual or unique quality, or the midwest, clean-scrubbed look, and gets the job. In commercials, we buy *a look!*"

At a discussion in her office, Doris gave me two photographs to look at and I contacted the woman on the eight-by-ten's—Hope Fitzgerald—for her own description of "the look."

"Why two photos? One is my 'commercial' type. The United States is fond of youth, vitality, and a wholesome quality that portrays a combination of innocence and trustworthiness. One photo—taken of me in a round-collared shirt and sweater, very little makeup and jewelry, and with my hair away from my face—*smiling*—I call my 'cheeseburger' shot. Would you buy a Big Mac from this woman?"

In a few years Hope will take other photographs, when she graduates to "the young housewife type," but she suggests that any actor or actress really understand exactly what their type is, to "go with your strongest suit."

"The other shot is for theater and film. I think it's the more 'essential me'—and there are very few things to identify me with one type or another. For instance, the absence of visible clothing, I believe, makes the viewer concentrate on my face and eyes for a clue about who I am. In 'real life' I'm a smiling person, so I smiled for the shot!"

On the subject of "type," Doris Gravert adds:

"Make up your mind what you want to be visually: ingenue? housewife? It may seem

vain, but you have to look in the mirror to get to know what you want to be, what you are, what your face can do. *Tell the photographer the look you want.* This is important."

She remembers one casting call in which she asked for gypsies, and she came out to the reception room to see over a hundred gypsies milling about the reception desk!

With the actor, possibly even more than with any other craft in our field except for the writer, the question of the agent comes up again and again. It is a sore point, and books have been written about the pros and cons:

★ The agents who favor the "stars" of their stable.
★ The advantages of a small agent over a large, successful one—or vice versa.
★ And how in the world do you get one in the first place?

One actor said getting an agent was like "making friends with a shark"! It isn't easy—but nothing is in this field, and it takes the same determination and follow-up (treading that thin line between contact and pest) that every other job hunt requires—but more so because there are lots more of you out of work. Doris Gravert comments on the subject of agents:

"I think the actor has to get an agent. Many agents attend showcases. When you are about to appear in one, call, leave a message with the information about time and place and what kind of showcase it is."

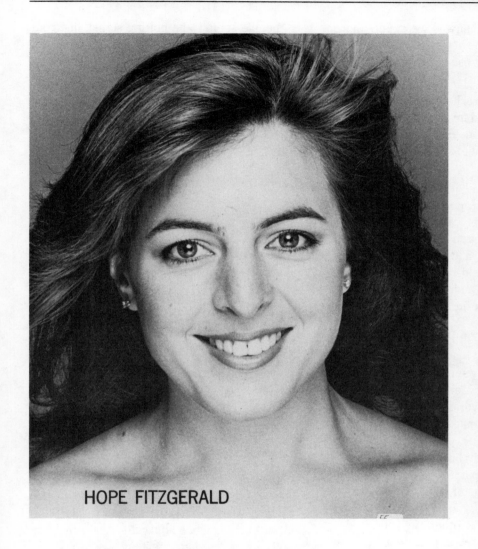

HOPE FITZGERALD

HOPE FITZGERALD

Young actress Hope Fitzgerald, who uses the shot on the left as her "essential me" and the one on the right as her "cheeseburger shot."

One thing most people agree upon is that the agent generally knows where it's all happening a lot faster and a lot more accurately than the rumor mill at the Broadway coffee shop, the round table on Sunset Boulevard, or the open-call ads in the trade papers. Casting directors also speak more honestly and more freely to agents whom they trust.

In addition, the agent's reputation is on the line—if he or she constantly sends just the right people to the casting sessions, there is a good chance for a lasting relationship with the people who cast, with the agency or with the networks. So being sent to an audition by a reputable agent increases your own chances in the talent contest. You may still run into the "cattle call" and all the other problems I've mentioned (and about which you already know), but narrowing the odds is what it's all about, isn't it?

On the subject of the "cattle call," incidentally, an old friend—once an agent but now a producer—commented:

"You'll never get rid of the cattle call. Too many fingers in the pie—five to ten in the control room, all of whom have something to justify their being there in the first place—the writer, producer, associate producer, art director, client, account supervisor. . . ."

Not everyone is perfect, in spite of what your mother said to you when you first decided to go to New York or Los Angeles and break into the world of the motion picture. As my wife, Sheryl, is fond of saying, "Just remember, fifty percent of all doctors graduated at the bottom of their class!" Why, then, should we expect more from any profession, be it architecture or the entertainment field. My friend continues:

"A lot of auditions are held by inept people. You've gotten dressed up for the audition, and the person running it doesn't even know how to use the tape machine!"

But you will survive. It's good experience.

If you are typical as an actor, in spite of your "type," you are probably also continuing your training in the craft, even while you consider yourself a professional and are out looking for work. In the acting field, there is a continual search for training, for additional schooling, and for the workshop experience that keeps your talent finely honed.

Unfortunately this situation also creates an opportunity for a great many schools to spring up and offers of coaching services by actors who, themselves, are finding it difficult to "make it" in the communications world. Some are good. Some are bad. Some are just perfect for keeping you in touch with your profession. It is no different from any other business or any other schooling offered as a part of continuing education. If you are looking for a school—or if you feel a need to continue your training, if only to keep in contact with the others in your field—Doris Gravert commented at our meeting about her own recommendations:

★ Don't just pick a school from the ads. Monitor a class. Do you like it? Do the people seem to be getting something from it? What about the instructor's critique?

★ After class, speak to the teacher. Come prepared with your best questions.

★ Don't go to one teacher for too long. You can get much more out of schooling and training by learning several techniques from different people.

★ Private schools are expensive. Check into the universities and colleges near you. For example, Northwestern and Yale have good acting schools.

★ While in your classes, you'll make contacts. They'll tell you more about the field than anyone else. Word gets around.

★ Try for off-off-off Broadway, summer stock, and regional theaters.

★ *Audition*. Go to as many as possible, even though some might be cattle calls. You bump up against people—and it gets you into the spirit and the pace of the city—be it New York or Los Angeles.

When we discussed the fact that "word gets around," I was reminded of my own casting calls, many of them "closed" to agents I knew. In spite of the limited number of prescreened actors that we had planned to see, calls *always* came in from people who had "heard" that we were looking for a midwest housewife with two and a third children for our sequence about a typical American family! Generally, as a courtesy, we would see them. Never can I remember any of them getting the job!

Though actors still flock to both coasts, and always will, for even I admit that's "where the action is," the out-of-town markets are sometimes denigrated or overlooked as places in which to make your first mark as an actor or even as a voice-over narrator for commercials or documentaries or business films. Another old friend in the business, dating back to my early days in live television when I taught school to make enough money to buy a three-vegetable plate at the Automat, is Chuck Tranum. He has been one of the top agents for voice-over talent for many years now, and he is a proponent of out-of-town experience before an attack on the major markets of either coast.

"I think that everyone should get their practice out of town—make a track record in Chicago or San Francisco or Detroit or even Dallas. When you audition, the agencies want to hear a tape of a *produced* spot. If you go to an agency or to a production house and use film or recordings of your own samples, they don't know if it took you one take or a hundred takes to get it right. It's just not like a real, professional sample of something you've done, even if you did it out of town."

Thus, the advantage of starting in the smaller markets and working slowly into larger and larger markets is that *everything* you have done will be of professional caliber, no matter what the city. The advice is not much different from that of people like Allen Zwerdling (page 65), who also thinks that the out-of-town markets present the best first opportunity for people just making their way up in the field. The problem, of course, is that all of us are in a hurry, and when we look at the numbers in this part of our industry, the proof is there, for the numbers always have—and always will—outweighed the jobs available. Chuck comments:

"The business mesmerizes people. All you need to hear is someone saying, 'Are you available?'—which doesn't mean you've got the job. It's just a way to ease you out, to make you feel good, and it doesn't even mean you're being considered . . . but it continues to give you hope. . . ."

As I said at the beginning, I look with awe at my brothers and sisters who choose acting as their part of our business, and I feel the empathy every time I touch your cold hand offered to me as "hello" or "good-bye" at an audition, and I am amazed at your fortitude, your drive, your tenacity, and your pigheadedness. Chuck Tranum says:

"How can anyone, unless they have great faith, go into an audition where twenty just as talented people are gathered, with only one who will get the job? What kind of person goes into those kind of odds—and what kind of professional ego is needed? If you don't have a monumental professional ego and great confidence in your ability, then leave the business!"

Which none of you will ever do! Just as those of us who work in production or editing or cinematography would never think of finding another way to spend our lives. Thus, I feel that I would like to leave you with one professional tip that will make it easier for you to keep from becoming discouraged. If I taught the production people how to get a crew of eight fed and out of an American restaurant in one hour, then I certainly owe the acting profession one piece of advice on how to get through to the people holding the audition and to set up an appointment, *when the line is always busy* (as it will be once the word gets out!).

The tip was given to me by actor John McEvily, a talented man who has impressed me at auditions with his charm and his professionalism:

"I learned the trick from the bookies! In an audition, when the phone is busy, use the trick that they do. Keep two quarters in your hand. When the line is busy, drop in the next quarter immediately and keep dialing. Do it until you finally get through."

Use the trick. It works. You've gotten through. The rest is now up to you!

MAKING IT ON YOUR OWN

Starting Your Own Production Company: In Las Vegas They Call It Gambling

It is not my purpose to begin an important section of this book on a firm note of pessimism. I, who am frequently criticized by my crew for being too optimistic about this business of film, might well be called a pragmatist—but a pessimist, never.

Nonetheless, I read with great interest some time ago that the firm of Wexler/Hall Productions had decided to go out of business after eight very successful years as producers of commercials. The Los Angeles–based company was a partnership of the well-known and innovative Haskell Wexler and Conrad Hall, the latter a successful director in his own right.

Now, if they had declared they were going out of business because of lack of work, I might not even have mentioned the item here. The small-firm competition is so keen in our industry that it is not at all unusual to see business fluctuations take their toll of production, postproduction, and service companies. First of all, we might as well face the fact that when the economy is suffering overall, the first place the budget generally gets cut is in the communications area. Executives can become instant heroes by slicing a $100,000 film out of next year's budget (even though their total shortfall is nearly $20 million!), and this reflects down to the agencies, the small producers, and then to the people who try to make a living.

When Pennsylvania's industrial complex of steel, coal, and aluminum was hit by a recession, the fallout of production companies became a torrent. Dependent upon training films, corporate image and stockholder films, and the flow of tape materials for employee communications, over *two dozen* small production houses folded in less than six months when the film/tape budgets were cut by clients.

The interesting thing about the Wexler/Hall decision is that the reasons given for dissolution were unusual—the kind not many of us think about when we decide to move our career in another direction and form our very own company, Round the Clock Productions (if that name is taken, you can use Rushed Productions). Hall commented: "I no longer want the headaches of collecting money or having to get into lawsuits and threats of litigation for nonpayment on jobs. I find this activity contrary to my nature. I am not a natural businessman."

Frankly, for those of us who have worked in companies, as beginners, as executives, or as partners who share the burdens with other unfortunates, it always astounds me that so many of us eventually decide to set off on our own, driven by the desire to control our own destinies, hoping that we can have still more freedom to do what we really want in film production, and guided by a dream that others have done it and it might be a good experience to try it for ourselves.

In my own case, it took almost thirty-three years to make the move and form my own little production company, Symbiosis Inc. Not only was I a "Depression kid" who was certain that this move would send me into penury almost at once, but I had been in film production with others for enough years to *know* what the pitfalls were. And still I went ahead and did it. Each day

I read of others who do the same—trained, experienced, qualified by years of guidance and preparation and absorption of business problems and solutions—they split off from the companies for which they work to begin again on their own. Back in the sixties and early seventies, MPO spawned a host of new companies, begun by their previous employees who wanted to shun the large production house syndrome to work in what they called "boutique shops."

Today, the large production facility, such as the old Wilding, Jam Handy, or MPO, has given way almost entirely to the small production house with somewhere between three and eight full-time employees and the balance of the crews made up of free-lancers. When I was with Wilding as president of their international division (1963), we numbered 432 full-time staff in seven cities with large, well-equipped studios in Detroit and Chicago to service our largest client, Ford Motor Company! Our overhead was probably close to the national debt, and the amount of business we needed to stay afloat reflected it in no uncertain terms.

The tape field has grown large enough and prosperous enough so that the same thing is happening in that part of our industry. From EUE, one of the giants of the commercials field, a tape postproduction house called Editel was organized. Eventually the employees of Editel, having learned their lessons well, split off one by one to form their own companies, not only in production, but in all the areas of postproduction—color correction, tape-to-film and film-to-tape transfer, editing, and other specialized services.

Being a "Depression kid" who always worries, I can only say that my own move, after fourteen years as a partner in a successful film company, has been rewarding both emotionally and financially, though I must admit that I constantly worry about "next year," and I am not alone. Every other small producer suffers from the same anxieties.

Although none of us can guarantee success, either for ourselves or for others, going into business for yourself is certainly a practical alternative or next step in a career path, whether you decide to do it in your first few years or after thirty-three years, as I did. But if you should decide to take the plunge, then I might be able to pass on some advice before reality overwhelms you.

In those first jobs, while you are still working for others, you have a superb opportunity to acquire experience not only in your selected craft as director or editor, but also in areas of business knowledge and client contact, be they corporations, motion picture moguls, foundations, or advertising agencies.

Keep in mind that owning your own business is an ongoing *selling* situation. Learn how first contacts are made, how budgets are constructed, how proposals are developed, and what overhead costs are and how they will affect your future balance sheet.

Wynn Nathan, who is now a vice-president with RKO Pictures, distributors and syndicators of both theatrical motion pictures and television series—such as *Sweeney Todd, The World of Survival,* and *Lena Horne: The Lady and Her Music*—began his own career by delivering mail at Universal Studios, moved to a job in the projection room, and then one day was invited by a man who ran his own production company to "come over and help run the office."

Wynn typed, ran messages, and, when Dick Powell's car needed washing, he washed Dick Powell's car. Well, his best experience in running a business came one day when he looked over the figures that the accountants had gotten together:

"I said to them, 'I really don't know much about accounting or bookkeeping, but isn't this dot in the wrong place?' They went over it and over it and over it and then said, 'You're right. We're broke!' And they promptly went out of business!"

Through his many years with Metromedia (where I first met him), Time-Life Films, Lionheart Productions, and now at RKO Pictures, putting the dot in the right place has helped him immeasurably!

In the area of personal contacts, Jeff Kleiser, president of Digital Effects (page 101) comments:

"While I was at Dolphin—and before I formed Digital Effects with Judson Rosebush—I learned some important things that we tend to forget in this field: how a director works with clients, presents options, handles them, allows the right amount of input while giving his own input. It's a delicate balance—it takes a special knack, and it stands you in good stead

Small production companies are thriving all across the country. Image Communications of Tampa, Florida, offers a full-service film and video production facility that includes sound stages, lighting grids, dressing rooms, conference rooms, set design, and building, as well as film and video support equipment and postproduction facilities.

for the rest of your career, especially when you decide to go into your own business."

The urge to go into your own business is not at all uncommon. For everyone, somewhere along the line, the thought comes to mind. In one of his columns for *Backstage,* Allen Zwerdling gave his most practical list of "musts" for anyone who decides to form a company on his or her own. Let me just list them and then comment where I think it will help:

★ *Try to have one or two definite, unshakable clients in your pocket to start.*

Make sure that they are, in fact, *unshakable,* since many corporations and agencies are loath to take a chance with someone new in the field. There are good reasons for this. Many small companies have gone out of business during production or postproduction. The film, original and work print, may be tied up in litigation or in the lab, the bills unpaid. The client is vulnerable because of the explanations due the executive board as to why a neophyte film company was chosen when there are so many solid film companies around (who, unbeknownst to the client, *also* go out of business).

In addition, you may have great relationships with an advertising agency, but the chances are that they will *not* move with you when you decide to open up shop yourself. The agency people claim that it's loyalty to suppliers, but my own guess is that agencies also don't take chances. As one agency exec was quoted as saying, "The concept of production companies working from lofts doesn't help. When you get down to it, they rent equipment, lease a director, and off you go. It's like putting your faith into complete strangers."

★ *Have enough money backing you so that you can operate without a single dime coming into the kitty from the business for the first six months.*

Carol Hale and Ed Schultz of Cinemakers in New York are even more adamant:

"You have to have resources that last a long, long time. There's a good chance that you will not be taking a salary. Not only that, but while you're producing, you somehow have to keep selling. The overhead continues. The costs mount up, and when the job is done, there's nothing in the house to continue the business. . . ."

They also suggest that the new group find a sales rep to work with you in the selling of your services. They have Beverly O'Reilly, a friend who dates back to my days at Wilding, and who has been with them for twenty years. Considering that they began with only one client, and now have a successful company that produces films, slide shows, programs, tape, and written materials, the move was a good one.

For others, the role of salesperson/producer is a natural one, since you are really selling *yourself* when you sell your services in the film/tape field. There is no single answer—it is something that you will have to decide, and frequently a partnership is formed, where one person sells and handles business management, while the other produces and directs.

★ *Be prepared to hear 100 reasons why you are not getting paid on time for your work or your merchandise or your services, and if you are a producer, depending upon an advertising agency or a sponsor, make that 101.*

This is such a critical area for the new business person that I have added a separate section in this part of the book that deals with just that problem. "Cash flow" is the name of the game.

★ *When you make up your projected expense budget for the first year, automatically double it, since you will find two dozen unexpected outlays.*

One factor that enters into the suggestion above is the item of *overhead.* When you project your rent, telephone, answering service, light, heat, and personnel who do not pay for themselves as producers, directors, editors, and so on, just keep in mind that these figures have a tendency to keep rising, and they do not show up on the screen, where the money *should* be spent.

I remember being with one company that had a lovely Fifth Avenue address in New York, and each time we figured the overhead factor into our budgets, it was almost impossible to come up with a figure labeled "Profit." A client

Foundations and social organizations use the motion picture for fund-raising and image-building. Director Ed Schultz of Cinemakers sets a shot with cameraman Phil Gries for the American Foundation for the Blind and assistant cameraman Peter Spera slates a scene.

walked in one day, looking for a new film company, looked around impressed, but then turned to me and said, "Well, who pays *this* overhead?" Calmly, I looked back at him without expression and said softly, "You!"

For some potential clients, especially in the large corporations and advertising agencies, the "flash" represents solidity, no matter how rocky the company's finances actually are. For others, it represents a waste of money. In either case, it is the *producer* who suffers the consequences of high overhead in trying to be competitive and produce films that throw off some kind of profit to tide the company over the quiet spots. Especially in the big cities, the rental of prime space is becoming exorbitant; many small companies are making the move into less expensive areas or out of the cities entirely and are discovering to their surprise that their customers like the idea of not being in the middle of the busiest sections in town. Restaurants are less crowded for business lunches, conferences can be held with less interruption, and much more space can be rented for the same amount of money spent for fashionable quarters in the middle of the "uptown" areas. The lower overhead costs also affect another important area: your bidding is much more competitive when you can keep costs down.

During 1983, in a very short period of time, more than *fifty* production houses moved from expensive midtown locations in New York to lower rent areas such as Soho, Chelsea, and west Greenwich Village. So many moved in so short a period of time, in fact, that one trade paper said that the only people who were getting rich in our business were *the moving companies*! Allen's list continues:

★ *Expect a two-year period before breaking even. Consider an eighty-hour work week normal for the first year.*

And finally:

★ *Above all, let's hope you're a lucky person. And even if you fail, the world will not come to an end and it's worth the risk. Also, keep your wife working!*

The last part of that advice brought Allen a letter from Dulcie Camp, who commented, "Great advice . . . but I think you should realize that there are lots of competent women in the industry, and it should have read, 'Keep your *spouse* working.' "

Which brings up a good point about our business. There are some women who own their own firms, and in the past ten years or so, the number of women who produce/direct and write their own films has increased. But *most* of the growth has been in the production area while either working for others or in partnership with *men*. It is an unfortunate reality that very few women actually *own* their own businesses. In terms of management, and especially at the very top, the film/tape field has not progressed very far in this area.

Possibly I am even more pessimistic than some of my female friends who own their own companies and who produce for major corporations. Some female producers insist that more and more opportunities have opened up for women on their own during these past ten years and that they now have more acceptance in the male-dominated corporate world.

Somehow *I* feel the numbers and the percentages have not changed very much and that the standards set for women in the field are still much higher than those set for men. Look, for example, at the Hollywood revolving door. The women who are chosen to direct feature films get one chance and one chance only, and then disappear from sight. My own dinnertime conversation usually revolves around the question, "What ever happened to Lina Wertmuller?"—a most talented woman who had one bad experience in Hollywood and then disappeared from view.

I somehow don't think it's much different in the world of the small company, for many of our client movers and shakers in the corporate world are still men who somehow don't trust women, no matter what they say for the public record about being equal opportunity employers!

And even when women do reach top levels in the advertising field, and in some cases form their own agencies, a great many of their clients are men. And for whatever reason, whether just "playing it safe" or because the odds are against the survival of any small production company, especially one owned by a woman, the major film/tape suppliers are male-owned or, at best, a male-female partnership.

As I said before, I am not being pessimistic. Possibly I am only being a pragmatist again—though a somewhat cynical one!

There is one other area that I'd like to

cover in terms of forming your own business. The job market and the potential for production and service companies have expanded greatly all across the country, and right at the beginning of this book I mentioned that this is an opportunity beginners somehow miss, given their mental thrust toward New York and Hollywood.

Joe Pipher, who has his own company in Cincinnati, Ohio, began his career in Los Angeles, but "the L.A. life-style was not for me." He took his family back to Ohio to live on a farm, then formed his own production house, Pipher & Company, and he's thriving in a business that caters to national advertisers who want to cut costs, as well as regional clients who want "the big city look."

Just as Tom Buckholtz (page 30) can provide the local color of New Orleans for his clients, Joe Pipher finds that a great deal of his work has to do with horses.

"I'm a horseman myself. I play polo, and Cincinnati is right next to the horse country of Kentucky across the river. It's amazing how just being there, in close proximity to a special feature, can bring business to the area. But if the client wants to shoot in L.A. or New York, we can do that, too—and at a lower overhead."

You've probably noticed that throughout this book I keep referring to filmmakers as "young" or "beginning," and at this point I must comment that the two are not necessarily the same. In our industry, insane as it is, there are people who begin their film careers very late in

Joe Pipher, another successful director/cameraman who has chosen to pursue his film career outside the major areas. His Cincinnati operation is thriving, and he manages to travel to all parts of the country to direct his spots.

life (just look at the lawyers at the networks and in Hollywood).

Al and Joan Harrison have been married for twenty-five years and have two grown children, both of whom are in college. Joan had had a career that began as a painter (not of houses, she says), taught art, and then got her degree in psychiatric social work, eventually became a psychotherapist with her own flourishing practice. Al, on the other hand, was a self-employed manufacturer and eventually became a manufacturer's sales representative in the field of industrial equipment.

"And so—after twenty-five years—midst child rearing, financial crises, identity crises, and in need of creative outlets and discussions about how we'd fill the vacuum created by the children leaving, we enrolled in the five-week intensive continuing education film course at NYU. . . ."

Which is where we first met, when I came to lecture. At a later date, I discussed their careers with them. The story is quite remarkable and, I think, indicative of just what can be done with experience garnered in *other* fields and then put to use in the film world.

Al was experienced in marketing and had contacts in the industrial world. Joan yearned to make documentaries "à la Charles Kuralt." They were advised by all who taught them to just "go and make films," even at their stage in life. So:

"We tapped our personal contacts, visited a lawyer, and $300 later, Vantage Point, Inc., was formed!"

The ad for Joe Pipher says it all. The answer to the question is that agencies will go anywhere in the country to find talented filmmakers.

Their selling took place among the companies that Al had visited as a sales representative. He convinced first one and then another that it might be a good idea to have a film that would show prospective customers just how their product worked. And, of course, he knew just the right film people to make that demonstration visual! They actually made some money on the third and fourth films, and they are involved in a new tape project at this point in their company's history.

I have one final bit of advice to those of you who plan to take this route, followed by some specifics that might just make a difference in determining success or failure as a new entrepreneur: *Incorporate!* The film field is tricky enough without making you personally liable for every mishap that befalls you along the way. A long talk with your accountant and your lawyer is probably a prerequisite for any plan of incorporation, and it would pay to investigate the subchapter "S" type of company, especially for the small owner.

And hopefully, after the first year and the next and the next, your accountant will call and give you the results with the words, "You did all right!" Which Ed Schultz translates into, "Congratulations! You stayed in business!"

Joan and Al Harrison, who started their small independent company, Vantage Point Inc., after their children were grown and had left home. They have just completed their fifth production.

Competition: The Bidding Game

If your career takes you into the realm of the business film or the commercial, you will eventually be confronted with all the complexities of figuring out just how much a specific project is going to cost. There are various games that are played by the buyer, each one more ingenious than blockbusters like Trivial Pursuit and Monopoly.

★ Someone will come to you and ask, "How much does a film cost?"
★ Someone will come to you and tell you that they have $75,000 and would like you to do their film.
★ Someone (probably an agency) will give you a storyboard and tell you that it is out for bids.
★ Someone will come to you and say, "I hear that film costs a thousand dollars a minute—and I would like you to produce our twelve-minute film!"

The small producer, no matter what his or her specialty in film, is always worried about the competition and about someone who might do exactly the same film for a lower price. In spite of what the advertising agencies and corporations proclaim, with some rare and outstanding exceptions, there is very little long-term loyalty to producers who have done a good job on prior projects. The reasons can vary:

★ You are working with a lower- or middle-level executive who likes you, is loyal, trusts you implicitly, and has worked closely with you for the years you have produced their films. An upper-level executive—possibly the president or chairman of the board—anxious to cut costs, insists that they look for someone less expensive, regardless of the results.
★ The company or advertising agency hires a "new boy (or girl) on the block." That person is now out to prove that everything ever done in the entire hundred-year history of the company has been inefficient, incompetent, and uncreative—and has cost too much money. *You* represent the past. The new producer represents the future.

I must comment here. Each time I have had a long-term working relationship with a client and am informed that at the next meeting they are bringing either a new assistant or new vice-president of marketing or advertising or public relations, I get minor knots in my stomach until I finally meet that person. Many times I find that I am quite taken with the new choice, and our relationship actually blossoms into a friendship that continues even after that person has left the company for another job in another city. On the other hand, I have had these meetings, made small talk with the new person, and have gone away knowing that the chemistry was wrong and that eventually the move would be made to another production company based in the city in which he or she previously worked. Generally, I have been quite right.

There is another reason:

★ Your favorite client or agency producer retires or moves to another company. The job is taken by someone with whom you have never worked—and very much like the "new boy/girl" syndrome, this person now—understandably—has to make his or her own mark. This is a common occurrence for those of us who have worked in the film field for many years and have grown up with our clients.

So this is a field where, unlike providing weapons for the Pentagon, there is a constant need to sell yourself, to rebid jobs even after you have established a reputation, and where you find yourself constantly competing with anywhere from one to seven other companies, all hungry for the contract. If ever we were to move light-years from the "glamour" of the industry, it is in this very pragmatic and difficult business area.

Let me, then, discuss the situations I outlined at the beginning and see if I can offer some tips when you meet them.

SOMEONE WILL COME TO YOU AND ASK, "HOW MUCH DOES A FILM COST?"

In the first place, of course, a film can't be budgeted until we know some facts: locations, objectives, shooting days, art work and animation, helicopters, crew size, travel and expenses, and other items that I've covered in the section on budgets. Nevertheless, you find that you are in a meeting with clients who are actually going to commit for a film. They are not kidding. They have had their meetings. *The budget has been approved* (in spite of their naiveté in asking how much a film costs).

In one quick session, before they go on to interview another producer who will give them a low price to get the job, you have to give them a "ball park" educated guess that will keep you in the running. Given years of experience, and given at least a one-hour meeting with your potential clients, you can probably come up with a fairly practical budget figure. But even here there are a great many pitfalls.

Many producers—your competition—will give a low figure in order to get the job. Then, when production begins, they send additional invoices for everything as "extras"—moving the budget up and over what *you* bid in the first place. The second area that takes some consideration is in deadline, the date the film is needed. It is a given in our field that a client or agency will devote most of a year to *deciding* to make a film and then want it the day after tomorrow. The same thing happens in the feature film: one or two years of negotiation on budget, star, production, and then a demand that the film be ready for the Christmas season—or cancellation because everyone has changed their minds.

My own commitment to film and to my clients has been to tell the truth—to give a budget figure that will hold firm unless they change the specifications drastically. And all of it must be spelled out in advance.

Actually, it can work. My own background as an accounting major in college has stood me in good stead when it comes time to give a "ball park" figure to a client. Some years back, when the Simmons Company was about to build its environmentally oriented corporate headquarters in Gwinnett County, Georgia, right alongside the Chattahoochee River, we were asked to follow the project from inception and design right through construction—over a four-year period—and we were also asked to give a budget to the top executives. All this happened at a luncheon, and they expected the figure right then and there.

Somehow I worked it out and projected everything I could think of, including an "expert" evaluation of what the inflation rate would be four years from the date we were meeting. I gave a figure and quickly downed a glass of wine to calm the fluttering and the doubts. At the end of four years, we found that we were about $1,000 off the figure we had given four years earlier!

It happened once again when the executives of Alitalia Airlines flew to New York to ask me to budget *eleven* films to be shot over a three- to five-year period! I had just finished a prizewinner for them, and this was to be my reward. However, instead of giving me some days or weeks to come up with the figure, they insisted that they had to fly back to Rome and could I not work it out right there so they would be aware of the budget?

Thus, while five of them chatted in Italian, I took a legal yellow pad and worked out a *five-year, eleven-film* budget (with my fingers crossed) and gave them the figure. When they translated it into lire, it was in the astronomical millions, and I calmly said, "It's not my fault that there are 620 lire to the dollar!" They laughed and left, and two months later we got the job. Interestingly enough, I had managed to project future inflation and costs so that we made exactly the amount of money I had forecast five years before! I would not like to try it again.

Most important of all, perhaps, is what eventually happens after you've given your figure. If you give the client a range that, for example, runs between $75,000 and $100,000 for the job, you can be certain that when the time comes to make the final negotiations and sign the contract, *they* will have heard $75,000 and *you* will be thinking $100,000!

SOMEONE WILL COME TO YOU AND TELL YOU THAT THEY HAVE $75,000 AND WOULD LIKE YOU TO DO THEIR FILM.

At first blush that sounds great. You have been working on your own low-budget jobs, and $75,000 seems like a fortune . . . until you hear the specs! One of the things that you must be aware of in your bidding for a film is the cost factor for any given set of specs. This comes with experience, of course, but I shall cover this in more detail in the following section on budgets. If the job entails a week's shooting in one nearby location, the chances are that you can do the job and turn a profit.

On the other hand, if they have plants in twenty-seven countries including Bangladesh and Hemlock, Ohio, the budget may not be enough to get you much past Kennedy Airport with your crew. Take the time to budget carefully and question the client group thoroughly.

SOMEONE (PROBABLY AN AGENCY) WILL GIVE YOU A STORYBOARD AND TELL YOU THAT IT IS OUT FOR BIDS.

This is probably the most difficult area of film bidding, since you never know just what factors are really entering into the bid.

Advertising agencies are, first of all, notorious for "setting up" a bid situation. I am not implying by that statement that there is anything illegal in what is being done—just a reality that borders on the unethical. You go into it—hungry for the job—and you actually have no chance to win. The producer has already been selected in the minds of the agency execs, and the "motions" of a bid are merely to prove that they have chosen the best team to do the job. Corporations are also not above doing exactly the same thing, and after a few years you are able to smell out the situation, but you go ahead and bid anyway, hoping that they will realize you are, indeed, the best (even if only your mother has thought that up to this point).

However, even when everything is on the up and up, which is probably true of the majority of bidding situations, many demands are made of the production company before the job is assigned.

I remember some years ago when I worked for a New York company called Transfilm-Caravel (before your time, indeed), I was called to an agency on a Friday afternoon about four P.M. to attend a meeting on an "urgent" bid situation. Excited, still having stars in my eyes about the growing field of television production, I arrived, expecting to be ushered into the office of the producer who had called and told me about the storyboard.

Instead, I was shown to a room that was *filled* with film producers, in a situation quite similar to the actor "cattle call." In front of the room were the agency people, with blackboard, chalk, and blowups of the storyboards, and the presentation closely resembled an air force briefing before the pilots were sent off to confront the Japanese at Midway Island.

We were told that the bid had to be done over the weekend and that it was to be delivered to the agency by eight o'clock on Monday morning, to be flown out to the client, who would make the decision within ten hours or some such time frame. The board was complicated. Questions were asked, and we didn't get out of there until about eight P.M.!

Possibly, without really knowing it at that time, this was a great turning point in my career, and it affected every agency contact after that time. I walked out of the meeting discouraged, depressed, and very disillusioned about the agency and the people who work for the advertising industry. Torn between my better judgment that it was all a waste of time and the guilt that would go with turning down the bid, I returned to my offices and telephoned some of my staff to tell them that we were all going to work over the weekend.

I won't go into the details of that time, even though I love to tell stories. Nothing was open on Saturday or Sunday, so getting figures together and making calls was a nightmare. Finally, on Monday morning it was finished. We delivered it to the agency, knowing that we had done our best, that the ideas and the budget were both competitive. And we waited.

And we waited. And waited. A week went by and we heard nothing from the advertising agency. Silence. I called another producer who had been there. He, too, had heard nothing. After a second week, I decided to call. The call was not returned. I called again. Finally, two days later, the agency producer got on the phone. "Oh, yeah!" he said calmly, "We sent it out to the client. And we decided that we weren't going to do the spot after all!"

There is a constant complaint about the agency bidding process that comes from producers who are active in our field. Many will never be quoted by name, since they depend upon the agencies for their livelihood, but in my conversations with friends who have made the television spot their careers, I have found there are two areas in which they are quite articulate in their condemnation:

★ A huge amount of energy is wasted in researching bidding, figuring, planning, meetings, with the job finally being awarded to someone else. Many times the producer spends more than a week trying to figure out ways to do the commercial efficiently, effectively, and at a budget that will get them the job. There is no remuneration for your work. You just hope you'll get the next one.

★ Even after you've lost the job, there are times you are not even notified—or if you are told that someone else got it, you are never told the reasons why. Even the military "debriefs," but the agencies have not yet learned the courtesy.

To make matters worse, agencies have now hired outside "cost consultants," with whom the producers now have to deal—this in addition to the normal agency complexities and people. The job of the cost consultant is to question the budgets submitted by the producers and ask such questions as, "Why do they have to do it this way?" or, "Can't they shoot it in two days instead of three?"

For the producer trying to deliver the most effective job, this can be a difficult time. One producer may bid on the storyboard and plan to use a crane or a helicopter. The other may bid after deciding to do the shot looking out from a manhole. Both might or might not be effective. One may be much more dynamic than the other. In both commercials and the business film, it is difficult to explain that the job you are suggesting will be more effective because of an expenditure of monies. Clients—and even agencies—are not as visual as we would like them to be, and it is we who are trapped by the competitive nature of the field.

Overall, though, I must comment that dollars do *not* equal creativity—and the "spoiled" people of our field, used to the most superb state-of-the-art technical backup, are not necessarily the most apt in putting a film together. For those of you starting out in the industry, these are all factors that you have to keep in mind—day after day, job after job. It is how we survive.

SOMEONE WILL COME TO YOU AND SAY, "I HEAR THAT FILM COSTS A THOUSAND DOLLARS A MINUTE—AND I WOULD LIKE YOU TO PRODUCE OUR TWELVE-MINUTE FILM!"

The people who have come to see you have done some homework, but certainly not enough. The $1,000 per minute figure comes out of the Great Depression. It has somehow remained with us and we suffer for it constantly. The only answer that I can give to anyone who drops that old chestnut in my lap (and believe it or not, I still hear it) is to quote the figures for *commercials* that are being produced these days.

If $1,000 a minute is the going rate for film, why has the cost of producing a thirty-second spot risen over 200 percent in the past ten years, moving to a production cost of well over $150,000 for that short *thirty seconds*? At that rate, then, the cost of a ten-minute corporate film or documentary would run somewhere near *$3,000,000!* Actually, the median range for other types of films in the nontheatrical field runs somewhere between $50,000 and $150,000—with some costs going up to $500,000 and more on what we consider the high-budget range for IMAX and other sophisticated presentations.

I would like to leave you with one note of optimism about this whole subject of the bidding game. Most of the time *it is not the low bid that wins*. Most smart business people are quite aware of the fact that "low" does not mean "good" (though it well may). Somewhere in that "ball park," a producer will be chosen, occasionally even the highest bidder of the group. But if that is the case, you may be certain other factors

have entered into the decision, and this is the area where you, too, may well have a chance to compete:

★ Personality. Don't ever minimize the chemistry aspect of a bid situation. The person making the decision has to have confidence in the final selection—and may even have to defend that confidence before his or her superiors.

★ Talent. A knowledge of the subject or the company or previous work in that area may well be the catalyst that moves the decision in your favor. Study the company, subject, or product before making your presentation.

★ A sample of your work. This advice goes for professionals as well as for film school grads. The sample may be just what they are looking for, or it may show off your talent in a situation quite unlike the one in which you are bidding. Just make certain that you give an adequate introduction before showing your sample: what audience it was made for, the prime objective of the film or tape, some of the history in both production and distribution, and the response from the audiences who had seen the film.

Even if you have made a generally good presentation, and are one of the people being considered for final selection, you will always be asked to "put something in writing." It is an unwritten rule almost everywhere, whether you are applying for a foundation grant, competing for a business film, or giving details of what your feature film is all about and why you should be the one to produce it.

The best advice I can give in the area of writing (aside from just learning how to write everything from a letter to a contract) is that you proceed on the assumption that everyone who is going to read what you've written is *nonvisual,* whether true or not. You'll have to learn to write in "pictures," and you'll have to learn to turn those pictures into production dollars, for every promise that you give on paper has to be translated to film—on budget!

Budgets: Some Lessons in Optimistic Juggling

Though I have a college background as an accounting major, and I have been in the motion picture and television business for thirty-five years, I still gag when I say the world "million." I get no picture of just how much money that is. I still have to count the number of zeroes when I write it. On the other hand, the feature business of Hollywood has no such problem. The word is bandied about flippantly, even when the newspapers report that Michael Cimino's catastrophic production of *Heaven's Gate* cost *$38 million!*

I read of *Annie* and *Star Trek* at $40 million, *Reds* and *Scarface* and *Blues Brothers* and *Apocalypse Now* all near $30 million or more. But I am also well aware that the winners make those figures look like two-dollar bets at the blackjack table in Atlantic City. *Return of the Jedi* grossed about *$250 million, Flashdance* neared $100 million—and there are hundreds of other films that play to packed houses of summer moviegoers, many of whom see those films ten and twelve times! It is no wonder that the goal of so many of our film school grads is to break into the golden jackpot of the industry. I fully understand it. I accept it if that's what you want. My only advice to you if you have gotten this far in the book is to *forget it*!

Whatever your eventual goal—and my wishes go with you in reaching it—your early years will be spent with the rest of us mortals who think in terms of "thousands"—and not too many of those at that. The majority of filmmakers who work in the field of commercials, documentaries, business films, and independent productions live their lives working with the sharpest of pencils, trying to cut down the figures for locations, travel, crew costs, hotels, number of shooting days, weather contingencies, and the mounting costs of van rentals, helicopters, and even food.

Above all, in spite of the fact that we know things are terribly expensive out there in the real world, we are all total and committed *optimists*! Either we unrealistically hide the true picture in terms of budget, or we are convinced that there is some other way to do it that will allow us to make our picture for the money we

have been given or promised. The fact that this never seems to happen is still no obstacle to our setting out for each and every production with total confidence that we will, somehow, make it. And somehow we sometimes do.

The budgeting of a film is a complex job, for there are so many factors that have to be considered, most of them unknowns. Certainly we know the cost of the crew when we start out. We also are aware of the cost per day for equipment, the price of air fares (though they seem to change daily), and film stock budgets from raw stock through the laboratory . . . but . . .

But . . . we never really know a great many other things, and much of our budgeting procedure is an "educated guess." In addition, as one student wrote to me some time back, reminding me of the Alitalia series I described:

"How do I determine the costs of a project that is to start one year in the future . . . when I'm budgeting it now?"

It is why we budget with the fingers of one hand crossed! Added to her question are the problems of not really knowing just how much film will be shot on location, whether we are realistic to think we could edit the finished film in five weeks, weather problems, and all the unexpected horrors of film production.

I have also learned in my own field that specifications given to me by the people who hire me are another brand of optimism that has its own unwritten rules. When one of my clients once asked me what it would cost to get "a couple of shots" down the Congo River and I told him that it would run somewhere near ten or twelve thousand dollars, he looked aghast and commented, "Only for a couple of shots?" Other clients tell me their specifications by passing them off quickly in their description so that they seem minor—and thus inexpensive. One person couldn't understand why it would cost so much money just to get a "subliminal" shot of the Taj Mahal!

A friend of mine, Truman Moore, one of the best of still photographers, tells me that in his field there is a similar problem in that clients generally pass off expensive production problems by suggesting that he "just put it under the lights"—or, better still, "have one of your people put it under the lights!"

But for us, the producers who must budget accurately if we are to survive, it is important to ask a series of questions—of ourselves as well as of those who are hiring us to produce their film or tape project. All of this transcends the usual budget listings, the obvious figures allotted to crew, talent, studio, raw stock, laboratory, music, sound, editing, transportation, per diem, overhead, contingencies—and, one hopes, profit. There are at least twenty-five or more budget forms that I might print here, but none of them will do you any good unless there is a logical basis for every figure you put down. I have, in fact, given up the printed forms and I now use a yellow legal pad, upon which I put as much of the philosophy of the film project as I do the straightforward figures.

Basically, every budget breaks down into preproduction, the shooting days necessary to do the job, and the postproduction costs. The place where we get into trouble first is in the optimistic evaluation of just how long it will take to produce the film. It is a good idea to "walk through" each phase of production, especially the days that you have allotted to put the subject onto film.

We generally think that we can shoot much more than we actually can. If a location is twenty miles from the next spot you've chosen to shoot, what are the road conditions, the transportation problems, the time of day—does the location close at five P.M.?

It is not my purpose here to give every possible situation you might encounter, a task that would, in any case, be impossible. I would suggest, though, that you begin to develop a technique of asking yourself the questions that will relate to your budget.

In answer to the young woman who wanted to know how to project for a year or more until she shoots the film, my only advice is to really think through the inflation rate in every phase of production, especially in air fares, hotels, and laboratory costs. But these are only a few of the things you might think about as you make out your first budget—or even your second and third. The only thing I can assure you is that it doesn't get easier, and each film project has its own specific problems to be overcome.

★ Are you realistic about shooting days? Are there enough weather contingencies in case you are rained out?

★ What is the crew payment rate? Does it include an eight-hour day plus overtime, or will they work for a "flat" ten hours before you have extra costs?

★ What is the length of the finished film? This counts considerably in the area of lab costs, matching, mix, and so forth.

★ Will it be cheaper to work with film or tape? What is the final use of the project? Doing simultaneous budgets for film and tape may well surprise you.

★ How many locations are required? Can you combine locations to save money on the budget? Many times several locations are chosen for "political" reasons—to show a corporation that they really care about their people in Hygiene, Colorado. I had one client who worked for Coca-Cola insist that we shoot at six plants for each film, even though every assembly line looked the same as the last one!

★ How long will it take to light an interior location? Though the advent of faster film stock has helped somewhat, most producers underestimate the time it takes to make an interior look good. It is not just a matter of having an exposure. The lighting has to be professional.

★ What about special equipment costs? Will a local wheelchair do instead of a Western Dolly? Look carefully at the requests made by the crew. They generally like to utilize every state-of-the-art invention. Can something be successfully substituted?

★ Do you really have to make a survey trip, or can you do it all by phone and letter?

★ What about animation and graphics? These are two areas—including titles—that can bring costs up considerably. In your original discussions, remember that computer graphics can be a wonderful suggestion, but it costs about $3,000 a second!

★ What is the time limit to produce the film or tape? The longer the film is in your possession, unfinished, the higher the costs will be—rentals, salaries, overhead.

★ Has someone suggested a "star" as host of your show or film? Remember that stars cost money and that some are difficult to work with, expanding your production time and thus your budget.

★ And about music—have you checked the costs of live music recently? Well, what about some small group you know—or what about a library score or just a guitar?

★ Most important to you: How many people will be involved in checking your treatment, script, dailies, fine cut, and answer print? The more people who are involved in a film project, the higher the eventual costs. For one committee of seven who had to come to New York from all over the country, I spent nearly *eight hundred dollars* in screening and interlock fees before the film was approved. (No, it was not in my budget!)

★ Is it better for you to pay the entire cost of crew transportation and subsistence or to pay your people a set amount of money, from which they will pay their own expenses? Remember that keeping a crew together is much more efficient than separating them and then rounding them up later on. The networks pay per diem. Most independents pay the total cost less liquor, phone calls, and laundry.

Here are some other areas that are frequently forgotten when making up a budget:

★ Insurance. Make sure you have both liability and negative insurance.

★ Pension and welfare (if necessary), social security (if you have a corporation), workmen's compensation, unemployment insurance.

★ Music royalties. Check this carefully. Most library music houses charge either one flat fee for the entire film or a "needle drop" fee, per selection—which can run into a large amount of money. This is in addition to hourly fees to help you select your music and transfer charges to 16 mm magnetic tape.

★ Hazard pay for crew members who have to fly in open helicopters or do some other feat that exposes them to danger.

★ Gratuities. Airport skycaps expect large tips from film crews and so do bellmen and doormen who handle your twenty-seven pieces of luggage.

★ Excess baggage at airports. These charges vary somewhat now that deregulations have complicated our film lives. Check the rates carefully. They can be very high.

★ Screening rooms. Straight screening can now run up to $100 per hour. Interlock screening goes for $200 per hour and more in the larger cities.

★ Don't let anyone convince you that the use of stock footage is a more reasonable way to produce sections of your film. By the time you add up search fees, lab costs, and the payment of rights, it may be better to shoot the footage yourself or drop the idea and replace it with something else.

Once you have it all together and you look at the budget carefully, and even sense that there may be a small profit lurking in there somewhere (even if you can't pay your own salary for some months), and the client or agency or foundation accepts the figure, you immediately run into another disease of our industry: *collecting the money they owe you!*

Payments and Contracts: The Ebb and Flow of Cash Flow

There are very few things of which you can be absolutely certain in this field, but here are two of them:

★ When a service is completed for you—edit, mix, lab, matching, whatever—an invoice will be in the mail to your company within twelve hours!

★ When *you* invoice someone who owes you money, you will not be paid for 30, 60, or 120 days!

Ours is not the only industry that suffers from problems of "cash flow," but we *are* one of the few where money comes in and goes out in huge chunks. In fact, this is an industry where a small business can easily go bankrupt, not because it has nothing in production, but because it is *too successful* and the bills have piled up while "the check is in the mail" from its own clients. It is a serious problem, and with the tightening of the economy some years back, the flow of money from client to supplier began to slow to an ooze.

I am not only speaking of small clients—many of them are the best in terms of their commitment to suppliers, and they pay quite well. I am speaking of the large companies of this country and of the giant advertising agencies who began to find that $25 million or $25 billion in the bank could draw interest at 10 percent or higher while the small supplier waited for the money to arrive. It began to occur more and more frequently, to the point where people no longer even told you that the check was in the mail. The invoice had not even been processed! Note, if you will, the statement made by Conrad Hall (page 175) on the headaches of collecting money.

Somehow, either I have been lucky or I have managed to get across to my own clients that I am a small supplier and that the contracted

payment schedule is important to my cash flow and my financial operation generally. I pay my film crews on time and I have tried to create the best of credit situations with my suppliers—labs, editing rental houses, tape editing, matchers, and so on. It is not always easy. However, many of my clients have worked with me to determine the pay schedules set up by their corporations, and for about five years to date, it has worked beautifully.

If you look carefully at the most critical times for a producer in terms of money flowing in and out (in those large chunks), they take place at specific times in your production schedules:

★ During and after the filming or taping of the project: crew salaries, rental of equipment, travel, and per diem expenses. To this, add lab costs.

★ During and following the editing process, music fees, mixing, matching, lab, answer print, and any other postproduction costs will pile the invoices up on your desk.

During the other parts of the project, the costs stay at a pretty constant rate—some travel, research, salaries, entertainment. But the panic begins to set in when the heavy production costs are there and the check—already sixty days late—is not in the mail.

Even if there is no real solution, there are some hints that may help you survive the cash crunch when (and if) it comes. A part of the solution is your ability to convince people who have gotten their weekly corporate or agency

salary check for forty straight years without a break that small suppliers are just not in the same position.

★ Find out the pay schedule that is structured into that company or agency. Ask if you can submit your invoice in advance, taking advantage of the time lag and thus giving you your check close to the due date. I had one client—one of the world's largest corporations—that agreed to that method of payment and then promptly "lost" every invoice that I submitted!

In scheduling your payment structure, try to break it down so that the cash will be there in advance of your large outlays of money. This requires a negotiation with some clients and an explanation as to why you have asked for payment in three, four, or five parts. Let me give you some examples. Let us assume that the contract is for $100,000:

★ One-quarter, or $25,000, on signing of contract. This, too, may not be paid for sixty days. If you can get the money, it puts you ahead at once.

★ One-quarter on completion of major photography. You have now been paid one-half of the contract price and should be able to manage financially.

★ One-quarter on presentation of interlock. At this point you are on the "thin" side of your cash flow, having paid your editor and assitant editor. And it will get worse because all of your postproduction costs are now to follow.

★ One-quarter on delivery of answer print. This will pay off the job, and there should be a profit (?) in the balance.

There are, of course, other ways:

★ One-fifth on signing.
★ One-fifth on presentation of treatment.
★ One-fifth on completion of photography.
★ One-fifth on interlock.
★ One-fifth on answer print.

Or:

★ One-third on signing.
★ One-third on photography.
★ One-third on answer print.

Occasionally the payments are made in sixths or even in a structure that varies with each payment. For example, you might *split* the last payment into two parts. It is all negotiable.

There are some clients—such as the U.S. government—that will not or cannot pay in advance or on signing the contract. What we generally do at that point, then, is to make the payment contingent upon some type of approval, such as a research and development outline or a first treatment outline.

In any case, the lesson is simple. If you are going to produce anything on your own, make certain that the cash flow is well thought out. I must say that, being a "Depression kid," it awes me constantly when I see the amounts of money

that flow out of my company's checking account at the critical production points of a film or tape. In tape, for example, the on-line editing costs for two days are the equivalent of eight weeks of film editing! You can imagine my shaking hand as I write the check.

CONTRACTS AND LETTERS OF AGREEMENT. Besides being a most talented producer, Frederick Wiseman is nobody's fool. Though he was trained as a lawyer and actually taught law before becoming a filmmaker, he lets someone else do his legal work. Even though the lawyers now run the Hollywood mills, they can't let well enough alone and are also involved in the contracting of films for small producers. Very few companies or agencies will contract without having you sign something that has been devised by their law firms. Many of the contracts are totally unrealistic and have nothing to do with the film field; be prepared for the legal onslaught. The government is even worse. You will learn to live with it.

Occasionally a letter of agreement is signed by both parties. More often, if the client is a large foundation or corporation or feature production company, network, or agency, there is a formal contract. Read it carefully. It will certainly be favorable to the client, and it may even protect *you* in some cases, should you and your client be killed in the same taxi accident in midtown Manhattan.

No two contracts are alike, of course. But I would like to list some things you might look for when you read those first legal documents, still euphoric about getting the job but suddenly

brought down to earth by "WHEREAS the parties desire to enter into an agreement for the purposes hereinafter set forth . . .":

★ Specify exactly what it is you are to produce, the time of that production, how it will be produced (tape, 16 mm film—color, black and white), and approximately what the subject is to be.
★ Stipulate exactly what it is that *you* are responsible for in preproduction, production, and postproduction, including which of the client expenses you might be responsible for, such as travel and per diem.
★ Give a delivery date. *But be careful!* If there *is* a specific date of delivery, make sure it not only requires *you* to meet the schedule of approved dates, but also commits *the client* to those same dates with a limitation on the number of days in which they can approve the treatment, fine cut, interlock, and so on.

I would like to add one more point. Sometimes—on rare occasions—a client will ask that you post a "performance bond." In other words, if you do not deliver on time, you are assessed a certain amount of money for each day or each week that you are late. To say the least, it is an unfair practice, and I have never signed one, nor will I ever sign one. Dates are dependent not only upon *me*, but also upon my client organization, and every client who has ever suggested a bond to me (generally lawyers themselves) have understood why I will not sign one. The other suggestion that I make to them is that if I am to be fined for each day I am late, then they should agree to pay me the same amount in addition to my contract for each day that I am *early!* I cannot guarantee the quality of their film, but you may be certain that I will come in at least two weeks before the due date!

Actually I have never signed a performance bond, but neither have I ever missed a deadline.

★ Include the information as to just what is owned by you and the client after the production is completed: picture negatives, sound, artwork, and so forth.

★ Include a clause that determines copyright, and if the client wants it, remember that there are details that have to be met with the Library of Congress, including the filing of two prints of the subject and a copyright line on one of the titles.

★ Of course, the payment schedule you have worked out *must* be in the contract or letter of agreement.

★ Spell out the rights that the client has purchased: television, nontheatrical, theatrical, whatever. Also spell out who pays residuals to any actors you may use in the film.

★ Include the fact that the client pays local, federal, and state taxes on the total price, depending upon the area in which the headquarters are located.

★ There should be a paragraph that includes the potential of laboratory price increases after a certain date—either for release printing in the future, tape copies, or new CRIs (color reversal internegatives). Remember, the labs seem to increase prices with each union negotiation.

★ Some reference to insurance coverage should be made with a cutoff point after production, after which insurance coverage goes from you to the client.

★ There should be some type of cancellation clause, with notice in writing, and a method of reimbursing you for costs already incurred or committed for the future. This is tricky, but generally it can be worked out to pay you for costs plus a small amount of overhead. Luckily I have never had to refer to this clause in over thirty-five years of production.

★ Make sure you know who is responsible for securing releases. In some cases a corporation will take care of releases (as in a film dealing with their employees). Normally, however, the producer is responsible.

★ Always include a paragraph that requires the other party to provide a person or persons who can make decisions on accuracy and detail during the various stages of production.

★ If you are dealing with unions, some reference to union contracts and your obligations should be in the contract.

★ An arbitration clause is generally included in case of disputes.

★ All contracts should have a "force majeure" clause—the famous "act of God" clause. It is my favorite one. It simply states that neither party is responsible for delays or an inability to fulfill any part of the contract because of wars, acts of God, fire, weather, strike, labor dispute, governmental action, delay in transportation, shortage of labor or material, or for any other cause not under the control of the party whose performance is interfered with.

Some years back, one of my ex-partners was negotiating a contract with a large new corporation, and the man who was reading the clause roared in disbelief. "Good God!" he exclaimed. "Why don't you put in revolutions, too?!" So they all laughed, and they did.

The crew left for Brazil on part of a South American trip, going from Rio to Brasília, and from there they were to make a connection to La Paz, Bolivia. They got to the airport, equipment checked in, and the plane never arrived. In La Paz, *a revolution had begun*. The crew was stranded for one week because the national airline of Bolivia stopped flying during that time. The client was notified. They didn't laugh—but they paid one week of crew time due to revolution!

Certainly, much of what I have written is a simplification, and in past years my relationships with my clients have evolved to a point where we merely write a letter of agreement that refers to a previous contract, rather than going through the motions again and again.

Keep in mind, however, that any contract or letter of agreement will take time, especially when it gets into the hands of the lawyers. Add that time to your deadline and schedule. I once had a meeting with a client who asked me how long the film would take to complete. I suggested six months. *"Six Months!"* he stormed. I guaranteed that the lawyers would take at least two of those months in nitpicking the contract, and I was right. I called him eight weeks later to remind him. He laughed weakly. The job took six months.

Whatever form you finally decide upon, there certainly should be *something* in writing (in case of that taxi accident!), and though I have never had to refer to a contract a second time in over thirty-five years of making corporate and documentary films, it is still a good idea to put everything down on paper. Just remember what Sam Goldwyn counseled so wisely: "A verbal contract ain't worth the paper it's written on!"

MAKING IT AS AN INDEPENDENT

Freedom in Abject Poverty

"I want, eventually, as I guess does every aspiring young filmmaker, to be able to make my own movies with as little hindrance from outsiders as possible. The more exposure I have to independent filmmakers, the more aware I become that the nature of film makes that peculiarly more difficult than in any other form of expression. Money, and big money, *is the continual stumbling block. . . ."*

—LETTER TO THE AUTHOR FROM
A FILM STUDENT

A short time after the publication of my first book, *Getting into Film,* I received a rather angry letter from Judith Wentzell of the art department at the Portland Public Library. (The quote above, incidentally, is not from Ms. Wentzell's letter.) Since I am generally a pragmatist who tries to counsel that the craft and the business of filmmaking should be close companions, I had given short shrift to the fields of experimental and independent films.

Certainly I do admire the lonely individual who works on new techniques—some of which may eventually find their way into my own films—and the free spirits with dogged determination who find some way to produce noncommercial features for very limited but very loyal audiences. But in a sense, perhaps I was too short with a part of our industry that has given us people like John Sayles, Frederick Wiseman, the Maysles Brothers, Anna Thomas, Gregory Nava, Peter Kinoy, Pamela Yates, and Frank and Eleanor Perry.

After a brief comment about how the new book would certainly fill a need, Ms. Wentzell, disturbed that I had devoted a great part of the section to an amusing story about a well-known experimental filmmaker, added:

"I must say, however, that I was horrified at your treatment of the independent and experimental film. I understand your minimal coverage of this aspect of film, but to have devoted twice as much space within the article to such an incompetent person rather than to the positive aspects of independents is sad. (Why did you hire him in the first place?)

At any rate, students need to be encouraged . . . why not have focused on the experimentation done by independents which have opened new roads for Hollywood? Why not have emphasized independents are artists? Why not have given independents their due as a rewarding (spiritually if not financially) alternative?"

Why not, indeed? As I analyzed the rather sharp critique, I realized that I had passed over this part of our profession so quickly because I felt (and still feel) that it is without doubt the most difficult area of the entire industry in which to make a living—or even to survive at what might be considered a minimally acceptable level.

On the other hand, she is quite right. Just because it is tough to make money in the independent field is no reason for me to have made it a stepchild in a book written to cover every aspect of this most complex film profession. Though I keep claiming that I am a pragmatist (too often, I suppose), I am just as delighted to read of a success story in which someone achieves a dream—whether in the corporate world or in motion pictures.

Nevertheless, if you are thinking of pursuing a career in the independent film world, take the advice of your peers seriously—and know what it is you are about to enter. Frederick Wiseman's counsel to "marry someone rich," though facetious at first glance, was expanded in a telephone conversation we had some time back:

"It's discouraging. It's a lot of work. And it will require you to hold two jobs at once—and spend half your time trying to raise money. It's debilitating, it's exhausting, it's degrading, it's denigrating. . . ."

But—he adds, for all those who want to work at it:

"It's well worth it if you decide that you want to do it!"

And many do want to do it. It would be simple for me to merely quote success stories in the independent field, covering documentarians like Wiseman or feature directors like Sayles. But I feel—and they agree—that the realities and practicalities of the field are too often missed or even blocked by the new filmmaker who sees only the dream of a finished project screened to the acclaim of a large and appreciative audience (possibly even at the Cannes Film Festival!).

Thus, I keep reemphasizing the financial problems, because without a realistic approach and the eventual funding of your films, the dream remains a dream. Even with funding, deferrals, and friends who work for you for no pay at all, the road is a long, hard, almost endless series of conflicts and disillusionments. And when it's all done, the problem of distribution still remains.

Robert Richter is one of the pioneers of the documentary, having worked in the field for over twenty-five years. Though he has worked for ABC News, *CBS Reports,* and PBS and has won three DuPont-Columbia awards, he was quoted as saying that "twenty-five percent of my time is spent in raising money. And that's with an assistant who spends 75 percent of her time fundraising. Meantime my overhead continues." Raising the money for his PBS documentary about corporate involvement with American agriculture, *The Politics of Hunger,* took him *four years*!

The stories are legion in our field. Almost every San Francisco filmmaker working as an independent makes the same complaint. New York filmmakers echo it, and before I become just a bit more optimistic about producing your own films in the independent field, let me depress you with just one more story, told to me by a student friend:

"I have a couple of friends who are working on a documentary. They are both twenty-six, have just married, and moved to New York from the West Coast. He has been working on the project now for over five years, and when he applied for a grant from the National Endowment for the Humanities at twenty, he was told over the telephone that they were awarding the full budget to the project. A few days later he received a letter of rejection!

Now, six years later, they're still looking for funds. Luckily, they're well connected financially and they think they're about to receive a private donation of $100,000—which may well cover the entire budget. By the time they're finished, it will have been perhaps *eight years in the making. . . ."*

There is but one further note of gloom. I find that young filmmakers equate the words "independent film" with the word "independence," and this is entirely understandable. However, they are by no means synonymous! The mere fact that you have decided to become an independent filmmaker does not, in any way, guarantee that you will have absolute and final say in every production phase of your filmmaking career. Though it may not be quite as bad as the "script mending" session that I described as U.S. government interference with a film project, the final distribution of the film may well bring people into it who demand (and sometimes get) changes, nuance revisions, and even the elimination of entire sequences as a negotiated compromise for agreeing to distribute the film or to show it on a television network. It may even come down to asking you to cut ten minutes of the film in order to fill a time slot. You have spent ten years on the project. Do you agree to cut the ten minutes of "your baby"? And if you do, *which* ten minutes of your blood and soul are you willing to part with?

Some years back, given "complete freedom" to do a network documentary, I came back with exciting footage from all over the world and was, indeed, given a great amount of freedom to put the film together in the way I wanted. However! However, this was in the sixties, even before the soap operas extolled cleavage, steamy sex, and raunchy plots, and I was told that the show could not go on the air unless I removed the word "circumcision" and an entire courtship sequence of the bare-breasted Giriama tribe in Africa! Of course, I made the trade-off. Possibly you might not have done the same.

Frederick Wiseman, when asked the question, insists that he has gotten freedom because "I demand it and because I know the subject better than anyone else." John Sayles commits his own funds to his films for exactly the same reasons. But too often the prevailing attitude is that of the executive at Home Box Office who was interviewed about the documentaries funded by the cable network. She was quoted as saying, "We have a lot of arguments with filmmakers. A documentary filmmaker often tends to lose sight of his original objectives, and it is our job [sic!] to keep him on the right track."

Nevertheless, in spite of the control demanded by HBO, most filmmakers would love to work for them, mostly because there are fewer and fewer opportunities available for the funding of independent documentaries, and many former, steadfast, more reliable sources have dried up somewhat in the past few years. What does remain is competed for by more filmmakers than ever before.

The Ford Foundation, National Endowment for the Humanities, the National Endowment for the Arts, the Corporation for Public Broadcasting, and the Independent Documentary Fund of PBS have all been cut back. In addition, federal grants have been severely limited in this area, something I consider rather unfair and even sinister in its implications. Accusations have been made (and promptly denied) that *subject matter* has been a factor in the final decisions of some grant boards in an administration that is wary of anything "too political."

It all means that independent filmmakers have had to become more ingenious than ever before. I once suggested that you even look deeply into the specifications for archaeological expeditions while searching for funds for films that you might want to do in Micronesia. Though I was not really being facetious, I didn't realize that I might be taken quite so seriously: this past year I received a letter from a filmmaker who lives in Guam. He told me that he had taken my advice, had searched the files for expeditions going to Micronesia, and was about to leave with one to make their documentary film!

The wonderful thing about independent film is that is attracts a very special breed of people. Those who are successful at it deserve a great deal of admiration and respect from those of us who are used to having our projects paid for by large corporations, advertisers, or major feature producers. John Reilly, the director of Global Village, a wonderful hands-on video production center and school in New York's SoHo district, comments, "The independent documentary is a measure of a filmmaker's dedication. . . ."

And to that he might well have added the independent feature filmmaker as well as the large experimental group who have given the film field much of the innovation in the short film form—from Len Lye and Norman McLaren to Carmen D'Avino and all the others who have managed to survive since the days of Cinema 16.

Some Tricks of the Trade

One of my dearest and most delightful friends in the early days of filmmaking was a man named Joel Holt, who died too young and who remains an inspiration to me when I find the practicalities of film beginning to overwhelm the emotional joy of producing and directing my motion pictures. Nothing—but absolutely nothing—could ever squelch his delightful optimism, especially such a minor thing as a lack of funds.

In the early fifties he went to Japan to produce his first feature film. The budget was $50,000. The film was entitled *Karate, Hand of Death,* and it is just possible that you have seen it on the late-late night television screen in glorious black and white.

The money was raised by convincing friends that this film about karate was ahead of its time (it was), by doing low-budget commercials for agencies that were just manging to survive the competition of Madison Avenue's big guns, and by digging deeply into whatever per-

Frederick Wiseman, one of the most innovative and successful of the documentary filmmakers.

sonal finances he had. The budget was low, even for those times. He wrote, produced, and directed the film, and since he also happened to be a black belt karate expert who could smash eight ceramic tiles with one blow, he decided to star in it as well.

When the film was completed, he met what most independent producers encounter in this world of "the bottom line." He could not get it distributed unless he gave away small percentages to everyone who offered to work with him. Like the ancient Asian "cuts of a thousand knives," he managed to give away the entire income generated by the film in order to see it play on television. But, as with all independents, just the fact that he managed to complete the project was enough for him, and in his own delightful way, he passed it all off to experience. Late, late at night, I would sometimes get a call from Joel: "Tune in channel four. They're playing *Karate, Hand of Death!*"

Well, Joel discovered many years ago what the major studios have just recently found to be a bonanza and a way to finance projects. At the time of the Brussels World's Fair, he telephoned to tell me that he had sold the idea of a film about the fair, and someone was contributing $12,000! "Twelve thousand dollars?" I exclaimed. "That's not enough to even pay the crew and take a plane to Brussels!"

I had not counted on the determination and ingenuity of my friend. Using the $12,000 figure as a fulcrum and armed with the vaguest of television commitments ("If the film is good and we have the time and we have nothing else to fill the space, sure we'll play it!"), he went from agency to agency and got some further commitments:

★ The storyline would be that of a young couple going to the fair. They would fly Sabena Airlines. For this he got free transportation.
★ He would show them getting into a Fiat car, and thus he got his crew vehicles on a swap.
★ They would carry Samsonite Luggage, easily recognizable, for which the fee would be an additional $1,000.
★ At the fair, the couple would stop at a soft drink stand and buy a Pepsi: $1,000 more.

Bit by ingenious bit, he built the budget for the film, with hotels, carry-on bags, recognizable products, clothing, until the entire plot was one jigsaw puzzle of sponsors for a film about the Brussels World's Fair. The budget, starting with the miserable $12,000, finally neared $65,000, and Joel not only made the film, but ended up with a handsome profit as well—in addition to his free trip to Brussels.

Today this is a common practice. There are actually companies that specialize in placing their client's products in feature films and paying a handsome fee for the exposure as well. The most famous, of course, is Reese's Pieces in the film *E.T.* after M&M Mars turned down the offer for their candies.

Interestingly enough, now that the major studios are being gobbled up by the multinational corporations, the game of product placement has changed in another way. For example, when Coca-Cola purchased Columbia Pictures, they sent a memo to studio executives forbidding the use of competing products in any of their films. The "hit list" was obvious: no Pepsi-Cola, no 7-Up, not even Miller or Löwenbräu beers, Stolichnaya vodka, or Frito-Lay potato chips. You may be sure studios that compete with Columbia will, in turn, forbid any production to show a Coca-Cola in a sequence.

For the independent, "deals" can still be made. They are much more difficult than when Joel Holt built his film out of product placement, but an occasional airline plug is still seen at the end credits of a film or a television show, and with deregulation it is easier for them to offer free transportation in return for a lovely shot of a 747 taking off into the sunset, theoretically carrying the stars of the film to some enchanted spot.

For the most part, however, the true independent does not want to be tied to a commercial product, no matter how subliminally it is seen in the film. Thus, many of the independents—in the documentary field as well as in the feature—try to raise their money in other ways. Foundations have already been mentioned, but these are quite limited because of competition and the drying up of funds. The complexities and time involved both in applying and in waiting can be debilitating. The networks still hold to the rule that they will produce their own documentaries, no matter how shallow or ineffective they are. Occasionally an independent does manage to break through, as David Wolper did in the fifties with his *Race for Space*. A few others have followed, but generally the independent has been limited to a showing on PBS.

There are other foundations that are generally overlooked, and it would be wise to check on every one you can locate to see if a film grant is available, just as my friend in Guam did about Micronesia.

But for the most part, independents are working in other categories in order to raise money for the projects that they really, deeply want to do. San Francisco independent Ernie Fosselius (*Hardware Wars*) says that he "wears a lot of hats" in order to make a living while he produces his independent films. He designs sets for industrials, makes commercial voice-overs, acts, and animates.

Jenny Bowen, who produced her first film, *Street Music,* with her husband, cinematographer Richard Bowen, worked as a sound engineer at Coppola's Zoetrope Productions during the three years it took to raise the money (though it took but one year to produce the film).

A large number of talented filmmakers are working right in the middle of the commercial world in order to do the films that tempt them most. Tom Buckholtz (page 30) puts in a full day at his successful commercial operation in New Orleans and then manages to find the time to work on a documentary about the Louisiana Cajuns with a grant from the American Film Institute.

Your application to a foundation might get more attention if your work as a filmmaker has gotten some recognition in another area. Previous awards, experience in the various crafts of film, and knowledge of sound, editing, or cine-matography might make the difference in the award of a grant, since you come off as a professional in the field. Given the overwhelming amount of good ideas and good intentions, that one factor may get you some of the money.

All across the country there are professionals working in other areas while making their independent documentaries. Again I stress that the work area need not be New York or Hollywood. Joe Pipher, who works out of Cincinnati and went there after eight years of experience on the West Coast, claims that "if you want to find out what film is *not* about, go to Hollywood!" Bob Richards is another director who is working in the Midwest in the commercials field in order to pursue his first love, the making of documentaries about the American Indian.

Born in England, Bob worked in New York for five years making what he calls "high budget beauty stuff." He married and moved to the city of Minneapolis, where he works successfully with Em Com.

"I decided to stay out here because I'm fascinated with the culture and the history of the American Indian in the Midwest. It takes a long time to gain trust, as you can well imagine. . . ."

He used his own money and a small grant from PBS to produce the film, *Amos and the Pipe,* about the spiritual significance of the peace pipe, and several other projects are in the works. I asked how he felt about working in the Minnesota area. Aside from comparing it to the America that Norman Rockwell used to paint, he said:

"If the winters weren't so hard, the summers wouldn't be so beautiful!"

Much of the independent movement is also budgeted through the use of deferrals, payments that will be made (one hopes) in the future when (and if) the film is in distribution. This is especially true of the independent feature.

Bob Richards of Em Com Productions in Minneapolis. His love of nature and his very special interest in the American Indian has kept him working in documentaries, commercials, and public television in the state of Minnesota.

If I have compared going into your own business with a gamble at Las Vegas, then the odds against making a successful feature must equal those of a state lottery that pays about $20 million to a winner who can choose six consecutive numbers. Nevertheless, some do make it. Wayne Wang (*Chan Is Missing*) nearly decided to go back to social work after producing his first feature. It played the New Director's Festival at Lincoln Center in New York, was seen and acclaimed by Vincent Canby of the *New York Times,* and was then picked up for distribution by New Yorker films, to go on to break house records as a first-run film. It is another example of the combination of hard-raised money and determination that keeps the independent looking and hoping.

Gregory Nava and Anna Thomas have shared a love of film from the time they met as film students at UCLA in the sixties. Though they have had some success with *El Norte,* their independent feature that has been called "a Latin American *Grapes of Wrath,*" they went through years of poverty; there was a time when Anna Thomas was so poor that she actually lived in a closet in a men's dormitory. Their first film, in 1973, *The Confessions of Amans,* was produced as much through persuasion as money.

They talked a Madrid costume house into renting them the costumes that had been made for the film *El Cid,* and for bargain prices at that. They convinced the curator of Segovia to let them shoot for nothing at Spanish national monuments. The cast worked only for expenses, and they shot the film with a three-person crew! The entire cost was *$24,000,* and the film won the best first feature prize at the 1976 Chicago International Film Festival.

The system of begging, borrowing, and deferring has not changed at all. Matthew Chapman called his film *Strangers Kiss* a "deferment picture." All salaries and fees were deferred, and a total of nearly $2 million in expenses are waiting to be paid when the film comes out—and if it is even moderately successful. The salaries of crew and actors were deferred, as were the postproduction costs. Even *a sushi maker* who catered the crew lunches and a young man who provided candy for quick energy on the set accepted deferrals. Over all, two hundred people now have an investment in the film! It was shot in twenty days, and Chapman commented in an interview, "You obviously can't pay them for very long. Otherwise they starve."

David Fishelson and Zoe Zinman made their film, *City News,* in East Greenwich Village in New York for $40,000, using borrowed equipment and money from a lawsuit settlement.

When Zinman was in high school, her teeth were knocked out in a car accident. Five years later, when she had almost forgotten about the incident, the money came through on her birthday. "It was a great birthday present," she commented, "but I wouldn't recommend it as a way to finance a film!"

If you look carefully at the credits of many of the independent features that play your small local theater, even the ones that are moderately successful, you will find names on that list that closely match the surnames of the producers of the film. The obvious reason is that money quite frequently comes from some of the wealthier relatives of the people who made the film. Several documentaries that have played the theatrical circuit, as well as some of the better known recent films, have tapped mothers, fathers, aunts, and uncles for some of the seed money to get started. It is certainly not something to be overlooked by the eager independent.

But one of the most unusual methods of fund-raising came to light about a year ago when my wife and I went out to dinner. In the West Greenwich Village section of New York is a superb and authentic Texas barbecue restaurant called Cottonwood Café, and though this is not a restaurant review book, we recommend it highly for starving filmmakers who don't mind the long wait for a table.

Walking into the second room one night, I noticed a large, plastic lemon juice jug on the shelf where dishes are stacked. Boldly printed on the front were the words "Doug's film fund— $500,000 or bust!! I could not resist getting the entire story, and luckily the time was early, the place was fairly empty, and I found the owner of the jug.

Doug Gowland came from Texas, where he got his BBA at the University of Texas at El Paso, plus an MBA in graduate school. Now thirty-five years old, he came to New York three years ago after working at odd jobs, studying voice, acting, and then putting in his time at Bill Peck's studio in Irving, Texas.

"Well, Bill was an old-time cameraman and he wanted to see how serious I was about film. So, the first day, they had me dig a ditch for a new air-conditioner pad. I said to myself, 'So *this* is the movie business!' "

From that time on, however, whenever they had a commercial to shoot, Gowland would end up as a grip or a gaffer, learning the terminology of film: what an Inky was, a Sun Gun, or a K-4. On one commercial he actually got paid $80. When he came to New York he met a fellow Texan, who owned the Cottonwood Café and offered Doug a job as a waiter to help pay the rent. Doug enrolled at NYU Film School but took only *one* course: How to Be a Producer. (He commented to me, "It was people like you who taught me how to do low-budget films!")

He now has a script for a feature comedy, and he is raising the money through investments of eighty shares at $5,000 each. His original estimate was $100,000 for the film, raised to $400,000 "when I saw the realities," and $500,000 on his famous fund-raising jug—just for safety. His company is called Apple Star productions (a combination of the Big Apple and the Lone Star State), and he calls his venture "the Boots project," after his mother's nickname. "After all," he told me, "Andrew Carnegie named his steel mills after his customers!"

Of course, raising the money is not his only problem. After the job is done, there is still the headache of distribution. And for that, he has three goals. He calls them his "three Cs":

1. Completion: I did it!
2. Creativity: a first film, something he can show as a sample even though it may be

Possibly one of the most unusual methods of raising production money for an independent film is Doug Gowland's large contribution jar at the Cottonwood Café in New York's Greenwich Village.

open to criticism. It may, in turn, open other doors for him.

3. Cash return to his investors.

At the Cottonwood, Doug meets a lot of people. He met his accountant and his lawyer there while they were having dinner. People inquire about the jug, just as I did, and Doug then sends his prospectus.

Has it been successful? Well, let's just say it's too early to tell. But in this crazy business, I will be looking carefully sometime in the future for an end credit that reads "an Apple Star production."

"When the Mountains Tremble": A Talk with Pamela Yates

There is no single case history in film that can be used to prove a point about any other production. The problem of raising money is solved in a hundred different ways, sometimes successfully, other times not too well, but always over an inordinate period of time, it seems. Whether I were to choose the story of the making of *David* *and Lisa, Northern Lights,* or *The Brother from Another Planet,* each solution would be quite different. The same holds true in the documentary field.

If there is one area in which we can make a general statement, however, it is in the raising of money and the distribution problems for films that deal with political subjects or documentaries about social change. It is probably the part of our field in which you will most often hear, "Oh, but you can't do a film about . . ." This, in spite of *The Battle of Algiers, Z, The China Syndrome,* and even *El Norte.* The same might also be said for *Holocaust, The Sorrow and the Pity,* and *Sakharov.* Occasionally we find room for films with ideas.

Since a part of my own career has been concerned with the social documentary, and having worked in some countries where the government was less than overjoyed to see a motion picture crew, I was particularly interested in two films that played at a small local movie house in Greenwich Village. Indeed, they had proven so popular with the public that they had been held over for some six weeks after being scheduled only for a limited run.

The double bill was *Nicaragua: Report from the Front* and *When the Mountains Tremble,* and I was especially taken with the handling of the second film, a documentary approach to the story of the real war in Guatemala. Both were perfect examples of what filmmakers can accomplish when they set out to tell a story to which they have a deep, personal, underlying commitment. In a sense, *When the Mountains Tremble* might well be one of the role models for the people who have attended my lectures and seminars and who have said to me, "What I would really like to do . . ."

Some time after seeing the films, both of which garnered excellent reviews, I telephoned Pam Yates, the codirector and sound recordist of the Guatemala film, met with her, and talked for a long time about the film, her background, and about the other people who work on her films with her. It struck me that there were several very good reasons to include her story here, in this section about independent filmmakers, because it underscores almost all of the points about film that I have covered in the previous sections of the book:

★ The film was a collaboration in an industry where that word is key.

★ The filmmakers had to raise funds for a political subject, never an easy job.

★ There was compromise involved in order to get the backing they needed.

★ All of the people involved work at other jobs in the industry during the time they are not producing their feature documentaries.

★ The film involved no small amount of danger, in that they were trying to give both sides of a story that had created turmoil, assassinations, and exploitation of the Indians in that country. Their "war stories" were close to being real rather than funny tales told over dinner.

★ To that end, they had to gain the confidence of local populations as well as government military people and "contras."

★ And after it was all done, they had to find some way to get the film into general distribution in an industry where summertime fare is on the level of *Gidget Goes to Grenada.*

The collaboration for the film dates back to 1976, when Pam Yates, Tom Sigel (codirector and cinematographer), and Peter Kinoy (producer and editor) formed their own company, Skylight Pictures. Pam explains:

"Other filmmakers of political films have a tendency to be too ponderous. We do political films, but we also work on others to learn creativity and what else is being done in the field. We do television documentaries, commercials, and advertising films, and we do rock video. It exposes us to other ideas, and it helps us build a base for ourselves. It's different from the attitude held by many young filmmakers—*me, the director*—instead of trying to develop a better working relationship and thus a better product by collaboration with other people."

Pamela had spent half her life in Latin America, something that would stand her in good stead later on in her professional career, since she speaks fluent Spanish. It is yet another lesson to beginning filmmakers that the talents you have in other areas outside film may well be your entrée into a job in later years. She started as a teenage fashion model ("one step above prostitution," she comments), but in the jobs she met photographers and learned as much about

COURTESY SKYLIGHT PICTURES

Filming Big Pine exercises in Honduras for Haskell Wexler's Latino. *On the left, Tom Sigel, and with the microphone, Pam Yates.*

photography as she could, then worked as a photojournalist in western Massachusetts, followed by a job for the Mexico City daily, *El Excelsior,* working all over South America for the newspaper.

In 1973 she returned to the United States and studied filmmaking at the University of Massachusetts and then came to New York, where she visited "every production house listed in the yellow book." One day she arrived at a company where they had just fired someone the day before (timing?), and they hired her on the spot. She got a job as assistant editor, worked there intermittently, and held a second job as a temp to survive.

I am always fascinated by just how we find our place in this field. Pam's view of editing is very much the same as mine, though she calls it the "kitchen" of the film industry:

★ You don't get to go on location.
★ You have to fix things that others louse up.
★ You have to be organized.

She got a job with Women Make Movies as national distribution director. It was a CETA project that helped her pay off her student loan.

"As soon as I had paid it off, I borrowed again, this time to buy a Nagra and to learn sound recording. On the job for Women Make Movies, I used all my vacation time as well as weekends to work free-lance, or *free,* on every film produced by one of my friends— just to get experience. Because I was fluent in Spanish, I was finally hired to do jobs in Latin

The crew on location for Latino: *Pam Yates, sound; Scott Sakamoto, assistant cameraman; Tom Sigel, cameraman; and a member of the U.S. Army.*

America, including Mexico and Puerto Rico. I'm a great believer that if you have something that is unique, take advantage of it!"

At Skylight Pictures, the partners worked on television network film reporting, notably for *CBS Reports,* and their first film collaboration was *Resurgence,* a documentary about the Ku Klux Klan and its intimidation of the civil rights movement. Since that time they have become expert in the production of films dealing with Central America, and two of their films, *El Salvador, Another Vietnam* and *Americas in Transition* (1981), received nominations for the Academy Award.

When the Mountains Tremble took one and a half years to make:

"But we went about it in a most unorthodox way. We went to the networks, because at that time no one could get into Guatemala, and we also knew CBS from our previous work with them. Since *they* couldn't get in, they had little choice but to work with us. However, CBS insisted on sending a network producer with the crew. We accepted the compromise in order to get the backing for the film. . . ."

It took three trips to Guatemala of several months' duration for each trip.

"Working in Central America, you have to know its history, its art, politics, economics, you have to know film techniques. You can't make a film in a vacuum. How on earth could

Young women from Nebaj, Guatemala, in the film When the Mountains Tremble, *produced by Skylight Pictures.*

you even *think* of going to Guatemala without understanding any of its history?"

The job was not easy. Much of the time was spent in the Indian highlands. They were the first film crew to photograph the guerrilla movement, and they were also the first people who managed to incorporate secretly filmed scenes of government repression. No film of this type is without their risks.

While in Guatemala, they were held up by young guerrillas who stole much of their equipment. They had to depend upon couriers to help carry the film footage out of the mountains, to be smuggled back to the United States for processing. Filming the "contras" moving into Nicaragua meant traveling two hundred miles, often without food and water, and carrying only limited film equipment. The achievement is to be applauded, while at the same time I have a weak feeling of gratitude that *I* was not a member of the crew on some of the more hazardous parts of the trip!

The films opened quietly. The reviews were good. Word of mouth helped somewhat, and bit by bit the distribution increased. By the time I met with Pam, the films had gone past their small showings at the Bleecker Street Cinema, and she was about to leave for the premiere of the films in Minneapolis. In addition, they were opening in six other cities across the country. Following that, she would be returning to Latin America to be sound person for a new Haskell Wexler feature film.

"When you look at my background in retrospect, it all seems planned. But it's otherwise.

MEISELAS/MAGNUM

The funeral of the assassinated neighborhood leader Luis Godoy, in When the Mountains Tremble.

Working for different directors as a sound person, I see the strengths and the weaknesses of every one of them. You can really learn by working with other people. You are constantly tempted to second-guess by saying, 'They could have done it this way or they could have done it that way'—until you start making *your own* films. It's a humbling experience!"

So I am always quite taken by the dreams of the filmmaker, and I read with delight the stories that tell me many of you manage to make it work out somehow. In each seminar I conduct, there is usually one person who is thinking seriously about taking that plunge with an independent project, in spite of the money problems, in spite of the distribution barricades, in spite of their lack of experience. Their questions revolve around the rental of used equipment, deferrals, crew selection (at less than professional prices), and the limitations in making a first film statement.

Not too long ago, in a class on directing at the New School, I was again a guest speaker, telling the "war stories" that had befallen me and my crew during the past six months. Two young people, Theresa Heinly and Kurt Remmers, spent about ten minutes with just such questions and then told me and the class that they were thinking of going to Caesarea in Israel on an independent film project that they wanted to produce. Did I think it was a good idea?

I told them to go, by all means, but to always remember that their finished film would be judged as a professional document and that audiences would not accept excuses and "war stories" as to why it just didn't accomplish what the filmmakers set out to record. But I guaranteed them that, if they could raise the money, the experience would be invaluable and that they would manage somehow to overcome the problems that would arise day by day, if not hour by hour.

A week later I received a note from Theresa, which read in part:

"Thanks for your well-placed advice and encouragement. And remember, it's *your* fault that we are going to Caesarea! Kurt and I will personally blame you for anything that goes wrong. If anything goes right, as well you know, it will be a fluke. . . ."

That was some months ago. There have been other classes, other seminars, other student questions, other words of encouragement to people who want to do their own independent films. Then, just this past week, a postcard arrived from Israel, decorated with two stamps carrying the portrait of someone named Leon Pinsker. The card, hurriedly scrawled in pencil, was from Theresa and Kurt, and all it said was:

"Dear Mel:
Have we got a story to tell!
Regards. . . ."

I can hardly wait for them to return.

MAKING IT HAPPEN

The most frequently asked questions about getting started and moving ahead in the film industry

Making It Happen

Through all these years of lecturing, counseling, and conducting film seminars across the country, I have made note of the questions that seem to come up most often from participants in these sessions. Somehow there seems to be a pattern, naturally based upon an intense desire to know the answers to getting a job and making a living in this highly competitive field. Though many (if not all) of the major questions are answered in this book, I thought it might be a good idea to cull them, condense them, and try

to answer them as succinctly as I can in this last section. If nothing else, it shows that you are not alone—that the doubts, the probing queries, the uncertainty and indecision are things that lie deep within all of us. And those of us who have "made it" (so far!) have also been in exactly the same situation throughout our careers.

Each of the questions that follows was, at one time or another, asked of me by a student, a seminar participant, or a correspondent who was either looking for advice or seeking a job with my company. The answers certainly do not represent *all* the solutions to those questions, and other filmmakers might well approach them differently. Possibly they will be of some help to you. One day soon, you may well have your own answers!

Up the Ladder

WHAT DO YOU MEAN BY "MAKING IT"? PRESTIGE? MONEY? BOTH?

For me, "making it" merely means finding a way to be active in the field, to make films that are exciting, and, above all, to make a living at it. For some, the ego is more important, for others the monetary rewards are crucial. But as one of my students once said, "If you want to make a lot of money, find another line of work!"

AFTER AN INTENSE SCHOOL PROGRAM (i.e., continuing education or a masters in communications) DO YOU CONTINUE SCHOOL OR GO OUT AND GET EXPERIENCE?

Though I prefer to hire people with field experience, I have also found excellent and talented people right out of school. My feeling about school is that you have only wasted your time if you do not come out with a personal *sample* of your work. In addition, the change in the field in the past years has put many more communications grads in the director's chair (Scorsese, Seidelman, Heckerling, Coen), as well as in positions of power (Coppola, Lucas, Spielberg), thus making the way into the field much easier for those who follow.

IS CINEMATOGRAPHY SCHOOL REALISTIC AFTER A FOUR-YEAR FILM STUDY COURSE?

My feeling is that the best experience you can get in the field of cinematography is to try to get a job at a camera equipment house while practicing your craft and learning to break down and put together every known make of camera and lens. Following that, a job as an assistant to a cinematographer will stand you in good stead, learning about the practical production problems on location or in a studio rather than concentrating on the aesthetics of photography, which is what I think most schools emphasize. There is no reason, however, that you cannot do *both* . . . and at the same time. All it takes is work.

WHAT ARE THE MAJOR MISTAKES MADE BY PEOPLE TRYING TO BREAK INTO FILM?

★ Setting your sights too high.
★ Setting your sights too low.

If you come out of school as a "feature freak," you are probably setting your sights too high at first. On the other hand, if you denigrate your other talents and your value to a production company, this, too, will come across to any interviewer. Make a realistic assessment of what it is you have to offer—and study the rungs of the ladder carefully.

HOW CAN I USE MY PREVIOUS EXPERIENCE IN OTHER FIELDS TO MAKE THE JUMP INTO FILM?

Frequently that is exactly the way to jump into film. Previous experience in almost every field might well land you your first job or move you ahead. This can include finance, fashion, styling, makeup, still photography, design and graphics, computer technology, music, and even sports like skiing, mountain climbing, or polo. We may just be looking for someone with your background. There are plenty of directors around, but not enough people who understand budgets.

HOW DO I MOVE FROM A SEEMINGLY DEAD-END JOB IN A FILM COMPANY (LEGAL, FINANCE, COMPUTERS, SECRETARY) INTO ACTIVE PRODUCTION?

I don't believe that any job need be a dead end, though I have often counseled that if it seems so after a year or more, move on somehow. But the beauty of even working for a large production company is that you constantly meet the people who control the job market in production. It is a natural adjunct of any job—just being there means meeting the right people. You need but one opportunity, one bit of right timing, to move upward. In one company, four successive receptionists moved up to production assistant and then to producer in a space of three years. Just by being there!

HOW DO I MOVE FROM A LARGE CORPORATION TO A SMALL PRODUCTION COMPANY?

Here again, meeting people is part of the job. If you are with a company that uses outside suppliers, you are in a perfect position to work for their clients. The same for advertising agencies. More people have moved into supplier production companies from ad agencies than from any other sources, I think. Find out who the suppliers are in the communications area, get to know them, and one day the opportunity might arise. I would only suggest that you do it carefully. Large corporations don't like the idea that their people want to move on to something else.

IS CORPORATE AUDIOVISUAL WORK AN OPPORTUNITY OR A DEAD END? WHAT ARE THE ENTRY LEVELS?

They are, in fact, wonderful places to learn and to make your samples for a future move. Many of the companies in the United States, Canada, and overseas have superb state-of-the-art equipment and facilities. Some are better than the networks. The entry levels are generally as a lower-category assistant to an audiovisual director, or corporate communications, advertising, or marketing. You may end up doing the dirty work on the annual report, but you'll also have an opportunity to work with tape and/or film.

HOW DO I MOVE FROM THE AREA OF "TECHNICIAN" INTO "CONCEPTUALIZING" AND WORKING IN PRODUCTION? ("I am trapped by splicers and trim bins. I believe the exposure one gets in the editing room is priceless, but I am not sure how to get out of it!")

I think that editors and people who work in labs and in equipment houses are in much better position to meet film people than someone still trying to knock down the doors to the industry. Just as the people who told their stories in this book—who worked for friends for free or little money—editors and technicians can do the same. Many editors that I know are now producing and directing. It is also quite possible for you to put together your own independent production as a producer/editor. Think of the costs you can save in the postproduction phase!

IS IT DETRIMENTAL TO LIMIT MYSELF TO FILM, ESPECIALLY SINCE SO MUCH VIDEOTAPE IS BEING DONE TODAY? IS FILM BECOMING A DINOSAUR?

Don't bury film yet—but learn as much about videotape as you can. There is still a great amount of "shaking out" going on in the tape field, with incompatibility being a major factor. Many people are also returning to film as they balance quality and cost. Tape is not cheap by any means, and I have devoted an entire chapter to the subject. If you want to make a living, *learn both*.

ARE THERE CLEAR-CUT AREAS OF WORK? CAN YOU FUNCTION IN TRAINING FILMS, DOCUMENTARIES, AND COMMERCIALS ALL AT THE SAME TIME?

Most filmmakers do many categories of films, moving back and forth as the demand requires. As you progress in the film field, you will find that your resume begins to include just about everything. The one exception may well be the feature film, where the incestuous quality of the field keeps people working (or starving) only in that area. But even here, many of the crew will work a feature when it comes to town and then go back to commercials the next day. Certainly you will find that you are quite able to work in almost any type of film—they all use the same equipment, film stock, editing machines, and labs. Only the thinking is different.

DO DOCUMENTARIES EVER USE AN ART DIRECTOR?

It is rare, but it happens. Usually if a film requires a specific design, or the title treatment is to be unusual, an art director may be called in. But more job opportunities are available in commercials than in documentaries. In the feature field the competition is quite keen, and most art directors do not work steadily. I have also covered this part of the industry in the text of this book.

IS THERE ROOM IN THE FIELD FOR PEOPLE WHO ARE MORE CREATIVE THAN STRUCTURED?

Yes, with some limitations. It depends upon what you mean by creative, one of my least favorite words. An old friend, Bud Wiser, used to say, "The essence of creativity is artistic and selective plagiarism," and I have always felt that the film field is re-creative rather than creative. But certainly some writers, directors, art directors, and musicians have an opportunity to exercise their creative muscles more than gaffers, grips, and camera assistants. Total freedom is reachable, but very hard to achieve.

DO DIRECTORS TAKE ON ASSISTANT DIRECTORS ON A NO-FEE BASIS?

In working your way up, if you find that you make contact with low-budget filmmakers who either defer payment of salaries or ask friends to work for them, the answer is "yes." On the other hand, in the strong union atmosphere of features, the answer is a definite "no." Most important, keep in mind that your climb will result as much from serendipity and luck as from talent, and you will no doubt know when you can make the jump from production assistant to assistant director.

HOW DID GOOD DIRECTORS AND EDITORS DEVELOP THEIR VISION AND EXPERTISE?

By work, by observation, by confidence, by constantly studying and learning about the field, by reading about it, keeping up with it through the trade papers—and sometimes by sheer luck. I was delighted to read an interview with Federico Fellini, who started his own career wanting to be a lawyer, then an actor, a cartoonist, and a writer of gags for screenplays. He said about the director, "When I was on the set and watched the director, I was really very disturbed by him—the chaos, the screaming, the arguments, the yelling. I found the movie director a very ugly person, to be so tyrannical, so powerful—he was just disgusting. I did not like and still don't like that kind of arrogant power . . . and now, I am exactly the worst of them. I am arrogant, capricious, hysterical, paranoid . . . at the beginning it was true, I was very shy, I was very different. I thought honestly that I did not have the character to be a movie director. But now I have to admit that I was wrong. I do have the character!"

AS A DIRECTOR, DO YOU THINK YOU NEED TO KNOW ABOUT CAMERAS, SOUND EQUIPMENT, EDITING EQUIPMENT?

I think you have to *know* about them, though I am not certain that you have to be able to operate them. There are various opinions about this, with some directors wanting to also shoot. I, in turn, feel that handling the camera would blind me to everything else that is happening around me. A prime example would be filming the carnival in Rio. With your eye glued to the camera, how would you know what else around you is ripe to shoot, with all the turmoil, dancing, and people in the streets? But I do believe, no matter what your choice as a hyphenated filmmaker, that you should know about equipment and how it operates. How else would you have an intelligent conversation with your cameraman in trying to decide on a particular shot or effect that you want—or, for another example, which editing machine you prefer to use: Kem, Steenbeck, or Moviola? I still have trouble threading an editing machine, but I sure know what they are capable of doing!

CAN YOU TELL US MORE ABOUT THE UNIONS IN THE INDUSTRY? WHO ARE THEY? WHAT DO THEY DO? MUST I JOIN ONE TO GET AHEAD?

I have discussed these questions in various parts of this book. However, I want to reemphasize that it is not necessary to join a union at the beginning, and it may never be necessary to join one. Strangely, as the time arrives, you will find that it all works out. People do get in. In the meantime, there are hundreds of film and tape projects being done by nonunion crews. Stop worrying about it—it seems to be a prevalent concern of beginners.

HOW DO YOU MEET PEOPLE IN THE INDUSTRY?

You will be surprised at how your list of friends and acquaintances grows. You will meet people right in the industry as you work, at screenings, at cocktail parties, on the beaches, sitting alongside of you on an airplane, through recommendations, and through all the other methods that people meet people anywhere in any industry. Ours is a small and incestuous field. We hear about one another, we meet one another, we work with one another at some time or another. Stop being in such a hurry. You *will* meet people as you go along.

WE HAVE AN OPPORTUNITY TO MAKE A FILM FOR A UNIVERSITY (WE BEING MYSELF AND THREE OTHERS). HOW CAN I CONVINCE THEM THAT OUR GROUP CAN DO IT BETTER AND CHEAPER THAN ANYONE ELSE?

First of all, I hope that "better" does come before "cheaper." This is one area where my constant pounding about having a sample would come into play. The "cheaper" is because you are just starting out and you have a lower overhead than a professional production company. The "better" takes salesmanship and a screening of your work to prove that what you say is true.

HOW DO I START MY OWN PRODUCTION COMPANY?

Starting is easy. After that, be prepared for

cash flow, sales efforts, competition. See Part Eight for a complete discussion of the subject. The important thing is timing. Make certain that you have at least one good client with you who can give you enough business to keep you afloat for a year or more, while you learn to swim.

Paying Your Dues

HOW DO I DO ALL THE THINGS I WANT TO DO WITHOUT HAVING A NERVOUS BREAKDOWN AND WITHOUT STARVING?

Probably by starving for a while (but, we hope, not having a nervous breakdown). One of the things that beginners seem to miss is that our field has other areas of "dues paying" in addition to the blockbuster multimillion-dollar feature or the network documentary. Herb Brodkin did training films for the army when he started. Joe Pipher, who runs his own production company in Cincinnati, began his career by making training films for hospitals, including such great subjects as *The Cleansing Enema, Making an Occupied Bed,* and *Naso-Gastric Intubation.* You'd be surprised at how many of us have the same type of background.

YES, BUT HOW DOES A YOUNG FILM-MAKER STAY BUSY DURING THE "SLOW SEASON" WITHOUT WORKING IN A RESTAURANT?

By working in a restaurant!

SHOULD SOMEONE IN THEIR THIRTIES TAKE A LOW-PAYING MENIAL JOB WITH A PRODUCTION CREW—OR TRY TO GET THEIR OWN GROUP TOGETHER TO MAKE THEIR OWN FILMS?

I don't see why you shouldn't be doing both! The experience you gain in any part of our industry will help you later on, whether it be in production or finance or distribution or just working with people on a crew. It all helps.

IS COMPETITION OVERWHELMING?

Only if you let it be. Everyone competes in this world, including lawyers and doctors and automotive designers. I will admit that it takes a certain determination and that you'll probably have to take a lot of jobs that were not originally your idea of the film industry, and that you'll no doubt be exploited from time to time. There is a marvelous line in the film *Terms of Endearment,* when the doctor tells Shirley MacLaine about her daughter's terminal illness, "We look for the best and prepare for the worst." To which she answers possibly the most brilliant line in the film, "And they let you get away with that?"

DOES IT PAY TO BE A PERFECTIONIST, OR DOESN'T THE WORD EXIST IN THE FILM INDUSTRY?

Oh, it exists all right, but it's usually combined with the word "compromise." The industry is a collaborative one, and it is controlled by business elements who insist upon being there when you least need them. On the other hand, there are people like Herbert Brodkin and Frederick Wiseman, who pretty much make the films

they want to make in the way that they want to make them. It just takes years to achieve.

DO WE HAVE TO LIVE IN NEW YORK OR HOLLYWOOD TO HAVE A FIGHTING CHANCE OF SUCCESS?

Absolutely not. I have again covered this subject in the book. There are people who are working happily and successfully all over the country—all over the world, in fact.

WHAT SHOULD I CHARGE FOR MY LABOR?

First of all, know exactly what the job pays when someone is a full-time union (or even nonunion) filmmaker, so that you are aware of the market. Anything below that becomes a fair target: free, half the fee, enough to live on for the next few weeks or months. It is a very personal area and one of the first questions might well be, "What does the job pay?" To which the producer will answer, "How much do you want?" It is a constant chess game even after you have years of experience. You don't want your fee to be nonnegotiable because you had asked for $500 and the producer was thinking about somewhere near $50. The whole thing takes on the feeling of a dueling match.

The Job Hunt

This question is probably the most asked of every experienced filmmaker:

WASN'T IT MUCH EASIER TO GET INTO FILM OR TELEVISION WHEN YOU "OLD-TIMERS" BEGAN?

No, it was not. First of all, there were fewer opportunities even if there were fewer people who were enchanted with the world of communications. I remember giving a lecture to a men's club back in the late forties and telling them that it was hard to believe, but "there are almost *one hundred thousand* TV sets in the United States today, and by next year we expect it to double!" We probably had exactly the same percentages against us, we paid our dues in exactly the same way (meaning that we worked for free or for very little), and we got to know our peers as they, too, moved up. It just seems easier to you—but we didn't think it was.

WHAT KIND OF THINGS DO YOU LOOK FOR IN A RESUME?

Frankly, I don't think that most of us actually *read* a resume carefully. We skim it or we don't look at it at all, except for the lead items. What I generally look for is what is in the cover letter—that it be a *personal* letter written to me and not to some title, that it be brief, that it have charm without being "cutesy," that it tell me quickly what it is the person wants to do. In the resume itself, I am generally more interested in some of the personal information than I am with the experience and the lists of previous employers. I also expect a follow-up at some point, if the person is really serious and not just mailing out two thousand resumes to the list of producers in his or her city. It takes real effort and it takes time on your part.

WHEN YOU'VE HIRED PRODUCTION PEOPLE, WHAT ARE THE QUALITIES THAT GOT THEM THE JOB?

In descending order: *Chemistry* first—the fact that I was certain that I could work with that person, that he or she would be a tribute to me and to my small company when clients or others were at a meeting. I mean, think of my reaction to a man I interviewed when I was looking for an editor. He arrived half an hour late with no excuse for his tardiness, he was dressed a la Hollywood with a blue shirt open to the belly button, gold chains dangling to his abdomen, and he introduced himself to me with, "Don't worry, baby, I've done this kind of stuff before," to reassure me that he could handle the film. Frankly, why would I even look at his experience?

Following chemistry, then, I would certainly look at experience, samples, and the personal recommendations of people I know in the industry. Have I ever been wrong? Of course I have. But the gut feeling at a personal interview is still how most of us work.

WHAT DO YOU LOOK FOR IN A CINEMATOGRAPHER?

I have always believed that a cinematographer can be more adept at one kind of photography than another, depending upon the personality. Some are great with people, others with machines and abstract images, some with lighting, others with a combination of all four. Most cinematographers would argue violently with my theory, but through the years I feel that I have proven it time and time again. Thus, I look at the samples of work that come to me in terms of subject matter, objective, production problems, lighting time, composition, and color quality. And—I still look for the gut feeling that he or she and I can work together.

IS IT WHO YOU KNOW, NOT WHAT YOU KNOW?

It is a combination of both. Many jobs are gotten from people you've never met before. Others come through the first contact being made by a recommendation. In either case, something has to be open. It will do you no good to meet someone and talk if nothing is available at the time. Nevertheless, I have always felt that meeting anyone to whom you are recommended gives you the distinct advantage of:

★ knowing someone for future contact
★ getting a recommendation to see someone else in the industry
★ getting good advice from yet another source

I always counsel that you don't need *twenty* jobs. You merely need *one* opening and *one* job—and the timing has to be right. I don't think you should turn down *any* opportunity to meet someone else in the field, but I don't think it's the only way to get ahead in the film business.

HOW DO I BEST PREPARE MYSELF FOR A JOB INTERVIEW? HOW DO I BEST PRESENT MYSELF?

I am amazed at the number of people who go for a job interview without trying to find out something about the company they want to work for. Make calls, speak to people, look at the film literature and production manuals to find out what kind of films or tapes they do, what their last few productions were about, who their clients are. And although it's easy for me to write "Be yourself," it is the single best advice that I can give to the job hunter. Trying to be something you are not cut out to be, trying to make more of your experience than is true, can only hurt you at some point during the interview. You never know when we look at your resume and find that someone you have listed as a reference is really a very good friend of ours.

ON THAT SUBJECT, HOW DO I MAKE THE MOST OF MY SMALL AMOUNT OF FILM EXPERIENCE?

By being honest. Remember that we also hire on the lower levels of the business. You are looking for entry-level jobs and free-lance work on the beginner's levels of the field. Don't denigrate yourself. Play up your positive qualities—attitude, willingness to learn, your accomplishments to date. Include not only your film credits, but achievements in other areas of your life as well. Sometimes a personal story will do more for you than your experience and background.

WHAT IS THE VALUE OF GRADUATE WORK IN FILM? DOES IT PROVIDE A SUBSTANTIAL EDGE FOR THE JOB SEEKER?

Only if your sample is better than the next person's sample. Only if your chemistry is right. Only if you don't denigrate the employer's profession because you are only interested in even-

tually making the great all-American feature film. I frankly don't think it gives you any edge at all.

IS TAKING A SALES JOB WITH COLUMBIA PICTURES A WAY TO GET INTO PRODUCTION?

I've included this question, almost a repetition of another one in a previous section, because the person who wrote it explained with a rather interesting story. Coca-Cola owns Columbia Pictures, and a friend who is with Coca-Cola is willing to set up a sales interview with an executive at Columbia. His final question was, "Am I spinning my wheels?" By now you know that I would heartily encourage him to make that contact, no matter how vague it seems. *Any* person who knows any other person in our field is a potential door opener. And yes, I do think that a sales job with Columbia would allow him to meet the right people in the field who, in turn, might move him into production.

I'M MOVING TO ATLANTA (DALLAS, SAN FRANCISCO, OMAHA). WHOM DO I CALL OR WRITE ABOUT MY GREAT TALENTS AND IDEAS?

Interestingly enough, we generally miss one of the great sources of information: the Yellow Pages of the city to which you are moving. After that, the production manuals, including the great production guide published by *Backstage,* will give you names and addresses. Remember to call to get the right person to whom you write if you can't find it in the book.

IS THERE HOPE FOR WOMEN TO SUCCEED IN THE VIDEO/FILM WORLD? OR IS IT AS DIFFICULT TO BREAK IN AS IT IS FOR WOMEN IN PHOTOGRAPHY?

The breaking in is easy. It is the climb up the ladder that is still quite difficult, once you get past the role of editor or even director. Though a new generation of women filmmakers is beginning to make itself known to the field, only 5 percent of all Directors Guild of America members are women. In addition, as I have already mentioned, the hurdles put up for female filmmakers are much greater than those for men: one flop and you're out! There is a glimmering on the horizon, and even with tokenism, some names have broken through: Sherry Lansing, Joan Micklin Silver, Martha Coolidge, Joan Tewkesbury, Elaine May, Amy Heckerling, Gillian Armstrong, and Susan Seidelman—as well as the veterans of the past—Ida Lupino, Dorothy Arzner, and Barbara Loden. However, I always feel that the minute we have to give examples to prove how great we are, things are not really so good. But it is improving, however slowly.

WHERE ARE THE "HOT SPOT" JOB OPPORTUNITIES FOR THE FUTURE?

Certainly in videotape, and in an expanding communications industry that includes videoconferencing, corporate audiovisual departments, and the expanded use of film and tape for training, documentaries, and education. When you look to the time I exclaimed that we had one hundred thousand television sets in the country and compare the industry then with the present day, you realize that it is *all* growing—and thus the job opportunities will continue to expand along with it, even as the film schools turn out so many would-be directors.

Life-Style

Here again is a subject that very little has been written about. We spend our lives in the film business, but somehow we never communicate what it's like to run our lives at the same time. It is a very special area of concern because of the demands of the industry. Thus:

HOW MUCH TIME DOES A SERIOUS FILM-MAKER ALLOT TO SPEND WITH A GIRLFRIEND (BOYFRIEND, WIFE, HUS-BAND, FAMILY)? I WANT CHILDREN, BUT I'M AFRAID MY CAREER WILL DEMAND TOO MUCH.

With the move of film to locations instead of studios, travel increased. With the increase in travel, time away from home expanded. With crews out of their city for days, weeks, months at a time, personal relationships broke apart. We have a separation rate and a divorce rate in our industry that is probably unequaled in any other field. Cinematographers, especially, can be away for up to eleven months a year. I know one person who was home *seven* days in a year. Under these circumstances it is rather difficult to maintain a relationship and to be a father or mother to children (no less to allot enough time for conception!). It is something that you will have to face if you plan to make this your career.

I received a letter from Larry Dubin the other day in which he outlined the reasons he finally decided to give up the film field after twenty years. His wife, Nancy Cook, was also a film-maker, becoming quite successful and well known as an editor:

"I didn't want to put my children on hold for twenty more years. Nancy was an editor. I was a production manager. She worked through the night. I left for work at 6 A.M. The only time we ever met was in the shower in the morning! We made tons of money—but we had no time to spend it."

In my own case, I have handled the problem over thirty-five years by working with my wife, by traveling together, and by deciding that children would be an impossible burden to the relationship if we were to survive the rigors of being apart so constantly. It is impossible for one person to travel, have adventures, and meet new people while the other spends the day at the supermarket, and then have something to say to one another when you finally have time together. It is something that you will have to work out for yourself. But it *is* a severe problem in our industry.

CAN I SUPPORT MYSELF STARTING FROM THE BOTTOM?

I have covered this in another area. The answer is "yes" if you are willing to do other things while pursuing the rather difficult practi-calities of the free-lance market. It will take dedication of monumental proportions, but others have done it, why not you? I know free-lancers who have made themselves invaluable in other areas of the field, enabling them to keep up their contacts while they earn a living. The woman who transcribes my tapes after a shoot is also a production manager. When one part of the field is slow, the other can be busy enough to give her an income.

WHEN WE COME FROM THE TV GENERA-TION AND UNEMPLOYMENT IS RAMPANT, HOW CAN WE KEEP GOING STRONG FOR WHAT WE BELIEVE?

That's exactly one of the reasons that books like this are written. Read the stories of the people I've interviewed on these pages—veterans, successful producers, designers, directors. They all started somewhere, and along the line a series of breaks managed to find them. My friend Wynn Nathan tells of his early days doing speedwriting for William Morris, and one day someone said to him, "We'd like you to take this new girl [sic!] we have and introduce her around the studios and to the right people—introduce her to everyone we know. Her name is Marilyn Monroe!" He took her to studio lunches and to parties, and while making those rounds he met the people who would give him his next job—that of an agent at Century Artists, where he handled some unknowns like Doris Day, Gordon McRae, and Jack Smith. Suddenly he was an agent. Today he is vice-president at RKO Pictures.

WHAT ARE THE "RULES OF THE GAME"? WHO PLAYS THE POLITICS, AND WHAT IS THE IMPACT OF THE CREATIVE INDIVIDUAL ON THE BUSINESS?

The question is complex. I have mentioned that this is an industry of collaboration and compromise. How much depends upon your eventual clout as a director or writer. But never forget that the business people run our industry, be it television, feature production, or business film and commercial. Too often in our field you have to tread the minefield of pleasing an executive rather than keeping an eye on the eventual audience. The best example I can give is that in making a film that will be shown to schoolchildren, it is the *teacher* who selects the film.

In dealing with Hollywood, the area of creativity generally takes second place. In working with corporations, their own image may be quite different from what you perceive. The field is a constant mixture of salesmanship, compromise, collaboration, trade-offs, and the eventual learning of how to give up very little in order to keep something that is terribly important to you as a filmmaker. I have covered more of this subject in "The Ethics and the Arrogance of Film" (page 148).

WHY IS THE TV/TAPE INDUSTRY SUCH A CUTTHROAT BUSINESS?

You've answered the question yourself by calling it a business, which it certainly is. It seems to attract huge egos, just as opera and theater do—but if you want to look at cutthroat businesses, you might also observe the fashion industry, airlines, real estate, trucking, computer development and design, gambling casinos, Wall Street, and most multinational corporations that swallow up their competition or threaten "greenmail" to turn a quick ten million bucks. By comparison, we are a delicate, gentle industry.

IS IT POSSIBLE TO KEEP YOUR IDEALS AND PRINCIPLES, TO KEEP DOING SOMETHING FRESH AND NEW—AND STILL MAKE A LIVING?

Strangely, to a great extent, it is. This is another subject covered in detail in the chapter about ethics, but I can answer here by saying that there *are* filmmakers who manage to do their work mostly undisturbed. It is just a matter of knowing where compromise is necessary and just what it is you are willing to give up in order to make your point.

It is also a matter, difficult at times, of making a decision that might well mean that you lose the job. You have to make those decisions, but don't complain about them after you've made them—either way.

IS THERE REALLY CREATIVE FREEDOM AT ALL IN THE UNITED STATES? BEING EUROPEAN, I OFTEN WONDER IF IT IS TRULY POSSIBLE TO MAKE THE FILM YOU REALLY WANT TO MAKE. HOW MUCH DO YOU HAVE TO COMPROMISE?

After all the discussion on this very subject, I can only ask a question in answer to the question: Is there really creative freedom in Europe?

Production

Much of what is written here has been covered in detail in my description of the "never-never land" of production. However, these seem to be the questions most asked by people who are just starting out, and I have culled the most important ones.

HOW MUCH TECHNICAL INFORMATION DO I NEED?

Jim Manilla, an old friend who now teaches at NYU, begins his classes by saying that he will ask a question, and if anyone can answer it, he or she will be excused from the rest of the course. The question he poses is "What is the difference between an 'A wind' and a 'B wind' optical track?" It is a question that plagues filmmakers even after thirty-five years. Joan Kuehl, a filmmaker who also teaches, mentioned to me the other day that many of her students feel it is not necessary to know the number of feet in a minute or the number of frames per second in order to make films. She and I both answer, "Balderdash!" (a phrase of contempt from the days of Lord Kitchener at Khartoum).

I don't know how you can even consider making films without knowing the technology that is so much a part of our field—and as much technology as is humanly possible. How can you hire crews, choose equipment, discuss problems with a lab, work on a mix, or determine the best and most reasonable way to print your final subject if you don't know the technical end of the business? There is no other answer.

HOW DO YOU KEEP UP WITH ALL THE NEW TECHNIQUES IN THIS BUSINESS?

By reading everything, by going to seminars when they take place, by attending demonstrations at the labs and at Eastman Kodak, by talking to everyone and anyone who works with you, by being curious and observant—and above all and through it all, by becoming a *professional* about your field.

DO YOU HAVE AN IDEA, A TREATMENT, OR AN OUTLINE BEFORE YOU SHOOT A DOCUMENTARY?

There is always something in writing, be it a treatment or just an outline. The most ineffective way to start on a shoot is to keep everything in your head. Every film crew should at least know what the objective of the film is and who the eventual audience is to be. After that, a visual outline gives you a road map when you finally have to shoot film (and watch the money disappear).

BUT IN DOING A DOCUMENTARY, AREN'T THINGS FREQUENTLY DIFFERENT FROM WHAT YOU IMAGINED THEM TO BE? DON'T THINGS CHANGE ON LOCATION?

Yes, they do change—and frequently. But that is where the good filmmaker takes advantage of the situation and shoots. If you were doing a travel film and you suddenly came across a rain dance in a jungle clearing, would you let it be just because it wasn't in your treatment? Of course not—you'd shoot it, budget be damned!

There is another aspect to this question. Many of us believe that the camera changes things just by being there, that people react differently when a crew arrives, that the camera itself *changes* the real situation. Others, like Frederick Wiseman, disagree. Fred says that the test of whether or not the camera changes behavior is your observation over a long period of time *before* you shoot. And when you do roll film through the camera, you already *know* what the behavior should be. The check is your previous observation.

In any case, even though you have written a treatment, you will learn when to break away from it and when to ignore the serendipitous event that is taking place unexpectedly.

HOW DO YOU SELECT YOUR FILM CREWS?

I balance compatibility with talent. I keep in mind that I have to live with these people, sometimes for as long as a month on the road— or confined on a ship sailing to Alaska, as we once did. Don't forget compatibility, but make sure your crew is talented, too.

EVEN IF YOU PLAN WELL, DON'T THINGS GO WRONG?

All the time! And we manage to work them out all the time. That is part of the joy as well as the trauma of the film business.

CAN'T YOU AVOID MISTAKES BY A SURVEY TRIP?

Sometimes, but things change from the time you survey the area until the crew arrives.

For a feature it is an absolute necessity, but for documentaries it is an expense that you generally cannot afford. And especially if you are assigned to cover an event that takes place but once a year, what good would a survey of the area do you, except to show you where to place the camera?

WHAT DO YOU MEAN BY "RAIN DAYS"?

As I've commented, every place in the world has unusual weather—and the rain days are merely the ones you set aside in advance (knowing it's going to rain) when you'll utilize the expensive crew by shooting inside. Rain days should also be considered when making up your budget. What if it rains all ten days?

WHERE DO YOU GET YOUR EQUIPMENT? DO YOU BUY OR RENT?

Generally we rent. Sometimes the equipment is owned by the cameraman or sound person, and we rent it, knowing that it is being maintained and should be in excellent working condition. Remember, if you rent from a supply house, you will need insurance. If you rent from your crew, the chances are that they already carry insurance on their valuable equipment.

On occasion, I do buy equipment, but only if I can project enough use to make it worthwhile. For example, we have just completed a long tape job for which I did buy equipment. To have rented it at $50 per hour would have mounted up to a figure twice that of the purchase price. Thus, the job is over and I now own the equipment, making it less expensive to do the next job. However, I will now have to figure for maintenance costs and insurance fees.

AT YOUR LOCATIONS, DO YOU GENERALLY HAVE A LOCAL CONTACT?

Yes, if we can. But we still do our homework and learn as much about the location as we possibly can. People who live in an area don't generally know much about hotels, weather, even good restaurants. But local people can help considerably, especially overseas. Remember my motto: *Don't trust anyone!*

HOW DO I WORK OUT A REALISTIC BUDGET FOR A PRODUCTION?

Read. Make calls to get figures. Speak to other filmmakers who have worked in the area. Stop being an optimist: every figure you put down will multiply by at least two.

The Big Questions

AFTER ALL THE STRUGGLE, IS IT REALLY WORTH IT?

If I have not convinced you of that in all these many pages, then I wonder at your grit in getting this far in the book. The answer, of course, is yes.

Yes.

Yes.

Those of us who have been in it for so long would not have chosen any other kind of work,

even if we first dropped into this remarkable industry by accident or luck. We would probably not, given a chance to do it again, live our lives any differently. You probably agree that it is a worthwhile pursuit, that it has its joys and its rewards in addition to its traumas and very special frustrations. And at the beginning, all of us know full well the emotion and the lonely cry that goes with the final, most important question of all:

CAN I MAKE IT?

You already know the answer to that. Yes, I think you can. Each of you will take a different path—and some will even drop out to pursue something else. In my first book about film, I ended with what I thought was a proper and heartfelt wish after writing with so much joy about a field I love so much—I said, "Good luck," and I meant it then . . . and I say it again now.

But since then, there have been a great many seminars and a great number of students to whom I have spoken and tried to give some advice. For you, too, coming to the end of a book written by one who, I assure you, is very supportive of what it is you want to do with your film life, I suppose that I can only quote a final line that comes from *you* to *me,* and to every other filmmaker who will see you, interview you, encourage you, and even hire you. It was a word written in large type at the bottom of a questionnaire turned in to me at a film class.

It was but a single word, but somehow I saw in it the universal cry of every beginner in our field, now faced with the practical task of

getting a job and then moving upward. The word leaped out at me and I laughed in genuine empathy. The word was:

HELP!!

And I hope this book will. . . .